The Middle School Experience

The Middle School Experience

Successful Teaching and Transition Planning for Diverse Learners

Jeanne B. Repetto
Kristine W. Webb
Debra A. Neubert
Christina Curran

pro·ed
An International Publisher

8700 Shoal Creek Boulevard
Austin, Texas 78757-6897
800/897-3202   Fax 800/397-7633
www.proedinc.com

© 2006 by PRO-ED, Inc.
8700 Shoal Creek Boulevard
Austin, Texas 78757-6897
800/897-3202   Fax 800/397-7633
www.proedinc.com

Library of Congress Cataloging-in-Publication Data

The middle school experience : successful teaching and transition planning
for diverse learners / Jeanne B. Repetto ... [et al.].
       p.   cm.
   Includes bibliographical references.
   ISBN 1-4164-0070-2 (softcover : alk. paper)
   1. Middle school teaching—United States.   2. Children with
disabilities—Education (Middle school)—United States.   I. Repetto, Jeanne B.,
1951–
LB1623.5.M543 2006
373.1102—dc22

                                                    2005022475

Art Director: Jason Crosier
Designer: Nancy McKinney
This book is designed in Birdlegs and Fairfield.

Printed in the United States of America

1   2   3   4   5   6   7   8   9   10   10   09   08   07   06

Contents

Illustrations

Figures

Tables

Meet Jason …
An insightful middle school student who possesses an awareness of himself, his world, and his expectations. As an adolescent with disabilities, his words speak volumes about his dreams and needs.

Jason

I am a good friend and a good thrower.
I wonder what I will get on my birthday, or how my life will turn out and what career I will have.
I hear the joy in voices.
I see the tragedies in people's lives; I also see the struggle in people trying to maintain a life.
I want revenge, the savage sweet, or the joy in success, the vastness of strength. I want popularity and friends.
I am a good friend and a good thrower.

I pretend I am all-powerful. I also pretend I can make a difference.
I feel good and bad. I feel cold and rejected or dark and evil. I feel an understanding of life. I feel offended and enlightened.
I feel good.
I touch into the inner heart of evil and suppress the spirit heart of death. I touch, the inner, S.O.U.L.
I worry about how my life and family will turn out. I worry about how I will live, my life.
I cry when I fail, when I fail in life.
I am a good friend and a good thrower.

I understand how the food chain in life goes, and I understand discipline. I understand despair.
I say that everything has a meaning, and I also say things that are not true.
I dream about what I shall be and what will happen in the future.
I try to make a difference in life.
I hope to make a difference in life, and I hope that I will turn out all right.
I am a good friend and a good thrower.

I have a good heart.

Foreword

At last! For years I have been wishing for a book focusing on the role of the middle school. There were times when I thought I might have to write it myself, but I never really thought I was the one to do it. Thankfully, some eminently qualified colleagues have stepped up and spared me from tackling the project in spite of my lack of true middle school credentials.

I was a junior high guidance counselor in Austin, Texas, in the early 1960s, but at that time the middle school concept had not emerged. I did see youngsters in Grades 7 through 9 every day, though, and that experience had an important influence on my professional perspective. Those seventh to ninth graders of just over 4 decades ago were probably much like the sixth to eighth graders of today—full of themselves, loud, and "squirrelly" one moment and serious the next; immature and childlike, then wise and insightful; exuberant about life one day, then despairing of themselves and others the next. A junior high music teacher once described eighth graders, in particular, as follows: "They don't like themselves or anyone else." That might have been a harsh generalization, but anyone working with these betwixt and between students knows what he meant.

Middle school teachers, for the most part, choose to work with this interesting and challenging age for various reasons. They see these young people as fun to teach and as a group that will never make teaching routine. They also see these students as undergoing a major transition in their lives—from child to adolescent—and enjoy working with these students who have so much to learn about themselves and life.

This book will give middle school teachers of diverse learners and students with disabilities an opportunity to gain new insight about their roles as teachers in the transition process and about these students' needs for the extra guidance and support that makes for better transitions. It is chock full of practical ideas and strategies to use with students and information on transition planning and instruction within the context of the middle school setting. But this book does more than provide useful information: It inspires, it encourages, and it calls the middle school teacher to self-awareness in ways that are not often found in professional books. For that, readers can all be grateful.

So, here it is—the long-awaited book that gives some order and structure to what has been an ill-defined, unmandated transition period in the educational life of diverse learners and students with disabilities. Additionally, encouragement, inspiration, and renewal of spirit are surprise bonuses that make this book truly special.

Gary M. Clark, EdD
Department of Special Education
University of Kansas

Acknowledgments

During the development, writing, and editing phases of our text, we have had the good fortune to work with a rich circle of partners. Drs. Gary Clark and Jim Patton helped us "sow the seeds" for this book, valued our ideas, and offered a constant flow of encouragement to us throughout the process.

We are particularly grateful to Dr. Kathryn Krudwig for sharing her expertise by writing Chapter 5, "Behavioral, Social, and Emotional Growth in Middle School." We believe that readers will find the strategies in this chapter practical and realistic.

We owe a great debt of thanks to the middle school students who were willing and excited to share their self-portraits and words of wisdom. We know our text would not have the student-centered richness without their contributions. We thank Richard Schrule (from Duval County School Board, Florida) and Susan Worthington (formerly with Bradford County School Board, now with Clay County School Board, Florida) for bringing their wonderful students' art to our attention. Both Rich and Susan were instrumental in obtaining students' and parents' authorizations to use the artwork in the text. A special thanks to Jason Schmidt for his insightful poem and accompanying artwork found in the beginning of the book. We also wish to thank J. Lee Miller (from Duval County School Board, Florida) for his sensitive account of a transition experience with a remarkable middle school student.

As we met to work on this project, we built a friendship with Hazel King, a senior clerk at Santa Fe Community College Andrews Center in Starke, Florida. Hazel made sure we had a place to work, answered questions, and offered us encouragement. She was "Mom" to our team of authors and helped us connect the geographic distances that separated us.

We would also like to thank the editors and graphic artists at PRO-ED, who gently guided us through this process. They not only were supportive but also shared our vision for the book.

Finally, we want to thank our families for believing in our work, sharing time, and cheering us on to completion. Our own children are past, present, and future middle school students. Taylor Rose, Emily, Nicole, Douglas, and Nikla, this book is for you and the countless middle school students who have touched our lives.

User Guide

Welcome to *The Middle School Experience: Successful Teaching and Transition Planning for Diverse Learners*. When you reflect back on the years you spent in middle school, you may remember a time that was particularly exciting because you were beginning to flex your first muscles of independence. On the other hand, perhaps the middle school years were painful or confusing and, looking back, you feel that you merely survived middle school. In reality, most of us probably experienced both ends of this emotional spectrum in middle or junior high school.

Whatever you experienced, we know you will agree that middle school is a time of change and tremendous growth. We want middle school students to embrace these changes, learn, and thrive during their middle school years. We extend this same desire to the professionals who teach middle school students. When teachers approach their students with expertise, enthusiasm, understanding, and commitment, both teachers and students are more likely to flourish and grow.

The purpose of our book is to support prospective or current middle school teachers so they will succeed as they work with middle school students who have diverse learning needs, especially students with disabilities. To achieve this purpose, professionals need tools and strategies that will help them build a framework geared for success. We have developed the middle school experience, or MidEx, model as an example of how professionals can integrate transition planning with age-appropriate instruction and emotional support to foster self-determination in order to maximize success for students with disabilities as they progress into high school and plan for adult life. The MidEx model serves a two-fold function: (a) to present information and resources to current and prospective professionals and (b) to demonstrate a model of how teachers and other professionals can present information and resources to middle school students.

Each chapter in this book incorporates the information from the MidEx model and offers strategies, grounded in universal design, for classroom implementation of the information presented. In Chapter 1, we provide an overview of the MidEx model and a summary of each of its components. Subsequent chapters make specific references to the MidEx model or offer information on the MidEx components. As you progress through the book, you will develop, enhance, and refine your knowledge, skills, and dispositions about each element of the MidEx model.

We developed the information in our book to facilitate growth for professionals who interact with middle school students. Current and future special education teachers, general educators, administrators, related service personnel, and parents will find information about middle schools and the diverse populations of students who attend them. Because of the wide variety of individuals involved in the transition process of individuals with disabilities, we have included information that will inform a wide circle of stakeholders.

Features

As we developed the book, we were committed to a student-centered focus. The MidEx model, introduced in Chapter 1, exemplifies this commitment; students form the core of the model, and all other components radiate from this center. The *student portraits* throughout the book serve as a reminder of the unique and remarkable characteristics of each and every middle school student. Middle level students with and without disabilities were asked to draw self-portraits for this book. Their art provides a glance into the self-perceptions of young adolescents. We found these pictures to be very revealing in their portrayals of self, socialization, and connection to the world. In addition, we begin each chapter with *quotations* from students and some of the stakeholders in their lives. We believe the quotations provide an additional glance into the characteristics of young adolescents as they relate to their world. We interviewed middle school students, their teachers, parents, and related service personnel to obtain these insights.

Following the quotations, each chapter features a set of *learning objectives* that will assist you in targeting the chapter's critical information. Every chapter includes ideas and techniques that align with current practices and descriptions of teacher characteristics that are the bases for the MidEx model. Furthermore, we have designed this information with implementation in mind because we believe that practical ideas and suggestions that are immediately useful to professionals are the most beneficial. To meet these objectives, each chapter includes the following:

- Descriptions of research-based practices

- Action planning to incorporate transition practices

- Resources for practices

- Strategies for effective inclusion

- Strategies for developmentally appropriate instruction

Activities throughout the book are designed to help you think about an idea based on your own experiences, practice a skill or strategy, or think critically about a particular topic. Professors may elect to use these activities as assignments or in-class activities. College students using this text to meet class requirements may find these activities helpful to gain competencies in class concepts. If you are reading this book on your own, the book's activities are designed to help you think about the information that is presented in the text. You may wish to jot notes directly in your book or in a separate notebook you use to record your thoughts about teaching middle school.

Several chapters have selections called "Middle School Tips." You may find these tips helpful as you work with middle school students, now or in the future. All of the tips are based on research-based practices, and they exemplify one or more MidEx components.

A vital component of the MidEx model is establishing your professional mission. At the end of the first chapter, you will write your mission statement as a middle school professional. In your mission statement, you will explain your role and purpose in educating middle school students. You might think of this statement as the answer to this question: *"Why do I get out of bed each morning?"* After reading each subsequent chapter, you will have the opportunity to revisit your mission statement and record your thoughts. The information from each chapter will help you reflect on any mission statement revisions, refinements, or enhancements. When you have finished the book, you will have a written record of your professional reflection and growth, along with your ideas for present and future implementation and expansion of your mission.

Our book is designed to explain the MidEx model in the context of areas you must address in a middle school setting. Each of the eight chapters has information about best practices and teacher characteristics that will help you provide support to middle school students and their families. We have summarized the content of each chapter to help you plan your learning experience.

@ **Chapter 1: Understanding Middle Schools.** This chapter features an overview of the foundations of middle level education and special education. We discuss characteristics of good middle level teachers and provide an overview of educational practices. We introduce and explain the MidEx model. The last section of this chapter introduces readers to an exercise in teacher reflection.

@ **Chapter 2: Understanding Middle School Students.** Chapter 2 addresses early adolescents' physical, intellectual, social, and emotional development. To address all of the unique needs of adolescents, we introduce middle school practices that include flexible structures, advisory support, and exploratory curricula, along with the collaborative partnerships. We discuss universal design and inclusive learning communities within middle school settings.

@ **Chapter 3: Transition and Career Development in Middle School.** In this chapter, readers will learn how to integrate career education and transition into middle schools. We describe components of effective transition programs, along with strategies to incorporate these practices. Case studies and real-life situations illustrate application of the practices.

@ **Chapter 4: Middle School Curriculum.** We introduce an array of curricula and the influences that define the curricular foundations and frameworks. We then explain how to develop a comprehensive transition-supported curriculum using the acronym I-CONDUIT. Finally, we demonstrate how professionals can digest the information, apply it to classrooms, and reflect on effectiveness.

@ **Chapter 5: Behavioral, Social, and Emotional Growth in Middle School.** Dr. Kathryn Krudwig, the author of this chapter, describes the social–developmental tasks of middle school learners. She explains strategies for organizing the physical arrangement of classrooms and for developing rules and routines. In this chapter, readers will learn about the myth of the magic bullet, and will read about effective strategies to support all students, including those who cope with trauma and family challenges. Krudwig offers ideas for enlisting families as partners in the educational process of middle school learners.

@ **Chapter 6: Transition Assessment.** This chapter highlights the Individuals with Disabilities Education Act's (IDEA's) requirements for assessment in terms of transition planning. A model for transition assessment practices is presented that focuses on collecting assessment data on the student and potential environments; emphasis is placed on using this data to make the best match for the student in terms of academic course placements, vocational experiences, and postschool goals.

@ **Chapter 7: Individualized Education Programs (IEPs) and Transition Planning.** Students with disabilities are guaranteed individualized services and accommodations under IDEA and Section 504 of the Rehabilitation Act of 1973. First, we review the requirements for developing an IEP according to IDEA. We also provide an overview of Section 504, along with the requirements for developing a 504 Plan. Finally, we include resources for understanding specific accommodations and assistive technology services.

@ **Chapter 8: Progressive Reflection.** In this final chapter, we discuss leadership and the need for reflection in education. We offer educators methods to be purposeful and reflective.

@ **Appendix A: Internet Resources.** This list of available resources compiled by Jeanne Repetto, Meridith Taylor, and Michael Palmer covers a variety of topics related to middle level education for diverse learners.

Suggested Uses of This Text

This text is designed as a resource tool for current or prospective middle school teachers who work with diverse learners in special or general education. The information in this text will be particularly useful to those teachers who are novice teachers, out-of-field teachers, or teachers who have changed to a middle school setting.

The opportunities for reflection incorporated within each chapter provide the practicing middle school teacher a tool for personal and professional reflection on the use of research-based best practices at the middle school level for students with disabilities. This book is intended to support teachers seeking to validate and extend their skills in working with inclusive and diverse middle school students, including those with disabilities. The text is appropriate for use by school districts with alternative certification courses, workshops, and in-service education for professionals who work with middle school students.

As teacher educators, we believe that undergraduate and graduate college faculty and students in education will discover that this book is a valuable text for courses that address transition, middle school teaching, or secondary education methods. The strategies, methods, and curricular frameworks are designed for the unique characteristics of middle school learners and the teachers who teach them. The text also provides information that may be used by school districts for alternative certification courses, workshops, and in-services for professionals who work with middle school students.

CHAPTER 1

Understanding Middle Schools

Why do you think we have middle school?

"To get you prepared for high school."

"To learn higher stuff than elementary."

Think of friends your age. How would you describe a typical middle school student?

"Energetic!"

"Out of hand!"

"Hyper"

"Lots of them at school act like they're all that and they think they're all grown up and do what they want to."

How would you describe the ideal middle school teacher?

"They listen to their students and challenge them."

"Nice, doesn't give that much work, and lets the class have parties."

"Nice and doesn't yell a lot."

"Friendly, no homework, gives parties, makes learning fun, and knows how to control the class."

Learning Objectives

1. To describe the historical and legal foundations of middle school education for diverse learners.

2. To identify the practices and teacher characteristics that shape effective middle school education.

3. To explain the components of the middle school experience (MidEx) model that will be presented throughout this textbook.

4. To identify methods to nurture your own professional growth.

Introduction

When you think about students in middle school, what labels have you heard to describe the group of students who are between 10 and 14 years of age—"hormones in sneakers," "middle school monsters," "tweeners"? As these stereotypes are uttered by parents, teachers, or other adults with some degree of strong emotion, these words may be accompanied with heavy sighs, rolled eyes, or a wry chuckle. Early adolescents may be considered as both children and young adults, and it is this mixed perception that is at the very core of how these students are viewed by society and how they view themselves. Historically, early adolescence has been marked by confusing, and sometimes dramatic, physical, emotional, and academic changes.

> For most 10- to 14-year olds, during the last century and a half the early adolescent years have posed basically the same set of problems in the areas of growth and development. However, since the mid-1970s the early adolescent experience has become more complex, and critical life issues have catapulted into the earlier stages. The media-influenced images of fashion, self-fulfillment, and sensual experiences coupled with the frightening warnings about smoking, drinking, sex, and even decibel levels and an evaporating ozone layer permeate their real and imagined view of the world. (Simpson, 1999, p. 5)

Who Is the Middle School Student?

Adolescence is marked by growth and development that is more rapid than at any other stage of life except infancy. Physical and emotional changes accompany the ability to have sexual relationships and the potential for reproduction (Jackson & Davis, 2000). Stevenson (1998) described early adolescence as a time filled with many changes that occur at distinctive times through a common sequence. Family, neighborhood, and racial–ethnic influences that affect adolescence appear to extend throughout life.

Given the challenges of adolescence, one wonders what leads educators to a career in middle school. The answer lies in a big-picture view of the middle school student. Early adolescence is an exciting time of great discovery. Students begin to discover their identities, passions, and life directions. Middle school students gain skills that allow them to have a greater capacity for complex thinking and to participate in a wider expanse of activities (Jackson & Davis, 2000). These students are able to "move into more formal operations that are marked by the move to higher-order, multiplicity functions" (Castle & Castle, 1999, p. 17). Early adolescents are curious, have a strong willingness to learn useful information, and have abilities to project thought into the future. They have also begun to understand the concept of metacognition, or the ability to learn about how they learn (Ross & Olsen, 1995). Chapter 2 explains more about what makes middle school students "tick."

What Is the Purpose of Middle Schools?

The overall purpose of middle level education is to provide young adolescents with a developmentally appropriate curriculum in a safe environment that supports their exploration of self in relationship to the larger world (Dickinson, 2001). According to Jackson and Davis (2000), the goal is to educate students in an environment that promotes critical thinking, industrious work, contributions to the community, and caring about oneself and others; the "whole child" who is taught in this way will mature into a contributing adult within society. Their definition of the "whole child" includes those students with disabilities and those for whom English is their second language. In addition, the Carnegie Council on Adolescent Development (1989) noted that the person leaving middle school should be a reflective and lifelong learner, good citizen, caring and ethical person, and healthy individual.

To foster this type of middle school graduate, middle level education must be developmentally responsive, academically excellent, and socially equitable (Lipsitz, Mizell, Jackson, & Austin, 1997). In *Turning Points 2000: Educating Adolescents in the 21st Century,* Jackson and Davis (2000) integrate research and practice to offer the following competencies for effective middle level schools:

1. Teach a curriculum grounded in rigorous, public academic standards for what students should know and be able to do, relevant to the concerns of adolescents and based on how students learn best.

2. Use instructional methods that prepare all students to achieve high standards and become lifelong learners.

3. Staff middle grade schools with teachers who are expert at teaching young adolescents, and engage teachers in ongoing targeted professional development opportunities.

4. Organize relationships for learning to create a climate of intellectual development and a caring community of shared educational purpose.

5. Govern democratically, through direct or representative participation by all school staff members, the adults who know the students best.

6. Provide a safe and healthy school environment as part of improving academic performance and developing caring, ethical citizens.

7. Involve parents and communities in supporting student learning and healthy development. (pp. 23–24)

How Did Middle Schools Evolve?

The unique needs of the diverse population of early adolescents have shaped the rich history of middle schools. This section offers an overview of the changes in middle school education to help you understand the unique developmental and educational needs of early adolescents.

Think back in your family's history. Do you know of a grandparent, great-grandparent, or other elderly person who completed the sixth, seventh, or eighth grade and then left school? If you know of people with this history, you may find that their educational paths were typical for adolescents in their age group. During the last part of the 19th century and early part of the 20th century, schools were organized to include an 8-year elementary and 4-year high school. This format allowed most students to receive an elementary education and an elite number of students to attain the preparation needed for college (H. A. Allen, 1992).

Do you know family members who attended a junior high school? Junior high schools emerged, in part, from the work the National Education Association's Committee of Ten, a group of university presidents who proposed recommendations in the 1890s. This Committee, which worked with an elementary school-focused Committee of Fifteen, believed that college entrance requirements needed uniformity and that 18, the average age of students entering college in the 1890s, was too high. In an effort to lower this age for students going to college and allow for the amount of information needed for college admission, the committee suggested that the seventh- and eighth-grade years could be used to prepare students for college (Dickinson, 2001). Although the effort was unsuccessful, the attempt at college preparation for 12- and 13-year-olds ultimately contributed to the development of the junior high school (Wiles & Bondi, 2001). School reform during the early 20th century centered on defining the functions and relationships of elementary schools and high schools (Manning, 2000). General dissatisfaction with the 8-year elementary and 4-year high school format influenced professionals as they recommended the development of junior high schools (George & Alexander, 1993).

The influx of immigrants in the late 19th and early 20th centuries was also a key factor in the structure of junior high schools. Often, immigrant children became disengaged and dropped out of school to join their parents as laborers in factories. Junior high schools were viewed as a means to reduce the growing numbers of immigrant students in elementary schools, to provide job preparation to these students, and to foster their assimilation into American society (Dickinson, 2001; Powell, Farrar, & Cohen, 1985). Therefore, to meet the needs of immigrant students and lower the age of students entering college, a differentiated curriculum was offered in junior high schools that included both college and vocational preparation.

Advocates for school reform from the National Education Association and other professional organizations charged schools to address the needs of early adolescents. The first junior high schools that educated students in Grades 7 through 9 were established in Columbus, Ohio, in 1909 (Manning, 2000). Many junior high schools at the turn of the century introduced a course of study, including subjects such as natural history, physics, foreign languages, and advanced mathematics, that was more comprehensive than when those grades were in elementary school (H. A. Allen, 1992).

Junior high schools that educated adolescents in Grades 7 through 9 were predominant until the 1960s. Because of the efforts described previously, students who attended junior high schools were prepared to enter the job market or a university. In light of these seemingly appropriate outcomes, why did the junior high school model fade from U.S. schools? According to Manning (2000), junior high schools failed to address "the unique social, personal, and academic needs of young adolescents" (p. 192). Middle schools emerged as an outgrowth of the junior high school model; the first middle school was established by the Bay City, Michigan school system in 1950 (Manning, 2000).

McEwin, Dickinson, and Jenkins (1996) list three vital components that shaped the development of middle schools and should be continued and expanded in future middle school endeavors. These include (a) knowledge about uniqueness, requirements, and interests of young adolescents; (b) knowledge about responsive curriculum and instruction; and (c) specialized middle school professional personnel preparation. Wiles and Bondi (2001) assert that the present-day middle school may be rooted in the work of John Dewey. In contrast to the traditional progression through a rigid and content-based curriculum, Dewey used progressive teaching methods in his Laboratory School at the University of Chicago between 1894 and 1904. "Over time, what emerged in the curriculum of the school was a kind of 'action learning' format where students investigated, reflected, and developed generalizations that would guide future decision making" (Wiles & Bondi, 2001, p. 7). Today's middle schools may include differentiated and exploratory curricula, interdisciplinary team organization, integrated themes, individualized instruction, and technology (George, 2001; Wiles & Bondi, 2001).

While reading this brief summary, you probably realized that the evolution of middle schools has been filled with changes and diverse philosophies. If you would like to read more about middle school history, *The New American Middle School* (Wiles & Bondi, 2001) is one of several books that offer an excellent historical perspective. (You will learn more details about the development of curriculum in Chapter 4 of this book.)

In Activity 1.1 you are encouraged to consider your own middle school experience. It can be useful to think about how your teaching can benefit from your personal experience in school.

What Makes Middle Schools Work?

What variables need to be present to build an effective middle school? To answer this question, you need to read about effective practices in middle schools and special education and about effective teacher characteristics, all of which we discuss in this chapter. Envisioning the total learning environment of a school, the National Middle School Association (NMSA) wrote a position statement in 2001 titled, *This We Believe … And Now We Must Act* (Erb, 2001). In this mission statement, NMSA outlined the following characteristics of effective middle schools:

1. Curriculum that is challenging, integrative, and exploratory
2. Assessment and evaluation that promote learning
3. Varied teaching and learning approaches
4. Flexible organizational structures
5. An adult advocate for every student
6. Comprehensive guidelines and support services
7. A shared vision
8. High expectations for all
9. Positive school climate
10. Educators committed to young adolescents
11. Programs and policies that foster health, wellness, and safety
12. Family and community partnerships (p. 3)

Through their position statement, the NMSA offers four curriculum elements needed to implement the effective characteristics. These elements are (a) milieu (i.e., standards, assessments, classroom placement, financial support, and community expectations), (b) subject matter, (c) student (both prior and learned knowledge), and (d) teacher. Perhaps these effective characteristics can be further grounded in attributes of middle school that include meeting the instructional needs of 10- to 14-year-olds, using proven techniques (e.g., advisor–advisee and interdisciplinary teaming or organization), building on skills learned in elementary school, and providing opportunities to explore unique abilities (Manning & Bucher, 2001).

Do you remember when you made the shift from middle school to high school student? What supports did you have in place as you made the shift? Another major component of an effective middle school is offering a transition program to students as they move from middle school to high school (Lancaster & Gildroy, 1999; J. Smith, 1997). Middle school transition programs have a positive effect on high school retention and experiences.

J. Smith (1997) used the base-year and first- and second-year follow-up data from the National Education Longitudinal Survey (NELS) to study 7,924 students from 702 middle schools across the United States. Of these students 1,980 had no transition programs available to them, 1,982 were involved in a partial program, and 3,962 participated in a full transition program. Transition programs work with students, parents, and school staff to assist students in moving from eighth grade to high school. Smith found that the most prevalent transition practice was to have high school counselors meet with eighth graders (83% of full and 74% of partial programs reported this practice). Other practices included eighth graders attending a high school class, high school students presenting information to eighth graders, parents visiting high school, parents visiting high school fall orientation, middle school and high school teachers meeting, middle school and high school administrators meeting, and middle school and high school counselors meeting. The impact of these activities on high school success was found to be positive, with higher retention rates and better performance indicated by students who had a full transition program available to them in middle school. Smith's work further expands the purpose of middle level education to include assisting students with their transition to high school and perhaps impacting their success in high school.

What Makes Special Education Work?

Middle school students with disabilities have the same characteristics and needs as their peers without disabilities. They are experiencing the same growth spurts, they have curiosity, and they are excited about exploring many different directions in learning. These students have the same need for peer acceptance and interaction. In short, middle school students want to fit in with other middle school students. Sadly, until the mid-1970s, many of these students did not have opportunities to explore options for adulthood, attend school with their peers, or receive special education services (D. D. Smith, 2004).

In a landmark effort to improve the lives of students with disabilities, Congress passed Public Law (P.L.) 94-142, the Education for All Handicapped Children Act, in 1975. This law set forth requirements to ensure that students with disabilities would receive appropriate services. This act was reauthorized in 1990 as the Individuals with Disabilities Education Act (IDEA), in 1997 as the IDEA Amendments, and in 2004 as the IDEA Improvement Act (IDEA 2004). The IDEA Amendments of 1997 and IDEA 2004 emphasize access to the general curriculum for students with disabilities, including participation in local and statewide assessments. Since 1990 IDEA has also mandated the provision of transition services to students with disabilities.

Under IDEA each student with a disability who qualifies for special education must have an Individualized Education Program (IEP). The IEP serves as a blueprint for an educational program that is designed to meet the unique needs of each student with disabilities. If a student has an IEP, his or her IEP is reviewed annually to determine progress on the student's goals. Middle school teachers and related personnel, along with students and parents, are responsible for developing students' IEPs and implementing the annual goals and objectives written on IEPs.

IDEA 2004 requires IEP teams to address transition needs of students with disabilities by age 16 and update the IEP annually. The IEP must include measurable postsecondary goals and the transition services (including the course of study) that a student needs to meet those goals. IDEA 2004 also mandates that IEPs reflect what each student's transition needs, preferences, and interests are in the areas of instruction, community experiences, employment, and other postsecondary goals. IEP goals for each student are developed based not only on how the student is performing but also on the student's preferences and interests (G. M. Clark, 1998). A detailed discussion of IEPs and transition services is presented in Chapters 3 and 7.

For students with disabilities to identify postsecondary goals by age 16 and the courses they will need to meet these goals, career exploration, transition assessment, and transition planning must take place in middle school. Therefore, as special education is discussed in this text, it will include the provision of transition planning and services. Best practices in special education are compatible and at times similar to the components of effective middle level education. One difference might be the heavy emphasis in special education on individual planning, diagnosis, and treatment of problems unique to one student. However, with the onset of inclusive programs supporting the education of students with disabilities in regular school programs comes a push for universally designed curriculum adaptations that will assist all students.

Researchers in the field of special education have identified best practices to include co-teaching and collaboration among professionals, individualized programming for students, student-centered curriculum, partnerships with families, curriculum that is thematic and infuses content learning throughout classes, instructional strategies, directive learning, outcome-orientated curriculum, interagency collaboration, and instruction in self-determination (Mastropieri & Scruggs, 2000; Mercer & Mercer, 2001; Sitlington, Clark, & Kolstoe, 2000). Specific strategies for assisting students with disabilities to learn can be broken into five main categories: (a) strategies intervention models (e.g. learning strategies, advanced organizers), (b) subject strategies (e.g., handwriting, spelling, math, reading), (c) behavior strategies (e.g., goal setting, behavior management, class environment), (d) content enhancement (e.g., concept teaching routine, selecting "considerate" textbooks), and (e) transition planning (i.e., transition assessment, community-based experiences, curriculum). Combining best practices with specific strategies will enhance the learning of students with disabilities, and the application of universal design will benefit all students. In-depth information about these practices is provided in Chapters 4, 5, and 6.

Activity 1.2 gives you the opportunity to list examples of teaching practices you think are effective for students in middle school and special education. You will add to this list in Activity 1.3.

Activity 1.2 Effective Teaching Practices

At this point, you probably have several ideas about effective teaching practices for students in middle school and students in special education. Using information identified in the literature and your own experiences, write some examples of good teaching practices.

Identified from Literature	Identified from Experience

Characteristics of Effective Middle Level Educators

I definitely believe middle level teacher preparation should be different from elementary or secondary. I spent time in elementary preparation courses and learned only through experience about teaching middle school students. After 10 years of experience, I hunger for methods courses that are specifically for middle school teachers. I have had to try to learn on my own or from other teachers. (Scales & McEwin, 1994, p. 470)

This sentiment expressed by a middle school teacher is validated in a study conducted by the Southern Regional Education Board (2000). During the spring of 2000, a survey was sent to 1,100 middle school teachers working in 28 schools throughout 13 states. Of the teachers surveyed, 30% held undergraduate degrees in content areas and 43% were elementary education majors. In addition, 80% of the teachers reported having little or no education in assisting low-performing students master content knowledge. Although this survey did not specifically target middle school teachers working with students with disabilities, it points to the need for educational materials and courses specifically designed for middle school teachers working with diverse student populations.

Throughout the middle school literature, an underlying message is that middle school students have unique needs that present educators with different challenges than elementary or high school students (Jackson & Davis, 2000; NMSA, 1995). These needs require educators to have a knowledge base in young adolescents' social, physical, and emotional requirements, along with methods to meet these needs in an educational setting. Being a middle school teacher requires the ability to negotiate peace treaties, calm a broken heart, engage an audience, inspire the lost, laugh at life, applaud success, and understand inner conflict (Wormeli, 2001). The teacher takes on these roles throughout the day while teaching content classes, collaborating with colleagues, communicating with parents, walking in the halls, riding a bus during a field trip, attending a school basketball game, and eating lunch. Middle level students are intense, needy, conflicted, inspired, and wonderful. These students are in the midst of one of life's major growth curves. As a teacher, there is no better reward than saying or doing just the right thing at the right moment that causes a middle school student's face to light up with understanding (e.g., "Aha! I get it!"). The following is one teacher's reflection about his experiences teaching a seventh- and eighth-grade class for varying exceptionalities at Highlands Middle School in Jacksonville, Florida (Duval County Schools).

Facing the challenge of teaching middle school students day after day takes the convergence of many skills and talents. Arth, Lounsbury, McEwin, and Swain (1995) developed a set of characteristics that defines an excellent middle level teacher. The list was developed based on the authors' collective knowledge, a literature review, and input from practitioners. Once developed, this information was validated by 48 middle level teachers and 24 principals across the country. Table 1.1 details the characteristics along with rankings given by the middle level teachers and principals. It is encouraging that among the top characteristics for both teachers and principals was the ability to be sensitive to individual differences.

Facilitators of Their Futures

by J. Lee Miller

All too often I believe that we, as teachers, can become so overwhelmed by the toils and challenges of our jobs that we become desensitized to the positive experiences that present themselves during our school day. As a fifth year teacher, I am keenly aware that I have to spend much of my time in pursuits other than teaching, and I believe this can be a disheartening reality for all of us. I believe that we all enter this field with the steadfast desire to make a difference in each of the lives that we touch, yet at times our burden veils us from reaping the rewards, often basic and emotional, we are sorely due. There is that occasional moment, however, that unexpectedly broadsides us and makes us ever aware that we, in fact, count. This moment in the life of a student whom we touch can serve to stimulate and revitalize each of us as teachers and make us aware once again of the reasons we embarked on this education journey to begin with. I had one such experience recently, and it is my hope that it can serve as a small, yet poignant, reminder to other teachers that their efforts can lead to changes in the students to which we are entrusted and that the work we do is not in vain.

"Mary" arrived in my class as a student who was so disinterested in school that she could barely keep her eyelids from fluttering in her often-pained attempts to stay alert. She was a student who, sadly, chose to pass her days in the classroom asleep rather than being an alive, participating member of our intimate education community. Every academic topic we broached in the classroom was met with a disinterested shrug of her shoulders and rarely did it seem that the class as a group could engage her enough to keep her from endless napping. I was often frustrated, for I felt that I simply was not reaching her, and I was concerned because it became increasingly easy to not worry about her since she did not present herself as a consistent behavior problem. It seemed as though Mary, at times, simply was not there, and I found myself a culprit in the denial of her presence. Mary, however, was never absent from school. Though other students would be habitually not present, through illness or otherwise, Mary, in her disinterested slumber never missed a day of school. I found this odd.

I was taking a course in which the focus was on transition, and one requirement was that we choose a particular student with whom we would administer different assessments that would culminate in a true, quality Transition Individualized Education Program (Transition IEP) that would focus wholly and completely on this student's needs and interests. For the longest time I struggled with the decision of with whom I could work, and it just did not seem that any particular student popped into mind as one I felt I could really reach. Then one day, things changed, as it occurred to me that Mary would be the perfect candidate. I figured that if there was ever any one student who was in need of some interested involvement by a significant individual in their life it was, indeed, Mary.

(continues)

I approached Mary one uneventful morning and asked her if she might be willing to talk to me about a certain matter. She looked at me in a somewhat alarmed manner, and I quickly surmised from her body language and averted gaze that she figured she was in some sort of trouble. I realized at this moment that even as I was innocently wanting to just speak to her that she assumed that I was taking some sort of punitive stance, and it bothered me. I wondered to myself if every time I had ever addressed her it had been in a corrective sense. I was experiencing a mix of emotions at the moment that I certainly had not expected.

I explained to Mary, in my best sincere, yet disarming, tone that I was interested in her and in her future, and that I wished to work with her in order to help her realize some of her goals. She shot a glance at me that spoke volumes, one that *screamed,* "You *must* be crazy." As I stumbled through my impromptu speech I realized that I had never really ever talked to this student at all, and she had every right to look upon me and my intent as suspect. I endeavored to win her graces, and it was certainly no small feat. I realized that Rome was not built in one day, so I simply left it at that, and told her I was excited about working with her on her Individualized Education Program for the year and that I wanted her to think for a couple of weeks about what was important in her life and what it was that she wanted to do as she matured into adulthood. She nodded weakly, and I could tell by her gestures that she thought that I might just be a little "off." I will never forget, however, that a slight, impish grin crossed her lips that said, softly, "Wow, is this man for *real*?? Does he really care about me?" That little smile was enough for me then.

I waited a couple of weeks before approaching Mary again, and when I did I was very direct and asked her if she might want to meet with me in my planning period to talk some about her life, her dreams, and her perception of where she was heading. I was completely blown away by her enthusiastic "Yes!" and before I knew it she was speaking very quickly and assertively (as I had never before heard from her) as she said, "I've been thinking about what you have said and I have some ideas about my IEP … When can we work on it? I think I might want to be a veterinarian when I get older." Taken aback by her confidence I muttered, weakly, "Great … soon!" Oh geez, what had I gotten myself involved with now? I smiled to myself as I realized that she was probably going to keep me on my toes from now on, which was a wonderful thing indeed!

In the successive weeks, Mary and I became much closer and I was truly reaping the benefits of our collaborative efforts. Mary began turning in assignments, completed, and actually stayed awake for my lessons. This was monumental. She would participate, and each day she would be one of the first students to greet me at my door. In our meetings she would tell me more about herself, and as our rapport grew deeper, I found myself glad that I had gotten to know her as a person. I was able to see her not as a student with little hope, but rather an individual with hopes and dreams who could accomplish much in this world.

Recently, I spoke with Mary and asked her if there was an animal hospital close to where she lives, since she had expressed an interest in work with animals. She immediately said there was one right down the street. I told Mary that perhaps she could get the phone number and together we could call them to see if they might be willing to speak with her regarding the possibility of summer help. She told me she would do it, and I thought nothing of it for a few days. However, the next week I was in for a real surprise.

On a Wednesday morning Mary came into my class before all of the other students, and I was amazed. Never before had I seen her in a dress, and she presented herself as a young adult who no longer looked quite so childlike. I asked her what the occasion was because I had never seen her look so well groomed and together. She said, completely unexpectedly, "Thanks to you I have a job interview. I went to the animal hospital myself and they told me that someone had just quit and they needed some help. I told them I would be available over the summer and they told me that I could probably work there and that I should come in for an interview." Now what could I possibly say to all of *that?* I was flabbergasted and elated for her. Mary said then, in a moment I will never forget, "I want to give you half of my first paycheck for helping me do this. Thank you." I was already paid in more ways than she would ever know.

I have learned from this experience that we, as teachers, are invaluable and indispensable in our students' lives. Perhaps it is that we are often unaware of the impact we are having on a daily basis, but the seeds we are sowing grow deep within them. We can serve as an inspiration for our students and can help them achieve greatness in their own, individual ways. What we may construe as a passing comment we make to a student in praise of them may serve as a wellspring and impetus for the changing and blossoming of their lives. We must be ever mindful of the impact we make to each and every one of them in every critical, precious moment we spend together. Our students look to us as guides for their dreams … we *are* the facilitators of their futures. (J. L. Miller, 2003, pp. 5–6)

This list of middle level teacher characteristics can be expanded to include having a sense of humor, being flexible, actively listening to and caring for students, placing students in the center of the learning process, and sharing one's love of learning (Knowles & Brown, 2000). Do you have some ideas about desirable characteristics? Does reviewing this list of needed skills and characteristics make the challenge of being a middle level educator seem within your reach?

Table 1.1
Teachers' and Principals' Rankings of Effective
Middle Level Teacher Characteristics

Characteristic	Ranking	
	Teachers	Principals
Establishes and maintains a disciplined learning environment that is safe and respects the dignity of young adolescents.	1st	7th
Is sensitive to the individual differences, cultural backgrounds, and exceptionalities of young adolescents, treats them with respect, and celebrates their special nature.	2nd	1st
Recognizes that major goals of middle level education include the development of human values, respect for self, and positive attitudes toward learning.	3rd	9th
Makes decisions about teaching based on a thorough understanding of the physical, social, intellectual, and emotional development of young adolescents.	4th	2nd
Understands and welcomes the role of advocate, adult role model, and advisor.	5th	6th
Is dedicated to improving the welfare and education of young adolescents.	6th	8th
Utilizes a wide variety of developmentally appropriate instructional strategies.	7th	5th
Ensures that all young adolescents will succeed in learning.	8th	4th
Is self-confident and personally secure—can take student challenges while teaching.	9th	3rd
Works collaboratively and professionally to initiate needed changes.	10th	10th
Acquires, creates, and utilizes a wide variety of resources to improve the learning experiences of young adolescents.	11th	11th
Is committed to integrating curriculum.	12th*	16th
Seeks out positive and constructive relationships and communications with young adolescents in a variety of environments.	12th*	12th
Uses varied evaluation techniques that both teach and assess the broad goals of middle level education and provide for student self-evaluation.	14th	13th*
Works closely with families to form partnerships to help young adolescents be successful at school.	15th	13th*
Has a broad, interdisciplinary knowledge of the subjects in the middle level curriculum and depth of content in one or more areas.	16th	15th

*Indicates tied rankings

Note. Adapted from *Middle Level Teachers: Portraits of Excellence* (p. 17), by A. Arth, J. Lounsbury, C. K. McEwin, and J. Swain, 1995, Westerville, OH: National Middle School Association and National Association of Secondary School Principals. Adapted with permission.

Characteristics of Effective Special Educators

Effective middle school, special education, and transition teachers employ practices that are germane across fields (Englert, Tarrant, & Mariage, 1992; Repetto & Webb, 1999; Reynolds, 1990). These practices require competencies in (a) classroom management; (b) assessment and instruction; (c) scholarship; (d) lifelong learning; (e) personal fitness; (f) caring about students, subject, and work; (g) collaboration; (h) legal and ethical principles; and (i) educational theories and systems (Lessen & Frankiewicz, 1992; Ornstein, 1990; Repetto, 1995; Reynolds, 1990). Each discipline requires additional competencies, such as the ability to develop individualized programs in special education, knowledge of content information in general education, and use of assessment data for transition planning. For example, deFur and Taymans (1995) validated a set of competencies needed by personnel in vocational rehabilitation, vocational education, and special education to be successful in assisting students with their transition from school to life after school. Their list includes competencies in (a) consultation/communication, (b) leadership, (c) individualized planning, (d) vocational assessment, (e) job development, (f) direct services, and (g) program evaluation. The Council for Exceptional Children (2002) has set standards for teacher licensure and preparation for beginning teachers in all grade levels of special education and for transition specialists. They include competencies related to having knowledge of (a) learner characteristics, (b) career and vocational assessment, (c) communication and collaboration, (d) managing student behaviors, (e) instructional content and practice, and (f) learning environment. These skills are not unique to any one discipline but rather can be shared to enhance curriculum through collaboration among all professionals.

Integration of Teaching Practices and Characteristics

After reading our descriptions of effective teaching practices and characteristics of competent educators, you may want to ask yourself several questions: How can I apply this information to shape my teaching career? How can I integrate this information into my current set of teaching skills to better educate my students? Will the integration of this information lead to a higher level of satisfaction as a middle school teacher? How do other teachers integrate this information? The remainder of this chapter offers (a) examples of integration of teaching practices and characteristics found in published case studies, (b) a model for combining middle school and special education, and (c) guides to assist you as you incorporate these practices and characteristics into your teaching.

Real Teachers with Real Students

You may be wondering how teachers actually blend and apply information about effective practices and teacher characteristics. A review of related literature about classroom and inclusion practices in middle school education revealed an interesting array of both teaching practices and characteristics (Arth et al., 1995; Kilgore, Griffin, Sindelar, & Webb, 2002). In classrooms with integrated teaching practices and characteristics, teachers encouraged students to do the following:

- Develop and post a set of beliefs about their school experiences in their classroom

- Engage in learning through inquiry and research

- Maintain a portfolio of their personal goals, schedule, and work

- Cover classroom walls with their work and photos of important events

- Work in cooperative groups to test one of their own science hypotheses

Also, teachers of these classrooms commonly do the following:

- Greet, recognize during class, and say goodbye to students using the students' names and add appropriate personal comments

- Perform magic tricks, with the assistance of student helpers to introduce science lessons

- Work together to plan and teach the curriculum to a student team of multiple ages (Grades 6–8)

- Laugh with students and have fun while teaching a lesson

- Provide one-on-one feedback to students regarding assignments

- Give in-service to each other to learn about varied areas of expertise

- Increase their repertoire of teaching strategies

- Share their failures and successes during team meetings in order to make a better learning environment

Activity 1.3 gives you the opportunity to revisit the list you created in Activity 1.2. For Activity 1.3, change or add any effective teaching practices or characteristics that came to mind as you read the text.

Activity 1.3 Your Ideas

You have probably thought about or implemented effective teaching practices. Add your ideas about practices and teaching characteristics to the list in Activity 1.2.

The MidEx Model: Components of the Effective Middle School Experience Model for Diverse Learners

Creating opportunities for students with disabilities to participate in a full range of middle school experiences is a challenge that requires teachers to draw upon their knowledge about effective practices and teacher characteristics. With a strong knowledge base, an assortment of tools and strategies, and an appreciation of the uniqueness of this age group, middle school teachers can have an exciting and renewing experience. Rather than merely surviving the middle school teaching experience, teachers will thrive and grow.

The MidEx model, shown in Figure 1.1, comprises the components that must be in place to provide valuable education to middle school students with diverse learning needs. These components include (a) effective practices; (b) effective teacher characteristics; (c) school, family, and community influences; and (d) stakeholder interaction with middle school education through engagement, reflection, and personal mission. The arrows on the model indicate the fluid nature of the components as they continually change in reaction to new situations and information. Central to the MidEx model is the middle school student, who is in continual interaction with the components of the model. The model components are as follows:

- *Middle school student*—The student is the centerpiece of the model because learner-centered instruction is one of the cornerstones of middle level education (McCombs, 2001; Orrill, 2001; Weinberger & McCombs, 2001). All of the model's components revolve around the unique needs of the middle school student.

- *Effective practices in middle school*—Practices such as learning communities, interdisciplinary approaches, and hands-on learning influence learning and successful student outcomes (Elmore, 2000; Flowers, Mertens, & Mulhall, 2000; Moss & Fuller, 2000). Throughout the book, we introduce a variety of effective practices designed to promote maximum learning environments for middle school learners.

- *Effective practices in special education*—Techniques such as strategic teaching, assessment, task analysis, assistive technology, and self-determination instruction (Gersten, Chard, & Baker, 2000; D. D. Smith, 2004) are considered effective special education practices.

- *Teacher characteristics in middle school*—Effective middle school teachers create positive learning climates, maintain high standards, build creativity into learning, and engage students in the learning process (Dieker, 2001; Hanna, 1998; Langer, 2000). Teachers who seek lifelong learning through professional and personal development are more likely to be effective teachers (Barresi, 2000; Langer, 2000).

- *Teacher characteristics in special education*—Attributes that make special education teachers effective include communication skills, problem-solving skills, decision-making skills, attention to students' prior knowledge, adaptability, and flexibility (Bradford, 1999; Klinger & Vaughn, 2002; Mostert, 2000). Other effective strategies are explained in subsequent chapters.

- *School*—Collaboration among school personnel and students is essential to student learning (Flowers, et al., 2000; Norton, 2001; Pardini, 2001).

- *Family*—A higher level of family involvement can be promoted through interactive assignments with family members, discussions about the transition to high school, and communication about student progress (Belenardo, 2001; Falbo, Lein, & Amador, 2001; Van Voorhis, 2001).

- *Community*—Connection of schools and community can be promoted through such elements as community service, real-life settings, technology, and global education (Caprio & Borgeson, 2001; Hensley, 2001; Langone, Shade, Clees, & Day, 1999; Weddle, 1999).

- *Engagement*—Students can become active participants in their own learning through instruction that focuses on student-directed learning, real issues in the students' environment, and connection to future goals (Lee & Ursel, 2001; Quaglia & Cobb, 1996).

- *Reflection*—Both students and teachers should contemplate learning experiences and determine benefits and areas of need. This component

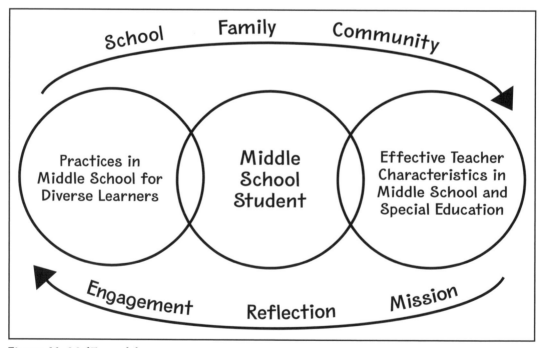

Figure 1.1. MidEx model.

includes openness and appreciation of differences, critical thinking, and the generation of ideas for future growth (Jay & Johnson, 2002; Loughran, 2002; Ukpokodu, 2002).

- *Mission*—An important component is the opportunity to develop and define one's purpose in life. For teachers, this component can be the reason they choose to pursue their profession. For students, this component can represent their life purpose and is supported by goals they write regarding the various areas of their lives (Bartels & Mortenson, 2002; Zimmerman, 1996). You will begin writing your own teaching mission in the following section of this chapter. As you proceed through the book, you will adjust your mission to reflect your growth, your experiences, and your philosophy.

Nurturing the Middle Level Educator

Although the main focus of this book is on how the middle school teacher can nurture and meet the needs of the middle school student, it is also important that the teacher focus on nurturing and meeting his or her own needs. Teaching in middle schools may result in curriculum-, administration-, and student-related stressors on teachers. Any of these stressors could easily cause educators to become disengaged with their teaching. This disengagement is illustrated in the following true story related to one of the authors by a fellow teacher educator. In relating the story, this individual indicated her struggle with how this event affected her personal legacy as an educator.

One night I was chatting with a neighbor who works as a teacher. As we were talking, a group of middle school students joined our conversation. After exchanging pleasantries with the kids, my neighbor excused herself and walked back to her home. One of the kids asked the group, "Doesn't she teach at our school?" Another responded, "Yeah, she's the burned-out teacher!" That's all they said about her! This scenario plagued me for days to come. Years of service boiled down to a single label. But it also triggered several questions in my own mind. What did I want to stand for as a teacher? When my students remembered my classes, what word, memory, or teaching picture would come to mind? What do I bring to the profession? What do I stand for?

Your Mission Statement

Each person is the sum total of his or her experiences. One person, for example, is (a) the student who experienced being in school as a young adolescent, (b) the teacher who earned a degree or is earning a degree in education, (c) the parent who attended an open house at a child's school, and (d) the community member who voted for a school tax increase. In addition, that person is a bike rider, runner, reader, daughter, sister, and wife. Through all these experiences and roles, the person learns who she is and how she acts or reacts to situations. Therefore, each experience has an impact on the individual's future experiences and actions (Dewey, 1938; M. Greene, 1991).

In your role as an educator, it is important to learn not only how to react to situations but also what influences your reactions (Hole & McEntree, 1999). This understanding of yourself and your practices as a teacher becomes your own life picture as an educator. An understanding of your mission will help you be more engaged in your teaching and less likely to be the teacher in the previous scenario that the students labeled as "burned out." Engaged educators are more likely to become lifelong consumers of effective practices as they strive to improve the education they provide to their students.

Hole and McEntree (1999) postulate, "the life force of teaching practice is thinking and wondering" (p. 34). They suggest that thinking and wondering about how and why events took place will lead teachers to understand their actions and perhaps see other actions that they as educators could have taken during the event. In their model for reflection on practice, Hole and McEntree ask teachers to (a) describe one actual teaching story, (b) explore why the events took place by reviewing current and past influences, and (c) consider how their teaching practices might change given new understanding.

As you read this text, we would like you to take time to think about your own personal life picture statement, or mission, and how this influences your actions as a teacher. Once you have developed your mission statement, you are asked to consider how the information presented in this textbook might change your mission. Activity 1.4 is a guide for you to use in this process. The worksheet is to be reviewed and changed as needed while you read and synthesize the information in this text. In each chapter, case studies, teacher tips, planning tips, and other activities will assist you with synthesizing the information presented. In Chapter 8 we ask you to revisit the worksheets to help you build a teacher portfolio.

At the end of every chapter, you will find a page titled "Impact of Information on Your Mission." This is an opportunity for you to think about what you have learned and record how this information impacts your teaching and your mission.

Summary

The aim of middle level education is to provide young adolescents with a safe environment for students to grow and learn. This is a time of exploration for students as each defines him- or herself as a friend, family member, student, worker, and community member. Teaching in middle level programs requires unique skills that allow teachers to guide and understand the needs of students, as well to celebrate their own professional growth. The components of middle level education are defined in the interactive MidEx model. Information presented in this book applies this model to provide educators with many of the tools necessary to work in middle level education. In addition, readers are asked to reflect on their current skills and how best to improve these skills so they can assist students and, at the same time, truly enjoy their work.

Activity 1.4 Mission Worksheet

YOUR MISSION STATEMENT FOR TEACHING

Write answers to these questions:

1. Why did I become a teacher? *or* Why do I want to become a teacher?

2. Why do I currently teach? *or* Why do I continue to pursue my teaching certificate?

3. At the end of my teaching career, how would I like to be remembered? What do I see as my role and purpose?

4. What is my mission statement for teaching? (Realize that this is a fluid statement that will change as you change.)

5. What keywords best describe my mission or what I stand for as an educator? (These words may change as your mission statement changes.)

There is something that is much more scarce,
something finer far, something rarer than ability.
It is the ability to recognize ability.

—Elbert Green Hubbard

Impact of Information on Your Mission

1. List your mission keywords.

2. Describe a story from your teaching or experience that relates to this chapter. Perhaps you thought of an event while you were reading this chapter.

3. What influenced your actions or the actions of others (e.g., students) in the story?

4. What information did you learn in this chapter that influences this story?

5. What teaching practices might you change based on this new information?

CHAPTER 2

Understanding Middle School Students

What is it like to be in middle school?

"You talk more on the phone than you used to."

"I get more zits."

"You can do things you couldn't before like walking and going places without your parents."

Teaching middle school is ...

"Having the feeling that I can be as crazy as the kids are and nobody notices."

What is it like to be the parent of a middle schooler?

"You're constantly 'in the know' without letting on."

"It's like living in a theme park: thrills, chills, spills, and bills!"

Learning Objectives

1. To describe an early adolescent and include the types of physical, cognitive, and intellectual changes that occur during the early adolescent years.

2. To explain how the social and emotional needs and development of a middle schooler differ from those of an elementary child or older adolescent.

3. To identify the types of developmental challenges that occur during early adolescence and the roles of the teacher, school, family, and community in addressing these challenges.

4. To explain and apply the types of middle school structures and instructional practices that support the unique physical, intellectual, emotional, and social development needs of 10- to 14-year-olds.

5. To describe how middle school programs and teachers address the unique needs of students with special needs.

Middle School Years

Other than during infancy, no other time in an individual's life span encompasses the degree of rapid change and growth than the period of development known as *puberty* or *adolescence*. Puberty signals the physical onset of adolescence—the biological and sexual maturation of an individual. Adolescence is the period of time between childhood and adulthood, roughly between the ages of 10 and 20 years, during which many changes take place in order to prepare for "life" as an adult. A myriad of biological, social, emotional, and intellectual changes intermingle throughout these years.

Early adolescence refers to the initial stage of adolescence, from ages 10 to 14, which sparks the journey toward adulthood. These years include the middle school years. Because you've lived through your own early adolescence, you no doubt bring many thoughts, ideas, and experiences about these years to your teaching. Take a step back in time and think about your middle school years; remember both good and not so good moments. In thinking about your own middle school years, you may recall a treasured friend, a significant adult, a unique or meaningful achievement, a disappointment, an embarrassing encounter, a special activity such as 4-H or band. Maybe you remember developing an interest in a new subject. Teaching is truly influenced by one's personal awareness and experiences, as well as by connections with and understanding of students. Activity 2.1 investigates perceptions and experiences that occur in the "tween" years.

Here are a few of the descriptions we brainstormed and heard from our students: *exciting, confusing, complicated, embarrassing, more responsibility, fun, harder, different, annoying, and interesting*. We found many of the same types of descriptors across age groups and generations. Did you?

Because predictable developmental changes occur during adolescence, you likely experienced joys and disappointments similar to those of the middle school students with whom you work. Note that the words and adjectives shared were no doubt varied, diverse, and certainly not boring. We believe that middle school students are among the most rewarding populations to teach. The purpose of this chapter is to explore (a) typical early adolescent physical, cognitive, and social–emotional development; (b) responsive developmental teaching practices; (c) effective middle school structures; (d) inclusive perspectives for students with disabilities; and (e) delivery of comprehensive middle school programs that build the foundation for transition.

Early Adolescent Development

Although today's early adolescents share growing pains and gains similar to those we did as early teens, they live in a world and culture that is more fast paced, global, media rich, mobile, and technological than we did during this stage. Their world is characterized by changing family structures; increasing economic prosperity for select sectors of society; continued poverty, particularly for children; greater access to information; shifting job markets; and global perspectives and pressures (Mather & Rivers, 2003; Queen, 1999).

The U.S. Census Bureau (2000) estimated a population of 20.5 million 10- to 14-year-olds, comprising 7.3% of the U.S. population. Although some individuals describe adolescence as a time of storm, stress, rebellion, and risks, today's youth, in fact, are actually healthier on many indicators than youth of a decade ago (U.S. Department of Health & Human Services, 2002). Nevertheless, many of the same types of risks to healthy adolescent development continue and new challenges emerge (e.g., Internet safety and predatory behavior). Table 2.1 provides a statistical snapshot of adolescence in today's culture.

Table 2.1
Snapshot of Adolescence in Today's Culture

- Of 9th graders responding to an international study in 1999, 50% reported participation in community volunteer activities (National Center for Education Statistics, 2003).

- Approximately 23.3% of children under age 18 live in single-parent households (Mather & Rivers, 2003).

- The status dropout rate of 16- to 24-year-olds declined to about 10.7% in 2001, yet it remains significantly higher for Hispanic individuals (27%) (National Center for Education Statistics, 2003).

- Youth with disabilities are three times more likely to drop out of school (Blackorby & Wagner, 1996).

- From 1991 to 2001 instances of reported sexual intercourse among teens in Grades 9 through 12 declined from 54% to 46% (Henry J. Kaiser Family Foundation, 2003).

- Of households with children ages 8 to 18, 86% report having a computer and 74% report availability of an Internet connection within the home (Roberts, Foehr, & Rideout, 2005).

- Half of youths ages 12 to 21 report they lack regular vigorous activity (Center for Disease Control, 1999b).

- Approximately 17% of households with children 5 to 17 years old speak a language other than English at home (National Center for Education Statistics, 2003).

- At least one adolescent age 10 to 19 dies of an injury every hour (Center for Disease Control, 1999a).

- Approximately 13% of middle school students indicated use of some form of tobacco, whereas about 9% report current use (Center for Disease Control, 2000).

- Approximately 14% of students in Grades 6 through 8 report some type of victimization at school (violent, property, or other) (National Center for Education Statistics, 2003).

- The number of students enrolled in secondary schools is expected to increase 3% between 2001 and 2011 (National Center for Education Statistics, 2002).

Physical Development in Early Adolescence

The most obvious transformations of middle school students occur in the physical realm and include pubertal development. Changes in height, weight, hair distribution, and maturation of primary and secondary sexual characteristics occur over a span of several years. Although all students eventually experience these changes, the intensity, timing, and duration of these changes vary greatly. Many middle schoolers also experience coordination problems. Different areas of their bodies grow at different times and rates (D. M. Walker & Lirgg, 1995); this asynchronous growth is common. A child may appear to be all legs or may indeed need to "grow into his or her feet." Many feel self-conscious as they trip and stumble around the school while getting used to their ever-changing bodies.

Look inside any classroom door at a middle school. If you were asked to guess the ages of the students without knowing their grade levels, you would no doubt identify some students as older or younger than they actually are. The vast difference in physical development provides for curiosity, interest, self-awareness, self-consciousness, embarrassment, and possibly status among students.

Growth Spurts

The adolescent growth spurt is the "accelerated rate of increase in height and weight that occurs during early adolescence" (D. M. Walker & Lirgg, 1995, p. 54). Suddenly, a child will seem to "take off" and sprout, without warning.

During middle school, young adolescents grow an average of 3 to 4 inches a year and can gain 8 to 10 pounds annually (Rathus, 2003; Santrock, 2001; Van Hoose, Strahan, & L'Esperance, 2001). By the end of middle school, students may be up to 12 inches taller than when they started (Steinberg, 1999). The weight spurt typically begins about 6 months after the height spurt begins (Rathus, 2003).

Girls begin their growth spurt approximately 2 years earlier than boys (Hyjer Dyk, 1993). For girls the mean onset for the beginning of the growth spurt is 9 years old and its peak occurs on the average at 11.5 years. The growth spurt continues gradually for another few years (Santrock, 2001). Many middle school girls, particularly between the ages of 11 and 13, dwarf their male counterparts (Steinberg, 1999).

The growth spurt in boys begins on average at 11 years of age, with a peak at 13.5, and continues for another few years (Santrock, 2001). Boys catch up to girls around age 14. Girls will reach 98% of their adult height by age 16¾ and boys by 17¾ (Rice & Dolgin, 2002). No two children, however, begin, peak, or end their growth spurts on a uniform clock. There will be wide differences in growth across students.

Bones grow and become denser during this period of adolescent growth (Van Hoose, Strahan, & L'Esperance, 2001). Muscles also develop. Boys will experience a leaner body fat ratio than girls, as well as greater muscular strength (Coleman & Hendry, 1999; Rice & Dolgin, 2002).

Sexual Maturation

During the middle school years, development and growth of the primary and secondary sex characteristics occur for students of both genders. *Primary sex characteristics* include development of the sex glands (gonads) and structures that make reproduction possible. For girls this includes the ovaries, vagina, uterus, and Fallopian tubes. For boys, the testes, penis, prostate gland, and seminal vesicles are the primary sex characteristics. *Secondary sex characteristics* are nonreproductive indicators of sexual maturity. These include breast development; growth of pubic, underarm, body, and facial hair; and voice changes (Rathus, 2003; Steinberg, 1999).

Girls begin sexual maturation 1 to 2 years before boys (D. M. Walker & Lirgg, 1995). The first menstrual period usually occurs between ages 10 and 16, with an average onset at around 12.5 years (Rice & Dolgin, 2002; D. M. Walker & Lirgg, 1995). Initial breast development occurs between the ages of 8 and 13 years (Hyjer Dyk, 1993). It may take as little as a few years or as long as 6 years for girls to complete their physical maturation process (Steinberg, 1999). To the dismay of many girls, a rounding and widening of the body contour happens, especially in the hips. Although these changes are needed to support reproductive functions, given the idealized images portrayed in the media and extolled by peers, young females may feel inadequate if they do not meet the perceived norm or ideal for "thinness" (Coleman & Hendry, 1999). Thus, many early adolescent girls express a level of dissatisfaction with their body image.

For boys, growth of primary sexual characteristics begins around age 11.5 and becomes more rapid by 13.5 years of age. This maturation includes growth of the testes, scrotum, and penis. Most boys experience spermache, or first ejaculation, around age 13 (Rice & Dolgin, 2002). Voice changes typically occur around age 14 or 15 (Rathus, 2003). Facial hair growth usually begins 2 years after the appearance of pubic hair. Boys complete their physically maturation typically between 2 and 5 years after onset (Steinberg, 1999).

For both boys and girls, these sexual and physical changes can generate curiosity, concern, or anxiety. Middle schoolers can be found peeking in the mirror at themselves or others. They observe and think about the many changes occurring in their bodies and compare themselves to others. Adolescents often equate physical attractiveness with body shape or build (Santrock, 2001).

Other Changes

Hormonal and bodily changes during puberty activate sweat and sex glands. The result is noticeable odor. We know of a few colleagues who keep a hidden stash of air freshener that is magically produced as needed. Personal hygiene needs to be addressed with students. Those 10- and 11-year-olds with antipathy to soap and water need to be approached with gentle dialogue and private discussion. Parents, however, report success with forcible threats, frequent reminders, and creative coercion.

Acne and pimples become an additional source of consternation for many middle schoolers, particularly for boys. Finally, changes and growth to the heart and the circulatory and respiratory systems also occur. These include increases in heart size and lung capacity (Steinberg, 1999). To fuel all of these physical changes, middle schoolers eat more than previously.

Table 2.2 provides a brief summary of physical changes that happen during early adolescence as reported by various authors (Merki, 1999; Rathus, 2003; Steinberg, 1999; Tanner, 1991; D. M. Walker & Lirgg, 1995).

Impact of Physical Changes on Classroom Life

In Activity 2.2, examine possible ways you may need to address physical growth changes in the classroom.

Considerations and Strategies for Physical Development

Did you think about the impacts that early or late maturation might have for each of these students? Perhaps you mentioned the importance of the peer group. Maybe you identified personal response and resilience factors. The following are considerations about and classroom strategies to address physical development.

1. Expect Early and Late Bloomers. Diana's early maturation might result in self-consciousness, isolation, and peer jealously or curiosity. Despite these impacts, not all early maturing girls will experience major threats to their psyche. Girls with a healthy self-concept and supportive networks weather these challenges. The research, however, indicates that many early maturing middle school girls do have a

Table 2.2
Summary of Adolescent Physical Development

Females	Males
• Growth spurt of 8 to 13 ½ inches	• Growth spurt of 12 to 14 ½ inches
• Development of breasts	• Growth and enlargement of external genitals
• Formation of mature eggs	• Beginning of sperm production
• Onset of menstruation	• Pubic, underarm, and facial hair
• Pubic hair and underarm hair	• Voice changes
• Increase in perspiration	• Increase in perspiration
• Acne	• Acne
• Narrowed waist	• Muscle development
• Wider hips	• Wider shoulders
• Increase in body fat	• Decrease in body fat

heightened sensitivity to their physical appearance. They can also experience negative impacts to their self-esteem. These young females report being less satisfied with their bodies and may be more withdrawn than their peers (Hyjer Dyk, 1993; Steinberg, 1999; D. M. Walker & Lirgg, 1995).

Late maturation can also pose some challenges. Oscar does not fit the typical stereotype of a late maturer. He has found healthy outlets for expression and recognition. He may, however, be avoiding dressing out for PE because of the "locker looks" and peer scrutiny. Late maturing boys often get labeled as less mature and may possibly have lower self-esteem (D. M. Walker & Lirgg, 1995).

Conversely, early developing boys often experience social benefits and status. They are viewed more positively by their peers and considered to be more socially mature by adults (Coleman & Hendry, 1999; D. M. Walker & Lirgg, 1995). These

Address Varied Rates of Development

- **Help middle schoolers develop positive body images.**
- **Provide recognition and acknowledgment of students' social, personal, and intellectual qualities to balance differences in physical development.**
- **Assist students in developing positive affirmations for social, personal, and intellectual aspects of their personality.**
- **Provide information about expected changes and the varied timelines for these changes.**
- **Avoid athletic competition as a group incentive.**

Activity 2.2 Magical Body Mystery Tour

Discovery is an excellent term to describe the impacts of the biological changes occurring during the middle school years. While students discover their "new selves," teachers also engage in a discovery process as they (a) recognize the variety of physical changes, (b) analyze the im-pact of these changes on individual students and groups of students, and (c) adjust and accommodate for these changes through classroom and school activities. If students become too preoccupied and concerned over these changes, learning is definitely affected. The main questions to consider in this activity are these:

1. How can these physical growth and sexual changes impact students emotionally and socially? Are there gender differences?

2. What types of adjustments or accommodations should I consider in my classroom environment or activities to address these impacts?

Imagine you have a classroom of 23 middle school students. Some students still appear as if they are elementary-aged, others are budding, and a few could pass for 17 or 18.

PROFILE 1
Diana

Diana is a seventh grader. She is well developed sexually; is tall, slender, and attractive, and has drawn the attention of high school boys. Although she has a few close friends at school in her band class, she tends to keep to herself a lot of the time in school. Diana volunteers in the media center during lunch a few days each week. After school she participates in several community activities, including 4-H and a youth group at her church. She has just begun dating a boy from her 4-H group, who is a freshman in high school. In locker conversations among the seventh-grade boys at school more than a few comments have been whispered about her imagined sexual activity. Vicious rumors have been perpetuated by some girls. Diana has a learning disability and receives some support in study skills and learning strategies in the resource room.

(continues)

PROFILE 2

Oscar
Oscar is also a seventh grader. The second of three children, Oscar is an active boy and is also involved in band and an extramural soccer league in the community.

He has several friends he "hangs with" during lunch and social activities. He has not yet hit his growth spurt, and in a lineup of classmates by size, he is often found at the rear of the pack. Oscar loves sports but he has not been dressing out for PE. He has a great sense of humor and enjoys jokes, which he shares often.

1. List the possible impacts of physical development for Diana and Oscar.

Physical and Sexual Growth

Possible Emotional Impacts		Possible Social Impacts	
Diana	Oscar	Diana	Oscar

2. List possible classroom adaptations and accommodations you might use to address these impacts.

students may also be more successful in athletic activities, given their advanced physical development.

2. Address Facts and Fantasy. Young teens are experiencing many changes. They need to be given accurate information concerning physical and sexual changes. It is mind boggling to consider that by the time they leave middle school, most girls will be able to conceive and boys able to father children. Although they have the physical capability, there are a number of important physical, social, emotional, economic, and ethical issues students should learn about engagement in sexual activity. Parents, counselors, and educators can provide the type of factual information and support that middle schoolers need. If students do not receive it from knowing adults, they often get inaccurate information from peers or, worse yet, seek answers through experimentation.

Support Factual Understanding of Physical Development

- Provide age-appropriate, accurate, and comprehensible information. Have varied resources that middle schoolers can access for answers to questions about puberty and sexual development.

- Be aware of school and district policy, as well as family preferences, regarding provision of information and resources on sexual maturation and activity. Connect with school health experts and the school guidance counselor.

- Address inaccuracies portrayed in the media concerning idealized body images and sexual activity and responsibility.

3. Nurture Nutritious Habits. Because students constantly eat and have expanded choices in fueling their bodies, it is important that they know about and practice healthy nutrition habits. Middle school students are hungry but may have particular food fetishes, especially for junk food (Ames, Ilg, & Baker, 1988).

4. Energize and Exercise. Middle schoolers need to move and stretch their growing bodies. It is critical for them to be given opportunities to move during both learning and leisure activities because many have trouble sitting still for extended periods of time. As students get older, there is a tendency to engage in a more sedentary lifestyle. They need to learn about healthy lifestyles involving exercise.

Focus on Healthy Habits

- Educate students on healthy eating and sleep needs, as well as habits for optimal health.

- Remember, students need to feed their bodies. Allow, as appropriate, healthy snacks in the classroom. Investigate choices in the cafeteria and school snack bar to ensure that healthy alternatives are available.

- Make sure students have access to water.

Motivate Students for Movement

- Educate students about the benefits of exercise. Establish varied fitness and exercise goals.

- Discuss, model, and connect students and their families to a range of leisure activities. Avoid stereotypical choices and options. Honor cultural activities.

- Allow frequent movement and support active learning strategies (see Chapter 4).

Intellectual and Cognitive Development in Early Adolescence

During the middle school years, classroom discussions and conversations become more interactive and expansive. Students are undergoing a transformation in their cognitive thought processes. They begin to experiment with the abstract, to explore possibilities, to reason logically, and to imagine the future (Mitchell, 1998; Wavering, 1995). Early adolescents begin to think about their thoughts and to explore their identities. To do this they try out many personas. For example, a child who adores the all-American hamburger one day may be a self-proclaimed vegetarian the next.

"Tweens" can swing back and forth between their childlike and more mature selves. Imagine for a moment a young adolescent in her hip huggers and "Princess"

Target Cognitive Connections

- Listen to and acknowledge students' ideas and viewpoints.

- Nurture interests and exploration through advisory and exploratory classes.

- Provide opportunities for inquiry and research in areas of choice.

- Support varied levels of cognitive development.

- Explore both the concrete and abstract aspects of concepts and ideas.

- Use a variety of learning activities, such as manipulatives, role playing, simulations, experiments, discussion, reflection, Socratic questions, hypothesis testing, reading, and writing.

Note. List compiled from material appearing in the work of Knowles and Brown (2000).

tee, sporting a removable tattoo and green hair. In her left hand she is holding her teddy bear. Middle schoolers want and need to experience new ideas, choices, responsibilities, and independence. They still, however, need to know they have their supports and safety nets in place.

Novel Ideas and New Possibilities

During adolescence students experience changes in conceptual thinking. Jean Piaget (1972) identified five stages of cognitive development, two of which—*concrete operational thought* and *formal operational thought*—are germane to students in middle school. Most middle schoolers begin sixth grade in Jean Piaget's stage of concrete operational thought (Schave & Schave, 1989). From the ages of about 7 to 11 or 12 years, children's thinking is characterized by the real, the concrete, the logical, and the specific (Schave & Shave, 1988; Van Hoose & Strahan, 1989). Children can classify using logical attributes and qualities. In this stage students need direct experiences to grasp concepts.

Eventually, most students move into the formal operational stage. This includes two distinct periods: early formal operational thought (from about 11 or 12 to 14 or 15 years of age) and late formal operational thought (from about 14 to 15 years of age on up) (Santrock, 2001). Formal operational thought is characterized by the abstract, the possible, the multidimensional, and the variable (Schave & Schave, 1989; Van Hoose, Strahan, & L'Esperance, 2001). At this stage students can reason hypothetically and deductively, investigate different perspectives, determine cause and effect, and examine personal thoughts. Middle schoolers are only emerging into formal thought. Many will see issues in black and white or may even tend toward overgeneralization (Elias et al., 1997).

Although most early adolescents enter into formal thought sometime during middle school, these changes occur at different times for different children in different areas of study. Some individuals, in fact, never fully develop formal operational thought (Rice & Dolgin, 2002).

Middle school students have a vast new world of ideas, possibilities, and experiences open to them. They typically are open to learning and are curious. They compare, they speculate, they argue, and they wonder. These students can be enthusiastic, passionate, confused, or overwhelmed when bombarded with new concepts, viewpoints, and ideals.

Egocentrism and Introspection

There is almost an obsession in middle school with the sense of being "watched" and "on stage." Middle school students constantly seem to be self-absorbed and self-conscious. They primp and pose. They cannot resist a sideward glance in the mirror in passing, and they expect others to be looking at them. Early adolescents are uncomfortably aware of any perceived visible flaws. They are also convinced that their thoughts, experiences and ideas are unique. Activity 2.3 gives you the opportunity to analyze students' comments that indicate self-interest and self-importance.

Did you find a number of examples of the growing self-interest of middle schoolers? Here are a few snippets we overheard: "I thought I was going to die." "Did you see ___ when ___?" "Oh my gawd, it was soooo embarrassing."

Activity 2.3 Windows and Mirrors

The conversations and behaviors of middle schoolers provide windows to their inner thoughts. These actions mirror feelings and ideas they have about themselves and their world. Without eavesdropping too obviously, note key phrases and words shared during students' informal conversations, or surreptitiously watch what students do when they have some down time. Observe them at the end or beginning of a period, waiting at the bus stop, or in the hallway between classes.

1. Make a list of words and phrases you heard or actions you observed.

2. Analyze your list. What do these words and actions say about students? About their thoughts about themselves? About their thoughts on their world?

3. Write your ideas below.

What I Heard or Saw	What That Means

Elkind (1981) described two terms related to the self-absorption of early adolescents. The first is the *imaginary audience,* or the notion that "everyone is watching me." The second is the *personal fable,* or the somewhat exaggerated view that one's thoughts, ideas, joys, and dilemmas are like none other in history. Students might think or say teachers, parents, or even peers, "Go away! You don't understand." "You can't possibly imagine what it's like to feel like I do." "This is absolutely tragic! I bet this hasn't happened to anyone else!" Students can become secretive; they may seek privacy and they definitely live in fear of shame and humiliation as they negotiate this phase.

Preoccupation with self may lead to risk-taking behaviors for some students. Beliefs in their uniqueness and invincibility may lead them to believe, "It can't happen to me!"

Social and Emotional Development

Social conformity and norms take on new meaning during the middle school years. The children who in elementary school had a sense of their own personal style in clothing and discourse are suddenly gone. Enter … the carbon copy. During early adolescence, tweens can and do search for personal identity; however, most do not want to stand out too much from the crowd. They still need some security while creating and exploring their emerging selves.

Middle schoolers crave a sense of belonging and seek social relationships and validation. They will forge new associations, build same-gender and cross-gender friendships, investigate romantic partnerships, and renegotiate their roles with parents, teachers, and other adults. Adults remain important, but the peer group moves to center stage.

In their growth toward adulthood, middle schoolers are at an advantage when equipped with a healthy self-concept and self-esteem. As they journey toward personal independence, they need these supports to make wise choices and decisions. They seek autonomy, responsibility, and a place in the world.

In this section, we touch on a few essential areas of social and emotional development: personal development and independence, peer relationships, and family relationships. More comprehensive information on the instructional and behavioral applications of social and emotional growth is provided in upcoming chapters.

Middle School Tips

Attend to Student Self-Interest

- Use activities such as interviews and discussions that provide opportunities for students to share experiences, beliefs, and feelings with peers and adults.

- Ensure that students have time for needed privacy.

- Address the facts and possible outcomes of risk-taking behaviors.

- Establish parameters and expectations for the classroom use or nonuse of personal care items (brushes, mirrors, hair products, combs, etc.).

Personal Development and Independence

Middle schoolers need to fuel their bodies and minds, but equally important are their spirits. Self-concept and self-esteem are essential building blocks that can cultivate or erode emotional growth and personal independence. *Self-concept* is "the perception(s) one has of oneself in terms of personal attributes and the various roles which are played or fulfilled by the individual" (Lipka, 1997, pp. 31–32). Simply put, it is one's self-image and self-perceptions. Self-concept is influenced positively or negatively by one's personal thought patterns, as well as by peer group members, friends, family members, and significant others. *Self-esteem* is the out-

Support Autonomy, Self-Concept, and Relationships

- Build personal relationships and recognize individual students.

- Use humor and see the lighter side.

- Help students to develop positive self-affirmations and identify positive personal qualities.

- De-emphasize group comparisons and competition, yet help students build connections with others.

- Support student autonomy, responsibility, and self-determination.

- Capitalize on the peer group by using appropriate opportunities for cooperative learning and peer-mediated instruction.

- Support student–school–family connections.

come of self-concept. It is the value or feelings one has about oneself (Lipka, 1997). Self-esteem has been shown to have an impact on achievement and motivation. Students who experience success feel more competent and capable. They are more likely to believe that they are causal agents and that their choices and actions have an impact on their successes or failures. These attributions are important motivational influences (Anderman & Midgley, 1998). Students need to feel confident, capable, responsible, and aware.

Many students' self-competence beliefs (Wigfield & Eccles, 1994) and self-esteem (Van Hoose, Strahan, & L'Esperance, 2001) take a dip during early adolescence. Some of this may be attributed to increased self-consciousness, to idealized comparisons, and to less personalized secondary school environments. Self-esteem for many students with learning and other disabilities can have other mitigating influences and impacts. These students may have lowered levels of self-esteem, fewer friendships, and less positive beliefs about their personal competence (Gans, Kenny, & Ghany, 2003; Smith-Horn & Singer, 1996; Wehmeyer, 2003).

Peer Relationships

Early adolescents are both influencing and influenced by their peer group. They are spending increasing amounts of time away from the family unit (Collins & Repinski, 1994). The peer group or crowd becomes their reference group. They begin to ask themselves questions such as "Who am I?" and "Where do I belong?" Membership in a peer group becomes an all-important part in building identity. Most early adolescent peer groups, or cliques, comprise those who are similar in age, gender, and socioeconomic status. These associations are most often formed on the basis of shared activities and interests. Middle schoolers may be members of several groups simultaneously and move in and out of these associations (Newman & Newman, 2001; Steinberg, 1999).

Students may also begin to develop nonromantic cross-gender friendships in the later middle school years. This often is a precursor to and assists in the transition to romantic relationships. Girls desire to develop romantic relationships earlier than do boys (Feiring, 1999).

Friendships are close, mutually beneficial relationships with other individuals. Unfortunately, not all middle schoolers experience these positive supports. Some students with low social status may not experience a sense of belonging, or they may feel that they are part of a group, only to find out later that they have been the victims of cruel ridicule. The ability to differentiate between sincerity and sarcasm is a skill adolescents are only beginning to develop. Lack of friendships or peer rejection puts students at risk for emotional and behavioral challenges (see Chapter 5).

Romantic relationships develop between some students during middle school, sometimes spurred by peer group pressure and norms. These relationships address a need for affiliation. Handholding is not an uncommon sight, especially among seventh or eighth graders. By chaperoning both a sixth-grade and an eighth-grade dance, one can gain an enlightened view of differences in social development across the grades.

Family Relationships

Although adolescents may at times seem antiparent, the family unit continues to play a necessary nurturing and supportive role for the middle schooler. Early adolescents may not let on in public, but they still want and need the encouragement, recognition, approval, and unconditional acceptance provided by parents and family members (Ames, Ilg, & Baker, 1988).

Because students are experiencing a natural process of independence, they are becoming more autonomous and less emotionally dependent on parents. Parents play an important role in providing safe opportunities for students to try out and evaluate their successes in new activities and choices. These ventures will have more or less successful outcomes. Conflicts happen as a natural part of this growing process.

Middle schoolers may publicly shun their parents. Arguments about typical routines, chores, or privileges will occur (Noller, 1994). Middle schoolers want to be more independent and self-reliant, but they still need their families to build these skills. In a typical day they will squabble with siblings; argue about bedtime and allowance; complain about mortal parental embarrassment; hug their mother, father, or caretaker; and want to be tucked in at night. Schools and educators can play an important role in supporting families as adolescents become more independent.

Developmental Challenges: Bumps in the Road

Most middle school students will exit adolescence without permanent injury and scars from their middle school years, although they may experience some developmental challenges. These include risk-taking behaviors such as unprotected sexual activity; tobacco, drug, or alcohol use; and gang activity. Other challenges, such as violence, abuse, harassment, and bullying, also can threaten healthy development. We presented some statistics earlier in this chapter. Although not all middle schoolers are at risk, some students will definitely face these challenges. Awareness, education, resources, and connections with others help middle schoolers address these challenges.

Middle School Structures and Best Practices

Early adolescence is a time of contrasts, extremes, and similarities. Adolescents are maturing, but not yet grown up, changing yet sometimes the same, independent but still reliant. Middle school structures and educators must be responsive to and dynamic in addressing the physical, intellectual, social, and emotional transitions of students. In this section, we outline middle school structures and educator best practices that meet the developmental needs of all middle schoolers. The middle school concept we support is one that creates a total educational environment for each and every student.

The National Middle School Association (NMSA) characterizes effective middle schools as ones that embrace and incorporate (a) flexible structures; (b) positive affective environments; (c) advocacy and support for all students, (d) challenging, integrative, and exploratory curriculum experiences; and (e) collaborative partnerships with families and community members (Erb, 2001). These practices are evidenced in the daily life of effective middle schools and in the curricula that teachers plan and provide.

Currently, the typical middle school student receives three years of core curriculum (language arts, social studies, mathematics, and science), physical education, exploratory curriculum (both required and elective), and advisory programs (Wiles & Bondi, 2001). Within these content areas or programs, effective middle school practices and philosophies must be incorporated to achieve the total school approach. Middle school programs and teachers must be responsive to developmental physical, intellectual, social, and emotional needs of early adolescents (Manning, 2002). Some adjustments need to be made to most middle school curricula to meet the needs of all students.

Flexible Structures

The term *flexible structures* refers to the type of organization that optimally occurs at middle school. This means that middle schools must be responsive to the varying needs of all students. Simply put, grouping, scheduling, and staffing practices should be designed to allow for the individual strengths and needs of a diverse group of middle school learners (Kashak, 2001). Using block structures and scheduling to deliver core curriculum is one type of flexible structure (D. C. Clark & Clark, 2000; Kellough & Kellough, 1999; Shortt & Thayer, 1999). In this structure the core content classes can be delivered in extended periods of time either singly (e.g.,

90 minutes of social studies content two to three times weekly) or in combination (e.g., 90 minutes of daily humanities class, with combined social studies and language arts content) (Wormeli, 2001). Identified teams of teachers (core curriculum teachers, specialists, and elective teachers) work with the same group of students throughout the day. Thus, teachers can make personal decisions about curriculum content, incorporate student interests, and attend to the unique strengths and needs of individual students. *Interdisciplinary teaming* (collaborative planning and curriculum delivery across groups of teachers) and *integrated content delivery* (curriculum integration across content areas) are two ways to support effective transition-supported middle school practices.

Advisory Programs and Support

Middle level teachers must also create and sustain *positive affective environments.* Creation of a safe and caring environment is essential for young adolescent success (NMSA, 1995; Wiles & Bondi, 2001). Teachers must create supportive environments and also engage students in social and emotional learning. Both general and special educators should provide experiences that (a) foster students' abilities to understand, manage, and express their feelings and (b) engage students in rewarding interactions with others (H. E. Taylor & Larson, 1999).

Advisory programs are another way in which middle schools can support personal skill development, peer and adult relationships, and individual attention for students. Advisory programs are weekly or daily programs that include a core group of students who interact with a common teacher or adult. The intent is to address the support, skills, and content needed for the personal, social, or civic development of early adolescents. One common structure is a 20- to 30-minute period of time in which a group of 12 to 15 students meets two or three times weekly with an advisor or mentor teacher (Wormeli, 2001). Advisory periods or programs provide connections and *advocacy for students.* In fact, the NMSA (1995) has identified advisory programs as one of the 10 essential elements of an effective middle school program.

Exploratory Curricula

Providing *challenging, integrative, and exploratory curricula* is also an essential component of an exemplary middle school. This practice involves addressing curriculum standards while balancing appropriate interests and needs of individual students and groups of students (Anafra & Brown, 2000; Stevenson, 1998). Connections across curriculum through integration of curriculum content strengthen active learning, promote understanding, and sustain opportunities for teachers to plan and deliver curriculum collaboratively.

Middle school experiences should also provide opportunities for students to explore and discover meaning. Young adolescents can explore new interests, talents, and strengths through exploratory elective classes and extracurricular activities. "The preadolescent's strong desire to be independent can be fostered in exploratory programs. The ability to weigh multiple options and make wise choices reinforces students' real-life decision-making processes" (Queen, 1999, p. 195). Exploratory curricula also provide students with opportunities to excel in varied areas and support self-awareness. Through a combination of required electives (e.g., physical education, technology literacy, home economics, art) and personal-choice elective or enrichment courses (e.g., industrial arts, foreign language, speech, music) students help refine and address their identities. Table 2.3 lists a sampling of middle school exploratory elective and extracurricular activities.

Collaborative Partnerships

Finally, *collaborative partnerships* among students, teachers, staff, and administrators, as well as with parents, families, and community members, are essential in providing an enriched middle school experience (Erb, 2001; Kellough & Kellough, 1999). These partnerships require the collaborative input of students, teachers, families, and community members. Parents and community members can also support curriculum by serving as role models, and by offering opportunities for support, service learning, and apprenticeships (NMSA, 1995). This collaboration is essential in transition-supported middle school curricula.

Table 2.3
Sampling of Middle School Exploratory and Extracurricular Activities

Exploratory Area	Examples of Content Focus
Vocational or career education	Woods, power, electricity, metals, graphics
Family and consumer sciences	Foods, consumer skills, clothing, childcare
Business	Keyboarding, typing, business skills, speech
Fine arts	Music (choir, vocal ensembles, band, orchestra), art, photography, drama, dance, journalism
Foreign language	Spanish, French, German, Japanese, American Sign Language
Technology literacy	Computer skills, text and graphics production, media and television production, technology programming, applications and problem solving
Extracurricular activities and clubs	Intramural and extramural sports; speech club; young authors club; readers club; chess or games club; cheerleading or pep squad; student council or student government; student yearbook; newsletter or newspaper; honor society; builder's or service clubs; Mathcounts, Geography Bee; Math, Engineering, Science and Achievement Programs; Family Math; Science Olympiad; homework club; Future Farmers of America; 4-H; Junior Achievement

Note. From *The New American Middle School: Educating Preadolescents in an Era of Change* (3rd ed.), by J. Wiles and J. Bondi, 2001, Upper Saddle River, NJ: Merrill/Prentice Hall. Copyright 2001 by Merrill/Prentice Hall. Adapted with permission.

Students with Disabilities

Students with disabilities are persons first. They have many of the same unique, changeable, perplexing, exhausting, exciting, and frustrating qualities of any middle school early adolescent. They *are not* labels. They *are not* exceptions. They *are not* yours to save or shelter. They are kids. They want to succeed, belong, and learn. They want to be ready for high school and for life.

It is outside the scope of this chapter to present lengthy discussion and lists of eligibility information characteristics. Excellent resources (e.g., Smith, 2004; T. C. Smith, Polloway, Patton, & Dowdy, 2004) are available to provide this information. We do, however, provide a portrait of current practices and services that are designed to support the specialized needs of middle schoolers with disabilities.

Universal Design

This text is written from a philosophy of *universal design* and *person first*. This means that school and instructional planning, decisions, and practices are designed with the notion that *all* students are part of the middle school "blueprint." The strengths, needs, interests, and abilities of all students, regardless of their linguistic, cultural, learning, physical, behavioral, and intellectual backgrounds or skills are incorporated from initial planning through reflective evaluation. There are no afterthoughts (Orkwis, 1999).

As you shape and refine your teaching practices for middle school teaching, we encourage you to do this with a comprehensive perspective. Look at the unique learning characteristics, individual strengths, personal desires, and private challenges of a student with a disability within the framework of the total middle school experience.

Who Are Students with Disabilities?

In the 2000–2001 school year, approximately 5.8 million students with disabilities ages 6 through 21 received special education services (U.S. Department of Education, 2002). To put this in perspective, 11.5% of students who are 6 to 17 years old have disabilities that require the support of special education services (U.S. Department of Education, 2002).

Most students with disabilities receive a majority of their education in the general education environment (see Table 2.4). Educators and advocates continue to strive toward serving students in the most appropriate and inclusive environments possible; therefore, both general and special educators need to work together to create and sustain successful positive learning experiences for these students.

There are 13 federal qualifying disability areas for special education services. Most students with disabilitites have *mild or high-incidence disabilities* (specific learning disabilities, speech or language impairments, mental retardation, and emotional disabilities). About half of all students receiving special education services under the Individuals with Disabilities Education Act are those with learning disabilities (U.S. Department of Education, 2002). *Low-incidence disabilities* are those

Table 2.4
Educational Environments of Students Ages 6 through 21
Served Under IDEA During 1999–2000

Environment	Percentage
Public school: Outside of the general education class	
Less than 21% of the school day	47.32%
21% to 60% of the school day	28.32%
Over 60% of the school day	20.29%
Public separate facility	1.88%
Private separate facility	1.02%
Public residential facility	0.39%
Private residential facility	0.30%
Home/hospital environment	0.48%

Note. Data from *Twenty-fourth Annual Report to Congress on the Implementation of the Individuals with Disabilities Education Act,* by U.S. Department of Education, 2002, Washington, DC: Author.

that occur less frequently. Teachers need to remember that eligibility classifications are merely labels and that their job is to teach *students*.

How Should Educators Support Middle Schoolers with Disabilities?

The use of an Individualized Education Program (IEP) designed for each student with a disability was discussed in Chapter 1. Through a process of collaboration, instruction, evaluation, and reflection, special and general educators can provide a middle school experience that addresses typical early adolescent development and the unique personal needs of students with disabilities. Services for these students might include the following:

- **Consultation.** Specialists or special educators work with general educators to plan and design learning and behavioral supports and accommodations delivered in the general education classroom.

- **Collaborative Teaching.** General and special education teachers of diverse groups of students co-teach or team teach in a single classroom.

- **Resource Room Support.** Special education teachers provide individualized instructional support for students with special needs in identified areas for a small portion of the school day. Typically, this support is provided for only one or a few school periods. It may include resource room support for reading, written expression, mathematics, study skills, or other learning needs identified in the IEP.

© **Self-Contained Classroom Services.** Special education teachers and service providers give individualized support for students with special needs for most or all of the school day (R. B. Lewis & Doorlag, 2003).

We discuss the process of making the individualized decisions about programming in Chapter 7. In the following section, we present important best practice principles and structures for making individual programming decisions in a total school approach.

Orchestrating a Total Middle School Approach

Addressing the varying developmental and individual needs of all middle schoolers for school and life success involves everyone. Teachers, students, parents, administrators, school personnel, families, school counselors, bus drivers, the lunch ladies, and even the owner of the local convenience store are important players. We have identified four key principles for laying this foundation: create connected, inclusive learning communities; build support systems; address individual needs; and keep an eye to the future. Practices that support each of these are shared in subsequent chapters.

Create Connected, Inclusive Learning Communities

"The most important characteristic of an inclusive environment is that teachers, parents, administrators, and students work together as a team and share ownership for all students" (Feichtel, 1997, p. 21). In other words, middle school teachers use practices that demonstrate a joint responsibility for educating all students. Activity 2.4 encourages you to consider what you believe an inclusive learning community means for middle school practitioners. As you read the remainder of this chapter and later chapters, we encourage you to revise and add ideas to Activity 2.4.

Inclusion is not a single instructional arrangement, grouping strategy, or place. It is a philosophy and the resultant practices that exemplify the ideas that all students belong, each person is important, every child has valuable contributions to share, and people are enriched by their diversity. When middle schoolers belong, they participate in the daily life of school activities, classes, and events (Halverson & Neary, 2001). Effective inclusionary practices can benefit students both academically and socially by reducing stigma, altering self-perceptions and self-esteem, and supporting improved academic achievement (Hines & Johnston, 1997; Kochar, West, & Taymans, 2000).

Creating inclusive learning communitites necessitates mutual trust and respect (Lenz & Deshler, 2004). Middle school best practices of teaming, instructional collaboration, and effective communication help support this philosophy. "Being a successful middle school teacher is a role characterized by a set of nested relationships" (McEwin & Dickinson, 2001, p. 13). Specialists and generalists must communicate

Activity 2.4 Construction Zone: Hard Hats Required

Creating an inclusive middle school community is an ongoing construction process. It involves examining personal beliefs and knowledge, analyzing instructional practices, evaluating school environments and structures, designing structures and supports to address student needs, and continued reflection and refinement.

Take a moment and look at your own beliefs and experiences. Jot down your ideas on each of the following.

1. What do you believe are the critical beliefs and practices of an inclusive teacher?

2. What are the characteristics of an inclusive environment?

3. What middle school structures support inclusive learning communities?

between and among themselves. They share ideas, suggest alternatives, use differentiated instruction, and support one another.

Interdisciplinary teaming is a recommended best practice for building an effective middle school learning community. Teams include teachers of varied disciplines who maintain responsibility for the learning and social development of a particular group of students. Most often teams are organized into grade-level groups, typically with two to five teachers. The classrooms of team members should be closely situated to support communication and interaction. There may be more than one team at any grade level. Team organization depends on the size, structure, mission, and philosophy of each middle school. Also, a common planning time is necessary for an effective interdisciplinary team (Erb, 1997; George, Lawrence, & Bushnell, 1998; George, Stevenson, Thomason, & Beane, 1992; Reiser & Butzin, 2000). At the sixth-grade level, a team might include educators who deliver math, science, language arts, and social studies instruction for a group of 120 students.

Teams should also include specialists, such as special educators, reading specialists, or fine arts instructors. These individuals can enrich the curriculum, provide broad perspectives, and lend varied expertise and supports (George et al., 1992; Kennedy & Fisher, 2001; Pugach & Johnson, 2002).

A good deal of empirical research supports the effectiveness of teams. For students, interdisciplinary teaming provides (a) gains in academic achievement, (b) improvement in school attitudes, (c) increases in consistent homework completion,

(d) connections among topics across the curriculum, (e) opportunities for social relationships and affiliation, and (f) models of effective collaboration and communication (Erb, 1997; Hough & St. Clair, 1995; Wormeli, 2001). For sixth-grade students transitioning from elementary school, interdisciplinary teaming has been found to be more effective for supporting academic achievement than the more traditional departmentalized structures (Alspaugh & Harting, 1997, 1998).

For teachers, interdisciplinary teaming does the following: (a) increases personal support, (b) delivers a sense of collegiality, (c) improves awareness of student needs and interests, and (d) encourages more positive dispositions about teaching (Erb, 1997; George et al., 1992; Hough & St. Clair, 1995). Table 2.5 is a compilation of important team qualities as described by Belenardo (2001), D. C. Clark and Clark (2000), George, Stevenson, Thomason, and Beane (1992), Pugach and Johnson (2002), and Wormeli (2001).

Table 2.5
Qualities of Effective Teams

Clear Definitions and Procedures
Teams must take time, preferably prior to the beginning of any school year, to clearly identify (a) membership of team members, (b) teaming structure and mission, (c) mutual goals and commitment, and (d) common policies and procedures. Teams can develop a team motto, create team rituals, and prepare a team handbook of common discipline, homework, and other expectations to solidify decisions and common practices. Teams should have a collective identity.

Decision-Making Frameworks
Each team must establish ways to make decisions and resolve differences. Sometimes a team leader or co-leaders are identified. Leaders become responsible for team meeting facilitation. They also serve as a conduit of communication with administrators and other school teams or professionals.

Structures for Organization
Teams need time to organize and communicate. A common planning time is one of the most often identified needs for effective teams. Ideally, a dedicated daily or weekly planning time is allocated for team members to share information, plan instruction and curriculum, discuss student concerns, and share personal growth.

Effective Communication Practices
Effective communication can make or break a team. Team members must use practices and interactions that support relationships. They need to have regular, consistent communication with one another, with students, and with parents. Teams should have some type of documentation of team meetings, decisions, and practices for later reference.

An Evaluation Plan
Teaming can be time and labor intensive. Team members need to assess the impact of their teaming efforts. Consistent evaluation and assessment of student progress and achievements should be examined. Teams also need to gather feedback from students and parents about what they perceive as "working" and "not working." Team members should evaluate the effectiveness of personal and collective communication and collaboration practices.

A Sense of Celebration
Successful teams celebrate. Team members celebrate student and team accomplishments. These are shared at the team, school, and community level. All students receive meaningful recognition throughout the year. Educators should also celebrate their own accomplishments by developing and sharing personal growth plans, sharing new ideas, and broadcasting successful teaching endeavors.

Build Support Systems

Inclusive support systems for students, teachers, and parents should be established. For students these scaffolds might be evidenced through advisory programs, school specialists, instructional classroom practices, extracurricular programs, and community agencies. Educators must also receive needed supports and resources to carry out their roles and responsibilities in collaborative, inclusive schools. Community members also play a key role in the service learning, community-based learning, and mentorship opportunities they provide.

Involving Families

It is absolutely essential for families to be involved as much as possible. Many parents become less connected during the middle school years (Billig, 2002a; Eccles & Harold, 1993). Parents have only 3 short years to learn the new structures and demands of the middle school. How do you believe parents and families are best supported for involvement in the education of their middle schoolers? Activity 2.5 is included for you to examine some of your beliefs.

Logistical constraints such as access to transportation and childcare, lack of knowledge on how to get involved, feelings of parenting inadequacy, and past histories of "horrible interactions" with schools are just a few reasons parents have shared for less involvement at the middle school (Eccles & Harold, 1993). Teachers and schools also lower parent involvement by (a) not providing needed information or opportunities, (b) using less sensitive communication practices, (c) ignoring parent ideas and input, and (d) utilizing involvement practices that are a mismatch for families (Eccles & Harold, 1993; Pruitt, Wandry, & Hollums, 1998). Your personal beliefs and practices about parent involvement are critical. The following strategies promote family and parent involvement.

Activity 2.5 Zap the Parent Trap

What benefits do you see in involving parents and families at the middle school level? How do you think parents and families should be involved during the middle school years? How do you find ways to involve parents effectively? Is this even feasible, given the fact that many preteens do not even want to be caught within 5 feet of their parents in any public location?

Create a list of parent and family involvement strategies you believe are effective for the middle school level.

Inform and Educate Parents

- Ensure that parents are informed about middle school organization, structures, and changes prior to the transition to middle school.
- Use informational exchanges such as open houses and classroom visits for parents to build relationships with individual teachers.
- Talk with parents about curricular choices and the impact of these choices.
- Provide letters and information about classroom behavioral expectations, homework policies, classroom curriculum, and grading policies.
- Inform parents regularly about student progress.

1. Keep Parents Informed. Parents and families can become overwhelmed with the changing demands and structures of middle school. Families need to become familiar with new schoolwide schedules, policies, procedures, and personnel. In addition to these changes, parents must beome familiar with multiple teachers who have varying expectations, curricula, and policies.

2. Make Involvement Meaningful. Some parents may want to get involved but are unsure of how to do so. Teachers must provide meaningful opportunities.

3. Offer Supports. Teachers and schools can provide access to and information on parenting and learning resources. These tools can assist families in supporting their middle school children.

Address Individual Needs

Society and classrooms are wonderfully diverse, but all students, including those with disabilities and unique needs, require the individual touch to flourish. Lenz

Involve Families Effectively

- Find out about the unique skills, talents, hobbies, and careers of parents and families.
- Establish ongoing opportunities for parents and family members to share special skills and talents through guest speaking or mini-courses.
- Create classroom assignments that provide parents with opportunities to connect to their child.
- Share schoolwide opportunities for parent involvement.
- Use culturally informed and sensitive interaction styles.

Connect Parents to Support Systems

- Provide supports that connect parents with information about tutoring skills or tutoring resources for their child.

- Ensure that parents have resources and support to understand and participate in educational planning for their child, including the IEP and transition processes.

- Offer a tip sheet of suggestions on how parents can assist middle schoolers with homework.

- Connect parents to community resources that provide parenting information about early adolescence.

- Recognize parents for their efforts and accomplishments.

and Deshler (2004) encourage teachers to develop an "inclusive pedagogy." Teachers must have a personal awareness of attitudes and skills that support inclusive practices. As needed, educators must expand their professional knowledge and skills to support diverse learners. (We discuss more about these practices in Chapter 4.)

Keep an Eye to the Future

Parents often exclaim, "I can't believe she is already in middle school!" "When did he get to be a junior in high school!" "What do I do with myself now that she's at college?" "Where did the time go?" Maybe you have experienced this thought as a teacher when encountering a former student after several years have passed. Teachers and parents have an important job to do, yet time does pass quickly. It is a privilege to have a small part in helping to build the future of a child.

Education is about preparing students for their futures. To do this, teachers must construct middle school classrooms and building-wide practices that prepare adolescents for their tomorrows. Students need to gain the dispositions, knowledge, and skills necessary to live responsible, productive, independent, and joyful lives. Educators can do this by infusing transition-centered principles and practices into middle schools.

Bringing the Pieces Together

Make Connections

Understanding early adolescents and teachers' roles in their lives can be likened to playing the childhood board game Chutes and Ladders. Players move forward or backward via chutes and ladders until they reach the winning corner. A player moves up the ladder by landing on a space that depicts a good activity or positive action. When the not-so-good happens, the player retreats down a chute and must try again to move forward. Middle schoolers are constantly up and down, back and forth, and side to side in their development. In Activity 2.6, consider how you can use the middle school practices discussed in this chapter to help move students across the developmental chutes and up the ladder toward adulthood. When students withdraw, how can you encourage them to try again?

Engage in Reflection: The MidEx Connection

Consider how the key information presented in this chapter relates to the Mid-Ex model presented in Chapter 1. In Figure 2.1 we outline several key concepts and principles supported throughout the literature. Note how these ideas reach across environments and middle school practices and impact multiple stakeholders. We hope that you have come to the conclusion that a total transition middle school approach is one that can sustain and nurture all students and support their developmental, individual, and unique needs as they journey toward adulthood. In the next chapter, we further examine how best to approach the transition needs of middle schoolers.

Activity 2.6 Chutes and Ladders

1. List the developmental physical, cognitive, and social–emotional chutes and ladders students must negotiate as they move through middle school.

   Examples: Changing body shape, emerging sexual characteristics

2. List adolescent experiences or occurrences that might hinder a student's successful forward movement.

   Examples: Self-consciousness, peer teasing, lowered self-esteem, inappropriate pressure for sexual activity

3. Describe middle school practices or structures that can address and support students as they resolve these developmental challenges.

   Examples: Advisory discussion on healthy body images; team meeting collaboration to discourage teasing; parent workshop on "What Really Happens in the Teen Dating Scene"; an open-door, welcoming policy in the school guidance office; weekly self-selected exploratory mini-courses

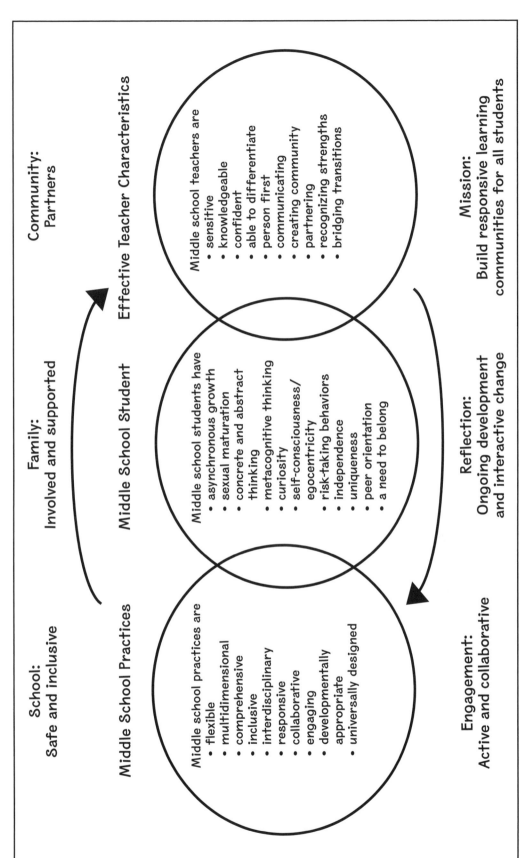

Figure 2.1. Middle school students and practices in the MidEx model.

Summary

Teaching the early adolescent necessitates an understanding of the unique developmental characteristics of this age group. Educators must support students through the myriad of physical, cognitive, and social–emotional changes that take place during the middle school years. Effective middle school practices, such as flexible organizational structures, advisory programs, exploratory curriculum, and collaborative partnerships with professionals and parents, address the needs of the middle schooler. Students with and without disabilities will experience a more successful journey through these years when teachers use inclusive and cohesive middle level practices that support transition-centered principles. By understanding and acting on knowledge of students and middle level best practices, teachers have the opportunity to shape more successful futures for middle school students.

How many children are discouraged from pursuing an education because teachers have taken it upon themselves to judge who can achieve and who cannot. I wasn't there to judge my students. My job as a teacher was to get their talents working.

—Marva Collins, former educator in
Chicago Public Schools and author of several books
(http://www.marvacollins.com/biography2.html)

Impact of Information on Your Mission

1. List your mission keywords (feel free to change keywords as you progress).

2. Describe a story from your teaching or experience that relates to the developing early adolescent and the role of the middle school general or special education teacher. Perhaps an event came to mind while you were reading this chapter.

3. What influenced your actions or the actions of others (e.g., students) in the story?

4. What information did you learn in this chapter that influences this story?

5. What teaching practices might you change based on this new information?

CHAPTER 3

Transition and Career Development in Middle School

What is the purpose of middle school?

Middle School Guidance Counselor:
   The purpose is to assist in meeting developmental goals and potentials.

Middle School Psychologist:
   The purpose is to provide adolescents with a safe environment to be adolescent.

Seventh-grade Language Arts Teacher:
   The purpose of middle school is to prepare adolescents for the high school experience. It also helps to prepare for life after high school and college prep.

Learning Objectives

1. To describe the historical foundations of career education and transition services.

2. To explain the models of service delivery for career education and transition services.

3. To describe the components of career education and transition services.

4. To give examples of how to assist students as they set postsecondary goals and plan activities to reach their goals.

5. To integrate transition planning and services into the middle school curriculum.

Is Transition Only About Work?

Several years ago Jeanne Repetto was the keynote speaker at a job fair for a local school district. Her audience was about 150 middle and high school students with disabilities. When she eagerly accepted this task, the organizer warned her not to be discouraged if none of the students listened to her because they tended to be poor listeners. Determined to enthrall these students, Dr. Repetto planned a presentation that would have the students sitting on the edge of their seats. Her plan was simply to discuss their futures. Dr. Repetto began by talking about a day in the students' lives 5 years after they graduated from school. They were asked to visualize waking up, turning on the radio, taking a shower, making breakfast, driving to work, working, paying some bills after work, going out to dinner and a movie with friends, and going to bed that night. This got the students' attention! Dr. Repetto then discussed goal writing and the skills needed to reach their goals. The presentation was not only fun but also prompted the students to think about their futures. It also helped them to realize that the future is not only about work.

Even if people work a 40-hour week and sleep 56 hours a week, they still have 72 hours each week to do other activities. Throughout the course of a week, a person takes on many different roles, including worker, friend, family member, consumer, athlete, and citizen. Most of the skills needed to perform these roles will overlap; however, each role may also have a unique set of skills needed for success. For example, a parent needs skills in general areas such as organizing schedules, communicating with others, and sharing affection, but a parent also needs to know how to discipline in a firm but loving manner. Assisting students to learn the skills needed to be successful in various life roles is key to the mission of career education.

Activity 3.1 gives you the opportunity to record how you spend your time during a week and how you learned to do each type of activity. You may want to ask your students to do this activity. They will learn how they are spending their time, and you may gain some more understanding of their lives.

What Is Transition?

Transition is mentioned frequently when professionals and parents discuss Individualized Education Programs (IEPs). Transitions happen throughout everyone's life. A person who moves makes a transition from one community to another. A person who changes marital status experiences a major transition in life. Changing jobs is a transition in employment. You can probably generate a long list of transitions that people undergo in life.

The idea of transition in education was initially linked to career education. The concept of career education was first introduced in 1971 by the U.S. Commissioner of Education, Sidney Marland, in response to high drop-out rates and lack of life skills preparation in U.S. schools (Brolin, 1996; Kolstoe, 1996). Although he introduced the concept, Marland did not provide a definition. The following two statements emerged later in the 1970s to better define Marland's concept. Both statements address the concept that career education is preparation for all the roles a person will assume in life. The second statement expands this concept by stressing the need for the coordination of activities to prepare students to gain fulfillment through playing these life roles.

> *Career education is the totality of experiences through which one learns about and prepares to engage in work as part of his or her way of living.* (Hoyt, 1975, p. 4)

> *Career education—a lifelong process that infuses a career emphasis in all subjects, grades K–12, including job training, apprenticeship programs, mentoring, career exploration, and the nonpaid work done as a family member, citizen, and leisure seeker.* (Brolin, 1995, p. 53)

In the 1970s the U.S. Office of Career Education sponsored demonstration grants encouraging school districts to develop and implement career education curriculum. It is important to note that this movement took place in general education and was not specifically targeted to students with disabilities. School district career education programs began to disappear, however, as the grant money terminated.

Transition Models

In 1984 the director of the Office of Special Education and Rehabilitative Services, Madeleine Will, introduced the concept of transition as a federal initiative for students with disabilities. She defined the concept by presenting what has become known as the bridges model (see Figure 3.1). This model illustrates three bridges

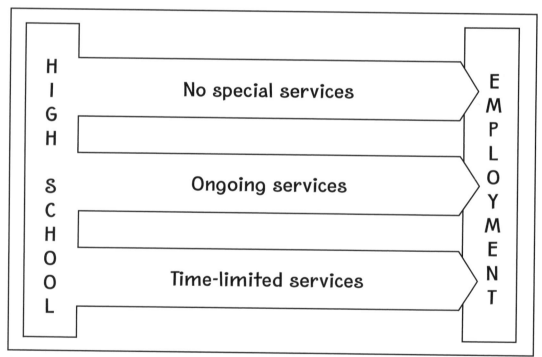

Figure 3.1. The bridges model of transition. *Note.* From *OSERS Programming for the Transition of Youth with Disabilities: Bridges from School to Working Life,* by M. Will, 1984, Washington, DC: Office of Special Education and Rehabilitative Services, U.S. Department of Education.

or paths to employment based on the level of support services a student needs (no services needed, ongoing services, time-limited services). The main focus of this initiative was to assist high school students with disabilities to successfully move into the world of work.

Results from studies (Hasazi, Gordon, & Roe, 1985; Mithaug, Horiuchi, & Fanning, 1985) showing that individuals with disabilities were experiencing poor postschool adjustment in all areas of life, not only employment, caused professionals to begin taking a broader view of transition. In 1985 Halpern introduced a model of transition that expanded the focus of the bridges model to include (a) employment, (b) residential environment, and (c) social and interpersonal networks as areas to address when assisting students in their move from school to adult life (see Figure 3.2).

The federal government adopted this broader view of transition with the passage of the Individuals with Disabilities Education Act (IDEA) of 1990, the IDEA Amendments of 1997, and the IDEA Improvement Act of 2004 (IDEA 2004) by mandating that transition services could encompass (a) instruction, (b) community

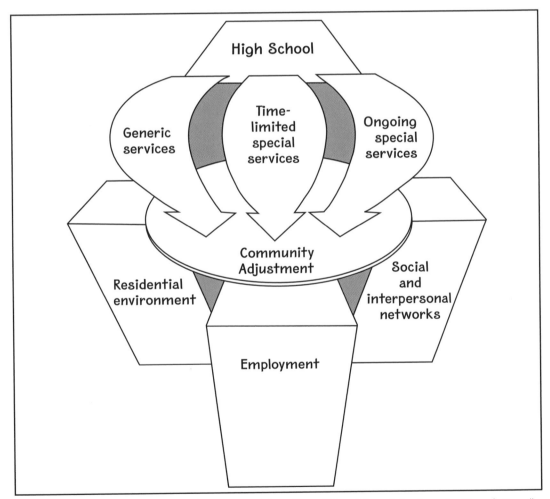

Figure 3.2. The Halpern model of transition. *Note.* From "Transition: A Look at the Foundations," by A. S. Halpern, 1985. *Exceptional Children, 51,* p. 481. Copyright 1985 by the Council for Exceptional Children. Reprinted with permission.

experiences, (c) employment, (d) postschool adult living skills, (e) functional vocational evaluation, and (f) related services. Transition services are to be based on individual student needs, preferences, strengths, and interests (IDEA 2004) and are to be designed within a results- and process-oriented program promoting movement into (a) postschool education, (b) vocational education, (c) integrated employment, (d) continuing and adult education, (e) adult services, (f) independent living, or (g) community participation.

Transition services need to be addressed in students' IEPs. IDEA 1990 required that a statement of transition services be included in a student's IEP by age 16, whereas the IDEA Amendments of 1997 required that a statement of transition services focusing on the student's courses of study be included in the IEP at age 14. IDEA 2004 has combined the language from these two requirements and requires a statement of transition services, no later than age 16, that addresses the following: (a) appropriate measurable postsecondary goals based on age-appropriate transition assessments related to training, education, employment, and independent living skills, and (b) transition services (including courses of study) needed to assist the student in reaching these goals.

The comprehensive transition education model (Sitlington & Clark, 2006; Sitlington, Clark, & Kolstoe, 2000) addresses the mandates of IDEA for determining students' transition needs. The model offers nine knowledge and skills domains: (a) communication and academic performance, (b) self-determination, (c) interpersonal relationships, (d) integrated community participation, (e) health and fitness, (f) independent/interdependent daily living, (g) leisure and recreation, (h) employment, and (i) further education and training. In the model this set of domains has two impact areas: (a) exit points and outcomes (see Figure 3.3) and (b) education and service delivery systems (see Figure 3.4). This model of transition further expands on previous models by infusing career education and career development components with transition concepts. For example, the comprehensive transition education model expands the transition focus on postsecondary outcomes to address all life outcomes, such as exiting elementary school to enter middle school education programs (Figure 3.3). The influence of career education can further be seen in the model's area of education and service delivery, which includes home and neighborhood, infant/toddler programs, and general education programs (Figure 3.4).

Another model of transition that uses choice making as its cornerstone is the lifelong model for choice building (Repetto & Webb, 1999). The term *choice building* replaces *transition* in this model and focuses on the ultimate transition outcome: the ability to plan and prepare for making one's own choices in life. Theoretically, the ability to make one's own life choices should foster a better quality of life because the person is in control of his or her actions. The lifelong model for choice building offers the following basic principles relating to transition and choice building:

- *Choices* are centered on an individual's needs, preferences, abilities, and interests, with transition services provided to assist the person to achieve his or her goals.

- *Transition planning and services* form the building blocks for life choices by providing the skills needed to achieve one's goals throughout life.

(*text continues on p. 63*)

Exit Points and Outcomes

Developmental/Life Phases	Exit Points
Infant/toddler and home training	Exit to preschool programs and integrated community participation
Preschool and home training	Exit to elementary school programs and integrated community participation
Elementary school	Exit to middle school/junior high school programs, age-appropriate self-determination, and integrated community participation
Middle school/junior high school	Exit to high school programs, entry-level employment, age-appropriate self-determination, and integrated community participation
High school	Exit to postsecondary education or entry-level employment, adult and continuing education, full-time homemaker, self-determined quality of life, and integrated community participation
Postsecondary education	Exit to specialized, technical, professional, or managerial employment, graduate or professional school programs, adult and continuing education, full-time homemaker, self-determined quality of life, and integrated community participation

Knowledge and Skills Domains

Communication and Academic Performance
Self-Determination
Interpersonal Relationships
Integrated Community Participation
Health and Fitness
Independent/Interdependent Daily Living
Leisure and Recreation
Employment
Further Education and Training

Figure 3.3. The comprehensive transition education model: Exit points and outcomes. *Note.* From *Transition Education and Services for Adolescents with Disabilities* (3rd ed., p. 27), by P. L. Sitlington, G. M. Clark, and O. P. Kolstoe, 2000, Needham Heights, MA: Allyn & Bacon. Copyright 2000 by Pearson Education. Reprinted with permission.

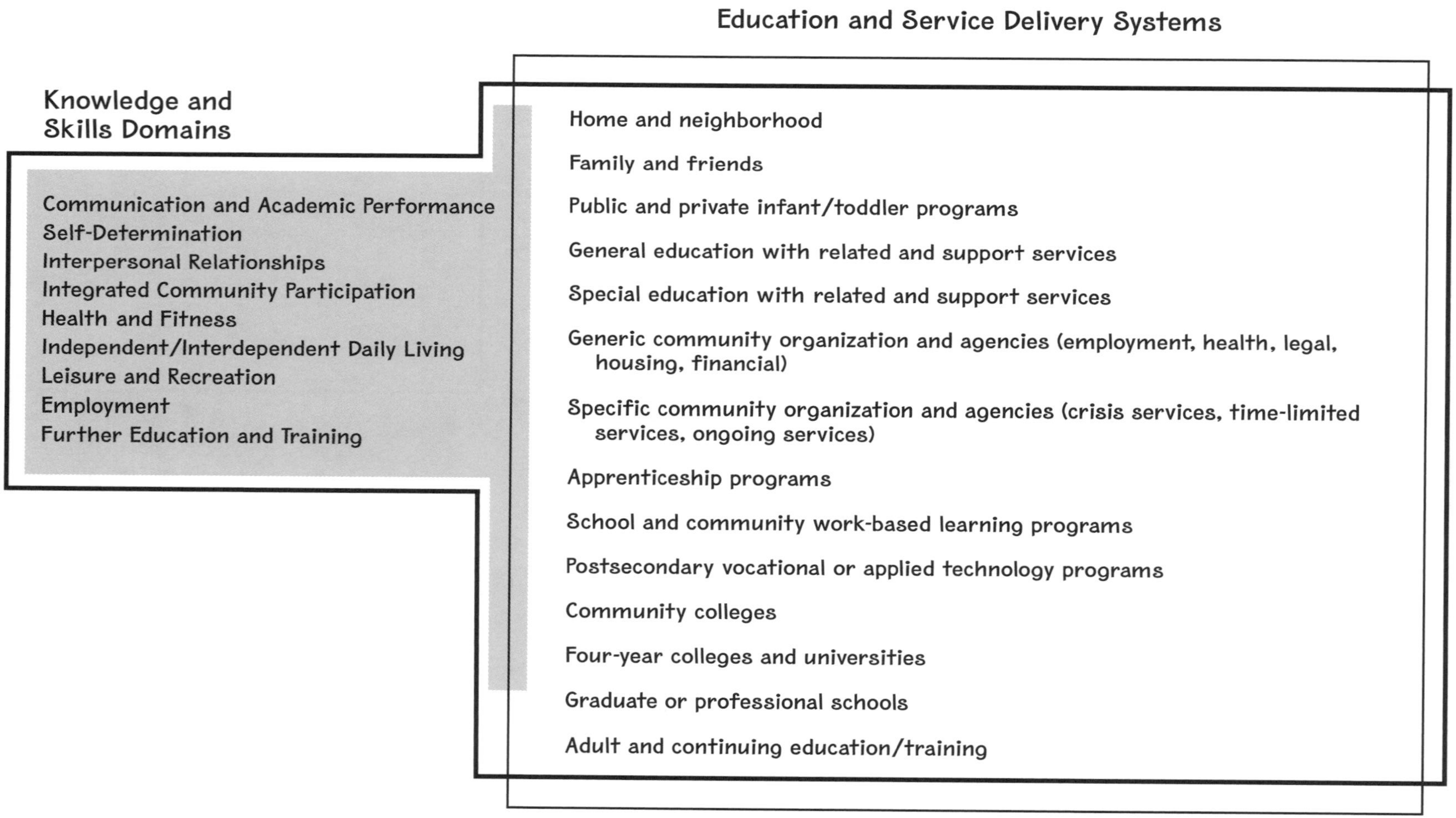

Education and Service Delivery Systems

Home and neighborhood

Family and friends

Public and private infant/toddler programs

General education with related and support services

Special education with related and support services

Generic community organization and agencies (employment, health, legal, housing, financial)

Specific community organization and agencies (crisis services, time-limited services, ongoing services)

Apprenticeship programs

School and community work-based learning programs

Postsecondary vocational or applied technology programs

Community colleges

Four-year colleges and universities

Graduate or professional schools

Adult and continuing education/training

Knowledge and Skills Domains

Communication and Academic Performance

Self-Determination

Interpersonal Relationships

Integrated Community Participation

Health and Fitness

Independent/Interdependent Daily Living

Leisure and Recreation

Employment

Further Education and Training

Figure 3.4. The comprehensive transition services model: Education and service delivery systems. *Note.* From *Transition Education and Services for Adolescents with Disabilities* (3rd ed., p. 28), by P. L. Sitlington, G. M. Clark, and O. P. Kolstoe, 2000, Needham Heights, MA: Allyn & Bacon. Copyright 2000 by Pearson Education. Reprinted with permission.

- The population of individuals who need transition and choice-making services is *all individuals from birth to death;* however, specific planning may focus on one life stage and the unique needs of one population (e.g., middle school students with learning disabilities).

- A person's goals and choices are *unique* and form each individual's distinctive construct of life.

- Transition planning is *active and ongoing* because people are lifelong learners, changing and making choices throughout their lives.

- Skills that are learned, such as self-determination, job hunting, and network building, are *applied to many situations* throughout one's life.

- Transition services are a *collaborative effort* among students, families, friends, special educators, general educators, and other service providers focused on assisting individuals to make choices and achieve goals.

- Transition and choice-making services *occur in many settings*, including school, home, community, and work.

Transition Definitions

By adopting the following definition of transition, the Council for Exceptional Children, Division of Career Development and Transition (DCDT) supports this broader view of transition.

> *Transition refers to a change in status from behaving primarily as a student to assuming emergent adult roles in the community. These roles include employment, participating in post-secondary education, maintaining a home, becoming appropriately involved in the community, and experiencing satisfactory personal and social relationships. The process of enhancing transition involves the participation and coordination of school programs, adult agency services, and natural supports within the community. The foundations for transition should be laid during the elementary and middle school years, guided by the broad concept of career development. Transition planning should begin no later than age 14, and students should be encouraged, to the full extent of their capabilities, to assume a maximum amount of responsibility for such planning.* (Halpern, 1994, p. 117)

In the DCDT's definition, career education and career development components are apparent. The importance of career development is addressed when suggesting that the foundation for transition is laid during the elementary and middle school years. Career education is infused into the definition by expanding adult roles beyond employment and postsecondary education to include maintaining a home and experiencing satisfactory personal and social relationships.

The DCDT definition exemplifies the broad definition of transition repre-sented in this book. Transition, as we use the term, includes components of career education, career development, transition assessment, and transition services and outcomes. In this text, although our focus is on middle level grades, transition is presented as a lifelong process beginning in infancy and lasting throughout life. We address services and skills needed by students to function in all of life's roles.

Is Quality of Life Important?

Many professionals believe that this broader definition of transition will help stu-dents to obtain a high quality of life. After analyzing 41 outcome studies on students with disabilities published between 1975 and 1990, Halpern (1993) developed three quality-of-life domains: (a) physical and material well-being, (b) performance in adult roles, and (c) personal fulfillment. A person's quality of life is determined by a balance among these domains. Data from research studies looking at employment, living situations, level of financial support, and involvement in leisure activities indi-cate that few adults with disabilities have adjusted well to adult life and obtained a good quality of life (Lichtenstein & Michaelides, 1993; Sitlington & Frank, 1993; Zetlin & Hosseini, 1989). Findings from the National Longitudinal Transition Study (Blackorby & Wagner, 1996) are more positive and show gains in employment rates, wages, postsecondary education enrollment, and independent living. However, con-cern was raised about the impact of continued low wages on the quality of life of individuals with disabilities. This concern points to the need for balance between the three quality-of-life domains. For example, a person may be performing an adult role by working, but his or her physical and material well-being will be impacted by low wages, thus affecting personal fulfillment.

Activity 3.2 encourages you to consider your own quality of life. You can adapt the activity for your students.

What Are Best Practices in Transition?

Throughout the past 3 decades, researchers and policymakers have identified best practices in both career education and transition. Various best practices have been organized and developed to guide transition programs (Brolin, 1997; Flexer, Sim-mons, Luft, & Baer, 2001; G. Greene & Kochhar-Bryant, 2003; Halpern, 1993; Kohler, 1993; Patton, 1999; F. Rusch & Chadsey, 1998; M. Rusch & Miller, 1998; Sitlington & Clark, 2006; Sitlington et al., 2000; Wehman, 1996). Identified best practices tend to fall into two main categories: (a) skills and competencies needed by students and (b) processes needed to support transition.

Skills and Competencies

One example of skills and competency best practices is the life centered career education (LCCE) model, which is a set of 22 competencies, categorized under the areas of daily living skills, personal/social skills, and occupational guidance and

Activity 3.2 My Quality of Life

1. Write a paragraph about your own quality of life, addressing each of the three domains—physical and material well-being, performance in adult roles, and personal fulfillment—defined by Halpern (1993).

2. List ways to improve your quality of life in each domain.

3. Do you think the concept of quality of life can be applied to your teaching? How?

preparation skills (Brolin, 1997). These competencies include skills such as paying taxes, buying and preparing food, and maintaining personnel relationships (see Chapter 4, Table 4.3). These competencies are used to guide instruction to prepare students for all life roles (see Figure 3.5).

A related set of skill competencies identified by the business community that have impacted transition programming was compiled by the Secretary's Commission on Achieving Necessary Skills (SCANS; 1991). These skills are needed by workers to successfully maintain jobs. The SCANS report also included letters to parents and educators, detailing the importance of their teaching these skills.

Transition best practices related to skills and competencies needed by students can be grouped into five categories: self-determination, academic and vocational performance, relationship building, consumerism, and self-maintenance (Repetto, 2003). These groupings (the first five listed on Table 3.1) are not meant to be all-inclusive because every student needs to develop specific skills to meet his or her unique needs. Teachers need to place varied levels of emphasis on these skills based on their students' individual needs and desired postschool outcomes.

(text continues on p. 68)

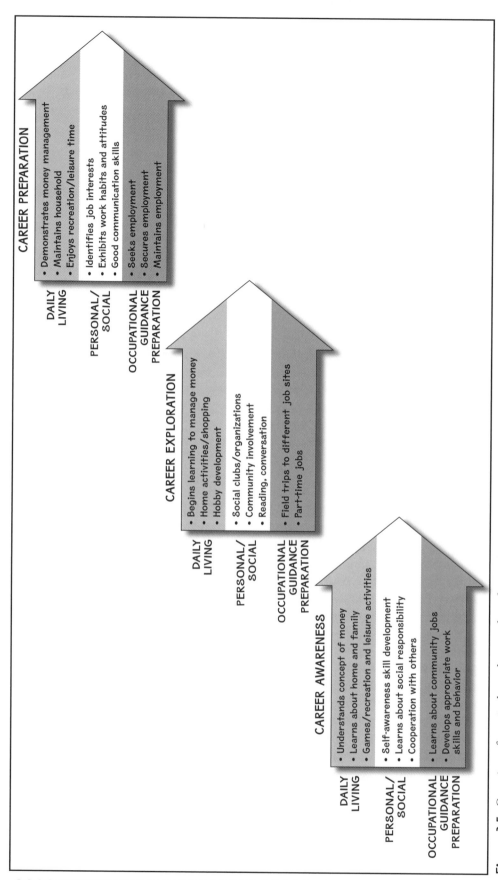

Figure 3.5. Overview of curriculum planning based on LCCE and the stages of career development. *Note.* From *Transition Manual: TRIAD Telecommunications Project* (p. 49), by I. D. Cook and M. Thurman-Urbanic, 1990, Institute: West Virginia Graduate College. Copyright 1990 by West Virginia Graduate College. Reprinted with permission. Originally adapted from *Life Centered Career Education* (3rd ed., pp. 10–12), by D. E. Brolin, 1989, Arlington, VA: Council for Exceptional Children.

Table 3.1
Transition Practices

Best Practice	Definition	Example of Use
Self-determination	Ability to determine a goal, acquire the skills to meet that goal, plan the actions to be taken, take the actions, and evaluate the outcome (Field, Hoffman, & Spezia, 1998)	Being self-determined allows (a) students to plan steps needed to meet their postschool outcomes with their IEP teams or (b) people to change jobs after acquiring new skills for a different, more self-fulfilling position.
Academic and vocational skills	Skills that include job-specific skills as well as general academic knowledge (Patton, Cronin, & Wood, 1999)	Academic and vocational skills assist an individual to complete a job application, program a computer, read a book, complete a college project, follow a cooking recipe, and surf the Web.
Relationship building	Ability to maintain a relationship with friends, co-workers, community members, and families (Brolin, 1997; Elksnin & Elksnin, 1998)	Relationship-building skills allow a person to visit with co-workers, complete group projects in school, enjoy parties, and report to the doctor why a child is not feeling well.
Consumerism	Skills needed to manage money and make good financial choices (Brolin, 1997)	Consumerism skills allow one to compare ads in the paper to find the best buy on a new car, pay monthly bills, and save for a vacation.
Self-maintenance	Skills needed to stay healthy, be able to work, and enjoy leisure time (Brolin, 1997)	Self-maintenance skills enable an individual to plan weekly menus, take care of clothing, access the community, visit doctors, and exercise.
Community experience	Access to the community through field trips, job tryouts, and paid and unpaid work experiences (Benz & Lindstrom, 1997; Brolin, 1997)	Community experience allows students to try out several jobs to learn what they like and do not like about various jobs.
Individualized planning	Planning for each student's desired postschool outcome based on his or her needs, interests, preferences, and abilities (Sitlington, Neubert, Begun, Lombard, & Leconte, 1996; West et al., 1999)	Through individualized planning, supports can be coordinated to allow a student to explore various careers in the community.
Family involvement	Inclusion of family in all aspects of the individualized planning process (Wehmeyer, Morningstar, & Husted, 1999)	Family involvement allows family's needs and desires to be heard and addressed.
Interagency coordination	Coordination of individuals' needs with agency services and supports offered while individuals are in school and once they leave school (Blalock & Benz, 1999)	Interagency coordination can assist a student who is going to a community college to link up with the support services available to help ensure his or her success while in college.

Note. Adapted from "Transition to Living," by J. Repetto, 2003, *Exceptionality, 11*(2), pp. 77–78. Copyright 2003 by Erlbaum. Adapted with permission.

Processes Needed To Support Transition

Processes that support transition include (a) interagency collaboration, (b) individualized student planning, (c) family involvement, (d) relationship building, (e) community connections, and (f) academic and vocational education. Patton (1999) developed a set of guiding principles to support transition: (a) start transition efforts early; (b) empower students; (c) include families; (d) utilize community-based activities; and (e) gain interagency commitment, cooperation, and coordination.

In Activity 3.3 you are asked to consider best practices in transition. If you are a current educator, assess your school's or program's current practices.

Activity 3.3 Best Practices List

List the best practices identified in the previous section for each of these areas: (a) skills and competencies needed by students and (b) processes needed to support transition. Put a check mark beside each best practice that you already have in your program and school.

Skills and Competencies Needed by Students	Processes Needed To Support Transition

How Does Transition Apply to Middle School Education?

Applying Transition to Middle School Education

You may have questions about how to infuse transition into your everyday teaching. What factors do you need to consider before you actually begin the process? How does transition impact your instruction in a middle school? Before you answer these questions, it is important to understand the full scope of transition and choice making. To recognize their impact and application in middle school settings, we provide examples in the areas of (a) delivery of services, (b) planning, (c) competencies, and (d) persons or professionals involved. Refer to the MidEx model presented in Chapter 1. Remember, the student is in the center of the model and is flanked by best practices and teacher characteristics. To further strengthen your understanding of how to incorporate transition into middle level education, we discuss how to build transition and choice components into your teaching. As this section unfolds, you may recognize many of the components of the MidEx model. If this process seems challenging or overwhelming to you, you are not alone. Many teachers have voiced concern about the task of integrating the large amount of necessary information into their teaching (Walsh, 2001), but once you understand the basic components, you will discover how naturally they fit into your teaching (Hapner & Imel, 2002; Otis-Wilborn, Winn, Ford, & Keyes, 2000).

Delivery of Services

At the middle school level, service delivery for students with disabilities is individualized through the IEP (see Chapter 7 for more information on IEPs). Services are provided to assist students to achieve their outcome statements or dream statements. These statements capture what students want to be doing 3 to 5 years after high school graduation. In middle school, these dream statements may be vague or global. As students near graduation, their outcome or dream statements will become more specific and detailed. To determine the who, what, where, how, and when of service delivery, the IEP team has to take into account the student's interests, preferences and needs. Both informal services (e.g., a field trip) and formal services (e.g., vocational evaluation) are delivered in many settings to help the student to meet his or her goals. In other words, services are delivered in any environment or setting that is appropriate to the student's goals. Delivery of services may take place in a home economics class, an after-school study strategy workshop, the family home, a community agency, or a bus. A variety of individuals may assist in delivery, and the time frame of service delivery may expand beyond the typical school day (see Table 3.2).

Activity 3.4 gives you an opportunity to consider the advantages of and challenges inherent in service delivery beyond school hours and settings. The case study in Activity 3.5 is for practice in designing a service delivery plan.

Planning

As you consider the planning process, think of planning in four career development stages: awareness, exploration, preparation, and actualization (Brolin, 1996; Halpern, 1985; Repetto & Webb, 1999; Sitlington et al., 2000). For each of these stages, we provide examples found in middle school settings.

Awareness. If you ask middle school students what they would like to be when they grow up, they often respond with one of the following: a professional athlete, actor, rock star, or the profession of a parent or significant person in the student's life. In the same vein, if you ask students about recreational choices, their answers often reflect preferences of their peers. In short, many middle school students may not have exposure to a wide array of choices, and when asked to voice their own choices, they may revert to what they know in life.

Table 3.2
Delivery of Services

Who	What	Where	How	When
Neighbor	Work on repairing a car	Neighbor's garage	Hands-on practice with expert advice of neighbor	Saturday mornings
Sister or brother	Volunteering	Nursing home	Reading to residents	Sunday afternoons
Friends	Talk about attending a ball game	University field	Phone conversations	Every evening for a week
Guidance counselor and other support service personnel	Learn about high school expectations and environment	High school guidance office	Conversation	During high school visit
School nurse	Explore health risks of certain jobs	Vocational classes	Conversation and presentation	During career exploration class
Speech and language therapist	Using an augmented communication device	Work, school, and community	Demonstration and guided learning	Various times throughout the week as directed by student

Note. From "A Model for Guiding the Transition Process," by J. B. Repetto and K. W. Webb, 1999, in Transition and School-Based Services, by S. H. deFur and J. R. Patton (Eds.), Austin, TX: PRO-ED. Copyright 1999 by PRO-ED, Inc. Adapted with permission.

Middle school teachers can help students broaden their awareness of the many choices available to them; however, teachers must take care not to invalidate students' initial choices in their attempts to expose students to other options. Consider the following example: Sam is a seventh-grade student who is reluctant to voice his preferences and dislikes. Your school is sponsoring an interests and hobbies day, and students choose three activities to attend. When you ask Sam what he has chosen, he shrugs and flatly recites the choices his friend John has selected. John, an artistic boy who enjoys creative, sedentary activities, has chosen activities that reflect his preferences. You know that Sam dislikes class projects that involve art but really enjoys his physical education class. You could respond in a number of ways:

1. "Sam, are you sure that is YOUR choice? You're just following John!"

2. "Sam, you KNOW you HATE art. Why in the world are you choosing that activity?"

3. "Sam, those are fun choices. Did you happen to notice the cooking, sports, and computer choices? Would you like to try any of these activities?"

As Sam's teacher, you must be careful to validate his choices but at the same time encourage him to expand his awareness of other options, as stated in response 3

Activity 3.4 Advantages and Challenges Related to the Delivery of Services

Spend some time looking at Table 3.2, Delivery of Services. You will notice an array of individuals involved in service delivery, a variety of activities and settings, and a range of times. What would be some advantages in expanding the service delivery beyond typical school times and settings? What are some challenges?

Advantages	Challenges

(Webb, 2000). Sam may truly want to explore his artistic self (see response 2) or he may be following the known choices of his friend (response 1).

Exploration. Typically, middle school students are in the exploration stage of planning, although planning is a lifelong process that continually cycles through the four career development stages. The exploration stage is a time of learning about one's place in the world of work, community, and family. In other words, exploration is a time for "trying on" choices to see how they fit. During this time, students learn about the skills, talents, and attributes they have and the skills they will need to learn in order to function in their chosen community setting, job, and family situation. Think of the development of middle schools you read about in Chapter 1. Many middle school models are built on a design in which students explore, investigate, reflect, and develop strategies that will guide future choices (Wiles & Bondi, 2001).

Imagine a seventh-grade student, Shalikia. When you ask her what she would like to do for work when she is an adult, she answers, "be a fashion model." In your efforts to help Shalikia explore this career, you can use a teaching tool, Webb et al.'s (1999) Circle of Possibilities (see Figure 3.6). Write her career dream in the circle. Ask her, "What are the parts of modeling that are appealing to you? What does being a model mean to you?" Write each of her reasons on lines that radiate from the circle. Then ask Shalikia to choose her three top reasons and list them as

Activity 3.5 Service Delivery Plan

Joey is a seventh grader in your class. He wants to take classes in high school that will result in a standard or general education high school diploma. He has expressed interest in working as an operator of heavy equipment and in learning how to swim and play golf. He also has expressed great concern about the number of lost and stray dogs in the community and says he would like to do something about the problem that would be "good for the dogs and people too." Design a service delivery plan that could help Joey explore some of his goals.

Who	What	Where	How	When

column headings on a chart like the chart in Activity 3.6. Next, brainstorm and list other careers that fit each reason. Shalikia can spend time and effort exploring any options that are of interest to her.

Preparation. The preparation stage of planning involves the action or effort made to achieve the goal that has been set. In other words, the tools or skills an individual needs are coordinated to the actualization of the goal. You might think of

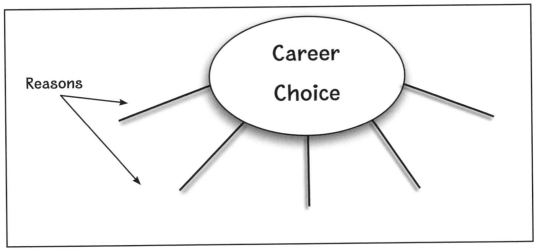

Figure 3.6. Circle of possibilities. *Note*. Adapted from *Dare to Dream* (2nd ed.), by K. Webb et al., 1999, Tallahassee, FL: Bureau of Instructional Support and Community Services, Florida Department of Education. Copyright 1999 by Florida Department of Education. Adapted with permission.

this stage as the *action* or *effort* part of planning. Preparation may require commitment, perseverance, and dedication to the ultimate goal, and students learn helpful information about the effort needed for goal acquisition. Teachers can play valuable roles during this stage by offering encouragement, showing efficient methods of effort, and rehearsing the actualization stages with students. During the preparation stage students learn a great deal about their abilities, talents, and needs. Teachers share in this learning process by bringing students' attention to their strengths and facilitating ways to meet needs. Students benefit from thinking about the changes

Activity 3.6 Career Brainstorming

Reason #1 Related Jobs or Careers	Reason #2 Related Jobs or Careers	Reason #3 Related Jobs or Careers

they may have to make and predicting how these changes will impact their lives. One method of assisting students in this stage is through Positive Path Behaviors (Webb et al., 1999, p. 23), which involves considering these questions:

- What can I do to make this dream happen?

- What changes do I have to make in order for this dream to happen?

- Who can support me as I take these steps?

- How will these changes affect my life?

Actualization. The actualization stage happens when students are ready to meet or attempt their goals. In your role as educator, you must be mindful that their initial attempts may not be successful. Rather than watching your students walk away from the goal while vowing to never attempt this goal again, you have an opportunity to teach problem solving, reflection, and resilience.

Consider this scenario as you think about teachable moments: Daria is an eighth-grade student who is interested in childcare and who loves babysitting. She mentions her interest at her IEP meeting and voices a desire to explore her interest. Several families would like to engage her as a babysitter but want assurance that she knows safety and childcare procedures. During Daria's exploration stage, she volunteers in a church nursery and job-shadows an older sister as she babysits. Daria spends time talking to childcare workers and finds out about several certification programs for babysitters. The program she chooses to pursue is offered in a Saturday workshop through the Red Cross. During the preparation stage Daria enrolls in the workshop and receives materials to read before the workshop. She brings the materials to school, and you suggest that she read them during silent reading time in your class. Days pass and you notice that she has not read her assigned materials in spite of your encouragement. On the day of the workshop, Daria is late to the session and still has not read the materials. On Monday she reports that she left the workshop before the final certification activity because "it was boring and those people were stupid." She seems very disappointed and turns to you for help.

At this point you want to investigate the following questions:

1. Is Daria still interested in the certification but underprepared?

2. Has Daria decided that babysitting and childcare are not among her preferences?

3. Would further preparation be beneficial and allow her to actualize her original goal?

Daria tells you she really wants to pursue the certification but she is scared of the process. You offer to help her (a) plan a schedule for reading the materials during silent reading, (b) arrange to rehearse the certification materials with her mom, and (c) plan to attend the workshop on time. Daria eagerly agrees with the plan and tells you she now knows what is expected during the certification activities. You congratulate Daria for her determination and ask her to tell you the important things she has learned about herself during this experience. She writes about her strengths and areas of need she discovered during journal time in your classroom.

Before actualizing her goals, Daria needed to spend more time and effort in the preparation stage. Teachers can play key roles in facilitating the successful movement between preparation and actualization by presenting this shift as a time for learning and growing, and then trying again with a new or remodeled set of tools. Teachers need to celebrate the learning and reflection accomplished by the students as much as the actualization of their goals.

Planning: Putting the Pieces Together. Setting postsecondary goals and a focus of study to meet those goals are key components of transition planning and services under IDEA 2004. Planning can be done formally through the IEP process or informally by students in journals, portfolios, and conversations. The essential part of planning is that students learn the process and apply it to the many facets of their lives. Table 3.3 presents several scenarios of the planning process for students.

Competencies

Competencies signify levels of mastery in essential life components within such areas as community, vocation, and academics (Repetto & Webb, 1999). You may find it helpful to think of competencies in the following way: A student first learns skills in self-determination. Because the student has a firm sense of knowing and valuing him- or herself, self-determination skills enable the student to set goals based on talents, preferences, and interests. The student makes choices to learn applicable knowledge that will assist him or her in obtaining personal goals. For example, if one of your middle school students wants to become a journalist, he must identify the specific competencies, or levels of mastery, needed to do this job. Although the student's language arts teacher could offer suggestions about the competencies needed for the job of a journalist, the guidance counselor, the high school journalism teacher, and a journalist with the local paper also could support the student as he determines specific competencies for the particular type of journalism he wants to attempt. In addition to the competencies he needs to become a journalist, your student must also acquire a set of competencies related to general work skills, such as dressing appropriately, interacting with coworkers, and managing time. One of your jobs as his teacher is to help him find key resource people such as the guidance counselor, a vocational teacher, or an employment specialist within a community agency.

The ability to determine competencies needed for any goal is a skill that will serve students in all areas of life. Once they become skilled at setting goals, finding resources, and breaking goals into the subsets of needed competencies, students are equipped with a strategy they can choose to use in many areas of life. Activity 3.7 provides an opportunity to determine competencies needed to help a student acquire his goals.

Persons and Professionals Involved

Have you ever sought the advice of family members, teachers, or health professionals? Perhaps you have gathered information from your peers or an employer.

Table 3.3
Transition and Career Planning

Awareness	Exploration	Preparation	Actualization
You hear about a new soccer team forming at your school.	Gather information about the requirements for eligibility, the coach, the costs of a uniform, and what kind of physical shape a participant needs to be in. Decide if you want to try out for the team.	Sign up for the tryouts and get in shape, review soccer rules, and make your grades meet team standards.	Try out for the team, do your best performance, and have a GOOD time.
Your teacher discusses high school with you.	Gather formal and informal information on the high school setting and decide what additional information you need to know.	Talk with school counselors, teachers, and other students.	Visit a high school.
A family friend is a cosmetologist and thinks that you might like to work in that career.	Since you just turned 14, discuss exploring the field of cosmetology in your next IEP meeting.	Write a goal to gather formal and informal information on the skills and work environments of being a cosmetologist. Information might be gathered from guidance counselor, school nurse, vocational educator, and cosmetologists.	Use information gathered to decide if your likes, interests, and abilities match this job.
You realize you are having difficulty reading and understanding your class reading assignments.	Meet with special education teacher to explore classes and methods to improve your reading.	Help your IEP team members write a reading goal to help you gain reading skills.	Apply your reading skills to your classes and everyday living.

Note. Adapted from "A Model for Guiding the Transition Process," by J. B. Repetto and K. W. Webb, 1999, in *Transition and School-Based Services,* by S. H. deFur and J. R. Patton (Eds.), Austin, TX: PRO-ED. Copyright 1999 by PRO-ED, Inc. Adapted with permission.

Most people have a network of contacts that might include friends, neighbors, family members, social workers, instructors, mentors, bosses, and other individuals. These individuals may offer encouragement or information. They may be casual acquaintances or paid professionals who help you. You may have connected with them by chance or through a formal system such as an IEP meeting. One of the most important roles you will play as a middle school special education teacher involves establishing collaborative relationships with other school professionals, family members, agency personnel, and community members. Furthermore, you will be modeling the importance of collaborating while teaching your students how to establish their own networks. As you facilitate your students' learning and devel-

Activity 3.7 Setting Competency Goals

Alexandro is a 15-year-old student in eighth grade. At his last IEP meeting, he shared his desired postschool outcome statement with team members. Alexandro shared that he wanted to learn to drive so he could get his driver's license, and he wanted to graduate from high school with a standard diploma. Use the following table to generate ideas for the competencies Alexandro could choose to pursue in order to acquire his goals.

Goals	Resources To Find Competencies	Needed Competencies
Get a driver's license		
Graduate from high school with a standard diploma		

© 2006 by PRO-ED, Inc.

opment, your collaboration may include professional relationships with school-based service providers, general educators, vocational educators, and personnel from high school, vocational rehabilitation, private industry, developmental services, substance abuse, mental health, blind services, and other public, private, or community agencies. Along with these formal linkages, family members, friends, and mentors are critical partners to you and your students. Students must know about these vital linkages and the services or supports each agency or person can offer. Armed with knowledge about their own unique interests and needs, your students will choose a group of people who will facilitate the foundation for a strong support network.

Activity 3.8 is a practice exercise for helping a student list people who could help him in achieving his goals.

Putting It All Together

Table 3.4 demonstrates the application of transition services offered to middle school students with disabilities. This same type of matrix could be useful to all students and could be used at many stages in their lives.

How To Teach Transition in an Age of Standards

Most states have implemented educational standards that are attached to high-stakes assessments. Under the IDEA Amendments of 1997 and IDEA 2004, all students with disabilities are to have access to the general education curriculum and be assessed accordingly. Students' IEPs must address this access, and the IEP team must determine how to appropriately assess students' growth within the general curriculum. As advocates, teachers want to ensure that students with disabilities have full participation in reform efforts and assessment (Quenemoen, 2001). On the other hand, many experts are concerned that the primary focus on academic skills may hinder growth in life skills, functional skills, and transition (Agran, Alper, & Wehmeyer, 2002; deFur, 2002; Edgar, Patton, & Day-Vines, 2002).

Table 3.4
Sampling of Middle School Transition Services

Population	Service Delivery	Planning	Competencies	Person/Professionals Involved
Ray, age 14	Intensive support services	Ray wants to attend sporting events at his high school next year and to learn to use the bus system in his city.	Gets an activity schedule from the high school; plans rides to get to the events; learns bus routes to places he wants to go	Family members Special educator Transportation personnel Occupational therapist
Lynn, age 12	Time-limited support services	Lynn wants to be a chef, make new friends, and be in the high school chorus.	Investigates high-tech program in high school; enrolls in a community education cooking class for youth; signs up for chorus in her middle school	Guidance counselor Family members Vocational education teacher Special educator Chorus teacher

Note. Adapted from "A Model for Guiding the Transition Process," by J. B. Repetto and K. W. Webb, 1999, in *Transition and School-Based Services,* by S. H. deFur and J. R. Patton (Eds.), Austin, TX: PRO-ED. Copyright 1999 by PRO-ED, Inc. Adapted with permission.

Activity 3.8 Establishing a Network

Jim is a seventh-grade student in your language arts class. He is quite shy and seems to lack confidence in himself. Jim has a supportive mother and a large extended family. You notice that he often eats by himself at lunchtime. Jim has difficulty with any kind of written assignment and sees the speech–language pathologist twice a week. During class he is quiet, does his work, and interacts fairly well with peers. Jim loves any outdoor activity and has told you about how much he enjoys "getting wood" with his neighbor for both families' wood-burning stoves. When you ask him about what he wants to do after high school, he tells you that he does not know but the job must involve being outdoors. Jim has a good relationship with the technical education teacher he had during his exploration classes, and Jim's math teacher has shared that she believes Jim has potential to per-form well in high school math classes. You want to assist Jim as he builds his network of support. List the individuals who are in his cur-rent circle of support. Next, think of individuals whom Jim could add to his network.

Current Network	
People	Reasons for Choice

Future Network	
People	Reasons for Choice

IDEA 2004 is aligned with the No Child Left Behind Act of 2001 and addresses the need for standards-based education in several ways. Students are to access and progress in general education and participate in all state and district assessments. The definition of transition services also addresses standards-based reform by stating that transition services are to be designed "within a results-oriented process, that is focused on improving the academic and functional achievement of the child with a disability to facilitate the child's movement from school to post-school activities" (IDEA 2004, Sec. 602).

Many teachers have infused the concepts of life and functional skills and transition into a standards-based curriculum. We think of this approach as "double whammy" teaching. Teachers can use standards to shape *what* they will teach. They can incorporate life skills, transition needs, and students' IEP goals according to *how* they teach the standards. For instance, if you were addressing the sixth-grade standard that "the student uses estimation in problem solving and computation" (Florida Sunshine State Standards MA.A.4.3, 1995), you could present the standard through grocery shopping, budgeting, consumer skills, or any other specific skills your students need. Additional resources to help you plan your teaching around these concepts include Kochar-Bryant and Bassett (2002) and Patton, Cronin, and Wood (1999).

Applying Transition to the MidEx Model

If you were a teacher assigned to teach health to seventh graders, you would consider best practices such as those listed in Table 3.1 as you planned, prepared, and taught. Suppose the standard you were addressing was the following: "The student analyzes the influence of culture, media, technology, and other factors on health" (Florida Sunshine State Standards HE.B.2.3, 1995). Activity 3.9 helps you to think through how you can apply transition to the MidEx model.

When you begin to think and teach using the MidEx model guidelines, the process may seem forced or even somewhat artificial. If the thought of adding all of the MidEx components at once seems daunting to you, try targeting one component per week. For example, if you want to focus on family involvement in your lessons, include the family component and reflect on the impact of your efforts. Next, you might embed opportunities for students to develop skills in self-determination. Eventually, you will find that you have expanded your teaching to many or all of the MidEx components. Your goal is to think and teach from a broader base that infuses transition components. Transition is *not* about adding additional work to your teaching workload, but rather about *how* you approach the content you are currently addressing. The benefits for this practice will help your students make smoother transitions to high school and adulthood and will contribute to your sense of well-being as a professional in middle school.

Summary

Career education and transition services are crucial components of the middle school curriculum. Because adolescence is a time of reflection and change, middle

Activity 3.9 Applying the MidEx Model

The lessons you are teaching direct students to learn how messages from the media influence students' health behaviors. Jot down some activities, ideas, or lesson objectives for this topic. Refer to the MidEx Model in Chapter 2 and use Table 3.1 to guide your responses.

1. Middle School Student: Consider your students. What are their individual goals? What IEP goals could be addressed in these lessons? In what ways could you and your students relate the content of the lessons to students' goals?

2. Practices in Middle School for Diverse Learners: Think about the transition elements in this chapter. How would you embed student choice and decision making? Self-determination? How would you incorporate the who, what, where, how, and when of service delivery and the elements of the planning process?

3. Teacher Characteristics in Middle School and Special Education: What distinctive teacher characteristics would help your students to successfully learn? What skills could you incorporate to encourage reluctant learners?

4. School, Family, and Community: How could you engage school personnel and peers in the lesson? What ideas do you have for family involvement and communication? How could you extend this lesson into students' communities?

5. Engagement, Reflection, and Mission: What ideas do you have that would encourage students to engage in their own growth and learning? How could you encourage students to reflect about what they learned and how they learned it? Finally, how would you assist students as they consider how this information relates to their own set of goals and their mission statements?

school teachers should provide students with opportunities to explore career and life roles. Connecting curriculum to current and future life roles will assist students as they define their roles in society. Teachers have a unique opportunity to engage students in learning by applying and infusing career education and transition components into the curriculum. This infusion aligns with the legal mandate to include transition services in a student's IEPs no later than the year the student turns 16 years old. To specify a course of study along with measurable postsecondary outcomes by age 16, middle school teachers must incorporate career education, transition assessment, and functional skill development into the curriculum to assist students in the career development and transition planning process.

If one advances confidently in the direction of their dreams, and endeavors to lead a life which they have imagined, they will meet with a success unexpected in common hours.

—Henry David Thoreau

Impact of Information on Your Mission

1. List your mission keywords. Feel free to change keywords as you progress.

2. Describe a story from your teaching or experience that relates to this chapter. Perhaps an event came to mind while you were reading this chapter.

3. What influenced your actions or the actions of others (e.g., students) in the story?

4. What information did you learn in this chapter that influences this story?

5. What teaching practices might you change based on this new information?

CHAPTER 4

Middle School Curriculum

The best thing I've learned so far in middle school is ...

"How to get my locker open real fast so I'm not late to class!"

A motto or belief I have for effective teaching is ...

"Teaching middle school kids is a bit like being a rodeo clown. You've got to be ready when they come out of the chute, step in when you are needed, catch their attention immediately, and guide them where they need to go. Of course, all of this needs to be done with a bit of humor and laughter."

I hope that middle school gives my child ...

"Teachers who care—about my child, about her learning, about her feelings, about her ideas, about her success. Teachers who simply care."

Learning Objectives

1. To define *curriculum,* including explicit, implicit, and absent curricula, and to explain how these impact students at the middle school level.

2. To explain the concepts and practices of curriculum access, accommodation, and modification, and to describe how these practices relate to curriculum and transition.

3. To identify curriculum areas and instructional practices that support transition-relevant middle school curricula.

4. To explain how teachers and schools infuse transition principles and practices in middle school curricula.

5. To describe types of collaborative partnerships that are needed for effective transition-supported middle school curricula.

Introduction

We explored the foundations and importance of early adolescence in Chapter 2 and important principles in transition planning and collaboration in Chapter 3. In this chapter we explain how to bridge developmental considerations and transition principles with middle school curriculum practices. The purpose of this chapter is to provide you with a curriculum framework for designing an integrated, systematic approach to transition support for all middle school students.

Perhaps as you read through the objectives at the beginning of the chapter, you began to formulate possibilities for designing your approach. Perhaps you generated additional questions about the *who, why,* and *how* of realistically addressing transition skills during the middle school years. Some of your questions may have included the following: How do we make transition more than a unit, seminar, or school visit during the year? How do we support transition without its being a "separate" area or class that only special educators address? Can we do this given the curricula we must already address at middle school?

Effective curriculum and instruction supporting transition for students at the middle school are rooted in an understanding of several dynamic variables. These include curriculum purposes and influences, middle school curriculum structures, individualized planning considerations for students with special needs, and systematic integration of transition opportunities into the curriculum. We explore each of these areas in this chapter. Activity 4.1 is a useful introductory activity for this chapter because it encourages you to examine the feasibility of addressing transition practices in middle school.

Activity 4.1 Perspectives and Possibilities

Consider the feasibility of addressing transition practices during the middle school years.

1. Ask yourself, "What is important for middle schoolers to know?" In other words, "What is important to teach?" Record your responses in the column labeled "My Ideas."

2. Ask a few colleagues for their ideas. Write their responses in the "Other Ideas" column.

3. Ask several middle school–age students and write their responses under "Student Ideas."

4. Analyze the responses for similarities and differences.

My Ideas	Other Ideas	Student Ideas

What Defines and Influences Middle School Curriculum?

Curriculum Definitions

What Is Curriculum?

If you were to ask a handful of individuals to explain what curriculum is, you would probably hear responses that range from a very broad definition—"everything we do with students to teach and support learning in and outside of the classroom"—to a more discrete or focused definition—"the teaching strategies, content or objectives, and materials we use to teach students what they need to know." Hoover and Patton (1997) summarize the work of curriculum specialists by stating that curriculum is the "planned and guided learning experiences under the direction of the school" (p. 6). It is critically important for teachers to keep in mind that the purpose or intended outcomes of curriculum are more than the results of a student's performance in a single content area or discipline. As Bigge and Stump (1999) caution,

> Teachers may lose sight of how what they are teaching connects with (a) what others in the school and community are teaching, (b) what outcomes of significance the students are learning, and (c) what has been set as an overall outcome of education—namely the development of skills and knowledge that students can apply in their daily lives. (p. 35)

Clearly, the importance of understanding what constitutes curriculum and what influences the delivery of curriculum is necessary for teachers to support transition skills for middle school students.

What Do Students Need To Know?

Think about the responses you collected in Activity 4.1. You may have documented a variety of targets or important areas. Many of the individuals' ideas may have been similar and others different. Figure 4.1 lists some possible responses.

The types of curriculum or knowledge identified in Figure 4.1 vary from content-specific information and skills to broad, life-based skills. Both of these areas are important elements of middle school learning, curriculum planning, and even transition instruction.

Hoover and Patton (1997) refer to three types of curriculum:

1. *Explicit curriculum*—Curriculum that is written and defined, such as curricular scope and sequence, written content standards or benchmarks, and content specific goals and objectives.

2. *Hidden curriculum*—Curriculum that is critically important for success or that is actually taught or expected. Hidden curriculum

What Is Important for Middle Schoolers To Know?		
My Ideas	**Other Ideas**	**Student Ideas**[a]
• Reading to find information • Sharing ideas clearly in speaking and writing • Mathematical literacy and problem solving • Staying organized • Completing homework successfully	• Reading and writing • Science and computer literacy • Being able to collaborate or work with others and to get along • Effective test-taking skills • Geography and history	• "How to learn math and science really well" • "How to get good grades" • "Yourself and your feelings" • "The latest fashion, who's going with whom, friends, and phone numbers"

Figure 4.1. Sample responses to Activity 4.1.

[a]Sampling of student responses from Mee (1997).

includes the content, strategies, methods, materials, procedures, and expectations used by educators in daily instruction and activities.

3. *Absent curriculum*—Curriculum that educators choose not to address or use, including content and strategies.

What Is Essential for Student Success?

Researchers have discussed the importance of understanding and addressing the unique *setting demands* required for student success (Deshler, Schumaker, Harris, & Graham, 1999). Setting demands refer to those unique academic and social demands required for actual success in school (Deshler & Putnam, 1996). Did you do better in some middle school classes and activities than others? What do you believe influenced a higher degree of success in some classes? What factors may have resulted in a lower level of achievement and satisfaction in other classes?

While students are gaining knowledge and developing skills in social studies, science, mathematics, literacy, and technology at the middle school, they also need to gain other types of skills necessary for them to succeed. Many changes in structure and expected independence occur once students leave elementary school. Some of these changes include increased school size, greater autonomy in selecting courses and activities, increased expectations for self-regulation of behavior and self-monitoring of assignment completion, expanded exposure to different models of peer interaction and behavior, and a necessity to adjust to a number of teachers and varied teaching styles (Cooke, 1995; Ferguson & Bulach, 1997; Lancaster & Gildroy, 1999; Perkins & Gelfer, 1995; Schumacher, 1998). Some setting demands important for consideration at the middle school level are listed in Table 4.1, which was compiled from requirements listed by Cooke (1995), Ellis (1996), Ferguson and Bulach (1997), Hughes (1996), S. P. Miller (2002), Polloway, Patton, and Serna (2001), Robinson, Braxdale, and Colson (1985), Schumacher (1998), Schumaker and Deshler (1984), Van Reusen (1999), and Wasburn-Moses (2003).

To understand and support learning for middle school students, teachers need to examine the interaction between individual student characteristics and the setting. By having an awareness of the explicit, hidden, and absent curriculum, as well as the setting demands required for learning at the middle school, teachers will be prepared to provide a more successful learning experience for early adolescents.

Curriculum Influences: Standards, Accountability, and School Reform

The explicit curriculum expressed in national, state, and district standards and measured in accountability assessment programs currently predominates the educational landscape. You may be familiar with some of the impacts of education reform programs on your own education or professional experience. In response to public and professional criticisms regarding school experiences and outcomes for students, recent education reform efforts center on the need to reaffirm and establish a

Table 4.1
Sampling of Setting Demand Variables

Setting Demand Area	Possible Skill Requirements
Organization	• Organize, locate, store, and retrieve materials including texts, notebooks, computer files, and supplies for several classes • Locate and navigate classrooms, lockers, and related school environments • Record assignments and monitor assignment completion • Plan, set, adjust, and monitor goals to address short- and long-term projects • Manage simultaneous or staggered completion of multiple projects and assignments • Access and use print and technology resources independently
Test-taking and study skills	• Understand and respond to different test formats • Understand how test performance affects grades and academic outcomes • Use effective study habits for tests, both in class and out of class • Apply appropriate test-taking strategies • Take effective notes and use them to study and review • Listen to oral lectures or presentations and identify, record, and retrieve significant ideas • Adjust to oral lectures and presentations from several teachers • Interpret and follow oral and written directions
Social and behavior	• Work effectively in pairs and cooperative groups • Seek or request assistance from peers, adults, and teachers • Address both positive and negative peer influences and interactions • Interpret social and situational cues, mores, and norms, and adjust accordingly • Select and apply different verbal and nonverbal communication styles for varied settings and audiences • Access and use resources, including networking skills • Share ideas and information appropriately • Use effective interpersonal and communication skills in class discussions and personal interactions • Know the consequences of both positive and negative behavioral choices • Understand and follow classroom, school, and districtwide policies and rules • Use effective decision-making skills • Accept and interpret peer and adult feedback
Cognitive	• Review and remember information from a variety of content areas • Apply an awareness of personal memory and learning strengths, needs, and strategies • Use skills of self-reflection to monitor or assess performances
Literacy and language	• Read content materials and textbooks independently • Answer questions from reading materials and textbooks • Identify and comprehend key ideas, convey their significance, and distinguish interrelationships across ideas • Provide legible, grammatically correct written responses on assignments and tests • Write essays and journal responses to show understanding of content or to pose questions • Use and understand varied media, including computer databases to access content information • Organize and complete independent research projects

challenging curriculum rooted in high expectations for all students (Nolet & McLaughlin, 2000). For middle school education, standards-based reforms provide equitable access to an appropriately challenging curriculum (Jackson & Davis, 2000).

To promote this change, policymakers and educators have been involved in identifying, implementing, and measuring content and performance standards. *Content standards* address specific curriculum content that has been identified at the state and district levels in disciplines such as reading, writing, science, social studies, and technological literacy. These standards are translated into basic requirements that students must know or be able to do in various disciplines as a result of participation in the general education curriculum (Thurlow, 2000). Content standards can be viewed as broad curriculum goals (Nolet & McLaughlin, 2000). *Performance standards* refer to criteria or indicators that state how well students must perform content standards to demonstrate understanding and skill (Thurlow, 2000). Benchmarks are set at various grades or years as targets for achievement. In Activity 4.2 you are asked to consider the benefits and challenges of standards-driven curriculum.

There is no doubt that for middle level education there are benefits to program standards, including equitable access to important curriculum for all students, regardless of the location of their school or the composition or training of the teaching staff (A.C. Lewis, 1999). Accountability programs also summarize student

Activity 4.2 Benefits and Challenges

Educators inevitably have thoughts, questions, and concerns regarding current education reform programs. Consider the following questions: What is the impact of standards and education reform for middle school educators and students? How does this impact the curriculum for students with disabilities? List the benefits and challenges of current standards-driven curriculum in the columns.

Benefits	Challenges

progress toward meeting these standards. Data in the form of test or assessment results and school attendance give educators and policymakers one gauge by which to measure the success of schools in delivering quality curriculum for all students (Nolet & McLaughlin, 2000).

Middle level general and special education professionals and advocates also express concerns, however:

- Will schools and districts narrow the curriculum or diminish the major focus in schools to address only those indicators articulated in written standards? (Thurlow, 2002)

- How do we blend (a) developmentally responsive curriculum that includes student empowerment and addresses the social and emotional needs and physical development of middle school students with (b) a standards-focused curriculum? (Anafra & Waks, 2002; National Middle School Association, 1995)

- Will the focus on current standards-based curriculum limit curriculum options for students who seek access to community-based education, career education, or vocational and life skills curriculum? (deFur, 2002; D. R. Johnson, Stodden, Emanuel, Luecking, & Mack, 2002)

The challenge for educators is to ensure access and success for each student in the general education curriculum while balancing developmentally appropriate curriculum suitable for early adolescents. Special educators must also incorporate and address unique individual needs and accommodations directed by the Individualized Education Program (IEP).

Middle School Curriculum Foundations

General Education Curriculum Practices

In Chapter 2 we identified key structures that support a comprehensive middle school approach. These structures included (a) flexible organization, such as interdisciplinary teaming and interdisciplinary content delivery; (b) advisory programs and support; (c) exploratory curriculum; and (d) collaborative partnerships with colleagues, families, and the community. These practices frame the middle school curriculum.

Integrated Content and Interdisciplinary Curriculum

Curriculum integration and interdisciplinary curriculum are middle school practices that support the varied cognitive, social, and emotional needs of early adolescents (D. C. Clark & Clark, 1994; Jacobs, 1989a; Wiles & Bondi, 2001; Wormeli, 2001). *Integrated curriculum* involves cross-curricular units or courses of study in which explicitly identified objectives and activities are planned around a central concept or theme. Jacobs (1989a) defines *interdisciplinary curriculum* as "a knowledge view and curriculum approach that consciously applies methodology and language from more than one discipline to examine a central theme, issue, problem, topic or experience" (p. 8).

Researchers have identified several advantages associated with interdisciplinary curriculum. These benefits include clearer connections across content areas, improved learning and retention of ideas, increased student motivation, and enhanced opportunities for active learning (D. C. Clark & Clark, 1994; George, Lawrence, & Bushnell, 1998; Hough & St. Clair, 1995; Vars & Beane, 2000). Increased teacher enthusiasm, added professional support, renewed energy, and improved collegiality are a few of the positive outcomes experienced by educators using an integrated curriculum model (D. C. Clark & Clark, 1994). When comparing the efficacy of integrated curriculum models to more traditional curriculum models, Vars and Beane (2000) found that students involved in interdisciplinary content do as well on state assessments as students in more traditional, discipline-specific instruction. Overall, interdisciplinary curriculum practices may provide added instructional, developmental, and professional advantages for both students and teachers.

The key elements of integrated curriculum involve (a) identification of a cohesive theme, question, issue, or topic addressed across subject areas and (b) specific objectives and related activities centralized around the common theme or issue (Tucker, Hafenstein, Tracy, Hillman, & Watson, 1995; Vars, 1993, cited in Hough & St. Clair, 1995). The themes, issues, and topics selected for these units should be based on student interests, concerns, and input (Hough & St. Clair, 1995).

Themes or issues can be generated for weekly, monthly, or even quarter-long units of inquiry and study. Identified themes or issues can be broad or more compact in focus. Some professionals assert that genuine interdisciplinary curriculum must occur across all of the disciplines in the school's curriculum (Jacobs, 1989b; Tucker et al., 1995); however, in the MidEx model, integrated or interdisciplinary curriculum is described as curriculum content bridged across two or more subjects or disciplines and centralized around a common theme or issue. For example, the "we are what we eat" theme in Table 4.5 later in this chapter could be integrated into the following content areas:

- Health: Learn food groups and daily requirements for each group

- Language arts: Write family histories

- Math: Calculate energy and calories; measure portions and body fat

- Culinary arts: Explore careers in cooking

Figure 4.2 depicts a planning or visual map of integrated curriculum planning, and Activity 4.3 enables you to examine a school-based example of interdisciplinary curriculum planning.

Were you able to identify content in Activity 4.3? Did you find this easy or difficult to do? Depending on your role (general or special educator), your familiarity with the discipline, and your interest or background in the theme, you may have found this task pleasurable and straightforward or distasteful and complicated.

Factors leading to more successful use of integrated content include strong administrative support, effective team communication structures, and adequate

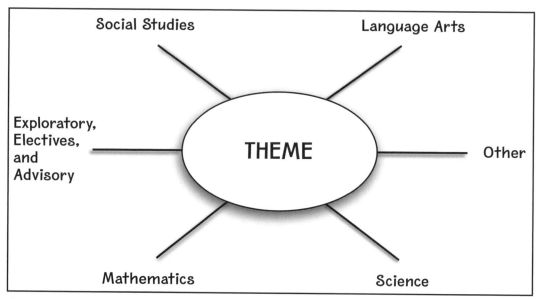

Figure 4.2. Integrated curriculum planning.

time to develop the curriculum unit (Howe & Bell, 1998). Both general and special educators can address the developmental and transition needs of middle schoolers in integrated content by (a) including inclusive opportunities for students to engage in unit content that has "real-life connections" and (b) supporting "themes" identified in the general education curriculum through special education instructional activities. An example of possible activities that might be part of the Traditions interdisciplinary unit is included in Appendix 4.A at the end of this chapter.

Advisement Programs

As discussed in Chapter 2, advisement programs address many of the developmental needs of middle school students and are an important part of the curriculum for all students. Advisement programs should include students in age-appropriate heterogeneous peer groups. We recommend an inclusive approach so that all students have the opportunity for peer support and role models.

Teachers have found that advisory programs offer opportunities to recognize the talents and unique abilities of students, as well as to support students academically. Students report that advisory programs are both valuable and fun. Activities such as celebrations of holidays or special occasions, supportive peer group discussions, games, and service learning projects are some of the preferred advisory activities identified by middle school students (George & Bushnell, 1993).

Exploratory Curricula

Exploratory curricula support student self-awareness and allow students to explore and refine current and future interests. The middle school curriculum provides required and elective courses, as well as integrated curriculum content that engages students in a process of discovery.

Activity 4.3 Exploration Station

Imagine a seventh-grade team of teachers and students. This team, the "Explorers," is composed of (a) content teachers in social studies, science, mathematics, and language arts; (b) resource and learning specialists in reading, special education, and bilingual education; and (c) representative elective and exploratory teachers. Each content and resource or learning specialist teacher has an advisory seminar involving 12 to 15 students on the team. These teachers are involved in a beginning of the year planning session to address the Explorer team's curriculum, procedures, expectations, and students.

The focus areas in each of the core content areas during seventh grade include these curriculum targets:

- Science: physical science and applied observation and inquiry skills

- Social studies: state history and geography

- Mathematics and language arts: state-mandated standards-based curriculum

All students on the Explorer team are also taking physical education. Students are involved in a number of electives or exploratory courses that may include music (choir or band), textiles and clothing, technology literacy, carpentry and woods, or journalism.

The teachers have decided that one way they will bridge content and enhance student learning is through the use of integrated units across disciplines. Team members have decided to begin the year with an integrated content theme titled "Traditions."

What ideas do you have for integrated content planning across curriculum areas? What types of content, questions, objectives, and activities might be possible for an interdisciplinary unit on traditions?

(continues)

Collaborative Practices

The familiar saying, "Two heads are better than one," holds true for curriculum planning and implementation. Practices that support communication and collaboration among all stakeholders (students, teachers, staff, administrators, families, and community members) are important elements of a total middle school approach.

1. Identify two or more discipline areas and list possible content in each of these areas related to the theme.

Content Area or Discipline	Theme-Related Content, Skills, Activities

2. What is the role of general and special education teachers in delivering integrated curriculum content for (a) middle school students and (b) students with disabilities?

Middle school practices that support a collaborative approach include interdisciplinary teaming, collaborative teaching, cooperative learning, effective family involvement practices, and service learning. Later in the chapter we investigate how these structures can support transition skills for students.

Additional Considerations for Students with Disabilities

There are additional considerations in curriculum planning and delivery for middle school students with disabilities. These include providing access to the general education curriculum, delivering appropriate curriculum adaptations and addressing individual curriculum needs, and preparing for and supporting effective transition needs and practices.

Curriculum Access

Educators must ensure that each child with an identified disability has access to the general education curriculum (Council for Exceptional Children, 1999). This requires that teachers consider the full spectrum of general education curriculum opportunities, including core, exploratory, advisory and other extracurricular opportunities available to students, when planning an individual's IEP (D. Fisher & Kennedy, 2001). Educators must document student involvement with and progress in the general education curriculum. Access, however, is more than merely having a foot in the door. It also means that schools and teachers provide the means by which students can benefit fully from the curriculum.

To ensure access, teachers must understand the purpose of *curriculum accommodations*. Nolet and McLaughlin (2000) state that accommodations are simply those services provided that support access to the general education content and experiences. To provide this access, teachers can make seating, scheduling, physical, materials, or structural adjustments in the instructional activities, timelines, or environments. These accommodations do not, however, include alterations of the content or standards for performance of competency. Thus, the integrity of content and performance standards is maintained.

When changes to curriculum content or performance requirements occur, altered expectations of student knowledge and skill may be evidenced. These are called *curriculum modifications* (or adaptations). Changes in the amount or complexity of curriculum content, in the focus of curriculum content, or in performance expectations fall under this category (Nolet & McLaughlin, 2000). Sometimes these adaptations may be short term in nature.

Additionally, students may have an *individualized or alternate curriculum*, such as life skills, study skills, career education, or vocational curriculum that is directed by decisions made by the IEP team. This type of curriculum "augmentation" might include providing students with instruction or skills "that enable them to more effectively interact with, and presumably progress in the general curriculum" (Wehmeyer, Sands, Knowlton, & Kozleski, 2002, p. 61). Wehmeyer and colleagues (2002) discussed the inclusion of curriculum that addresses strategy instruction, self-regulation or self-management skills, and self-determination skills for students. Support in these areas can lead students to increased access to the general education curriculum.

General and special educators are faced with decisions about curriculum access, accommodation, and modification for students. Figure 4.3 provides a synthesis of these curriculum considerations.

Universal Design for Learning

Orkwis (1999) stated, "Teachers must ensure students are actively engaged in learning, that is, the subject matter is cognitively challenging them, regardless of their developmental level" (p. 2). This principle of curriculum access, as discussed in Chapter 2, is known as the principal of *universal design*. Universal design for learning means that curriculum and learning experiences are designed, planned and delivered for maximum participation and benefit of *all* learners, regardless of language, sensory, physical, cognitive, or communicative abilities. The concept of universal design is also explained in the Assistive Technology Act of 1998 (29 U.S.C. § 3002) as a concept or philosophy for designing and delivering products and services that are usable by people with the widest possible range of functional capabilities, which include products and services that are directly usable (without requiring assistive technologies) and products and services that are made usable with assistive technologies. For middle level educators, this means that instructional

	Special Education and Related Expanded Curricula		
General Curriculum			
No Accommodations/ Modifications	**Accommodations**	**Modifications**	**Alternate**
No changes to • Curriculum content • Performance expectations • Sequence and timelines • Instruction	No changes to • Curriculum content • Performance expectations **Changes to** • Sequence and timelines • Instructional environ- ment, presentation, or learning activities	Changes to some or all of • Curriculum content areas • Performance expectations • Sequence and timelines • Instructional environ- ment, presentation, or learning activities	• Individualized curriculum goal (e.g., learning strategies, study skills, vocational education) • Separate functional curriculum

Figure 4.3. Special education and general education curriculum options. *Note.* From *The General Education Curriculum: Including Students with Disabilities in Standards-Based Reform* (p. 13), by V. Nolet and M. J. McLaughlin, 2000, Thousand Oaks, CA: Crown Press. Copyright 2000 by Crown Press. Adapted with permission.

accommodations and supports must be included in the design of lessons, units, and activities.

Universal design for learning (UDL) necessitates using varied materials in teaching and learning activities, using multiple teaching strategies, and delivering appropriate learning activities that support the abilities and interests of diverse learners. Effective middle level educators realize there is no "one size fits all" approach to curriculum or instruction (Bremer, Clapper, Hitchcock, Hall, & Kachgal, 2002; Hitchcock, Meyer, Rose, & Jackson, 2002; Orkwis & McLane, 1998).

A first consideration in UDL is the provision of multiple means of representation. Concepts, information, and lessons should be provided so that all students can be engaged in learning important content. Teachers should provide information in more than one manner. Because language and literacy skills and physical abilities can present barriers for student participation, teachers must address these aspects in the design of lessons. All students will then be able to participate actively in learning activities.

A second area of UDL involves student expression. Teachers must provide students with a menu of opportunities to express themselves. It is safe to say that a majority of learning experiences provided in today's middle schools requires that students participate or express themselves in class discussion or in a written response. Unfortunately, for some students this type of teaching may close doors for successful learning.

Finally, to ensure UDL, teachers should also employ multiple means of engagement. Teachers must structure, support, and scaffold curriculum content to provide appropriate challenge for each student (Nolet & McLaughlin, 2000; Orkwis & McLane, 1998). Table 4.2 includes a list of considerations and options in planning for UDL (adapted from Roja, 1994). Activity 4.4 engages you in a planning process using UDL. Sample UDL ideas for this lesson are included in Appendix 4.B at the end of this chapter.

Individual Curriculum Needs

Although the general education approach to curriculum may lack individual focus, the content of special education curriculum can become watered down (Pugach & Warger, 1993). The balance that educators must strike is to provide students with challenging, appropriate, meaningful, and relevant curriculum that helps them succeed both now and in the future. Educators must carefully consider special education students' access to the general education curriculum. The hallmark of special education has been the provision of *appropriate* curriculum to meet *unique* or *individual* needs resulting from a student's disability. This means

Table 4.2
Sampling of Options To Include in Universal Design for Learning

Multiple Means of Representation	Multiple Means of Expression	Multiple Means of Engagement
Oral Format Lecture, discussion, questioning, read alouds, stories, direct instruction, peer presentations, interviews	**Presentation/Graphics** Word processors and presentation software, talking word processors, word prediction software, voice recognition software and programs, graphic organization visuals or software, concept maps, diagrams, photography, drawing, outlining	**Scaffolds and Supports** Concept anchoring, templates, guided visual or textual notes, study guides, highlighting tools, cooperative groups, peer tutoring, learning strategy instruction, mnemonic strategies, study skills, advance organizers
Visual Formats Pictures/graphics, charts, transparencies, chalkboards, white boards, videotapes or DVDs, captioned media, role-play scenarios, large-print materials	**Oral Presentations** Individual, small or large group presentations; debates; student-led discussions; role-playing activities; demonstrations; poster presentations	**Varied Pacing** Tiered assignments, learning contracts, activity packages, curriculum compacting, learning centers
Interactive Formats Demonstrations, think alouds, dramatization, simulation, construction, manipulative use, cooperative learning	**Models and Manipulatives** Lab demonstrations, teacher and peer demonstrations, computer- or digital-mediated demonstrations or simulations	**Student Interests and Motivation** Choices in learning activities, varied structures for inquiry, demonstration and assessment
Media and Materials Digital media, Internet, videotape or DVD presentation, audiotape and CD books, tape-recorded lectures, alternate textbooks, computer and text readers, E-books, television, newspapers		

Note. Adapted and expanded from *The General Education Curriculum: Including Students with Disabilities in Standards-Based Reform,* by V. Nolet and M. J. McLaughlin, 2000, Thousand Oaks, CA: Crown Press. Copyright 2000 by Crown Press. Adapted with permission.

Activity 4.4 Opportunities and Options

Read the following scenario. Decide how you would initially incorporate principles of universal design for learning (UDL) in this lesson.

Classroom: Eighth-grade language arts and social studies blocked class

Students: 28 students: 15 female and 13 male students; 3 students with limited English proficiency, 2 students with attention-deficit disorder; 2 students with specific learning disability; 1 student who is hard of hearing.

Content: How a Bill Becomes a Law

Learning Objectives: Students will be able to:

1. Identify steps by which a bill becomes a federal law.

2. Discuss the roles and functions of a congressional lobbyist.

3. Identify one or more issues affecting American citizens and discuss problems or circumstances that make this an issue.

4. Identify their district's U.S. Representative and their state's U.S. Senators.

5. Identify three local government officials.

6. Identify at least three national or local special interest groups related to an issue of choice.Create a list of your initial lesson ideas for UDL in the chart below. Consider how you will design your lesson information, presentation, and activities so that all students can experience success.

Create a list of your initial lesson ideas for UDL in the chart below. Consider how you will design your lesson information, presentation, and activities so that all students can experience success.

Options for Instructional Presentation or Representation of Ideas	Options for Student Expression	Options for Student Engagement

© 2006 by PRO-ED, Inc. Adapted from Roja (1994).

that educators and IEP team members need to select and implement curriculum modifications or deliver alternate curriculum. Because a student's success in the high school curriculum can rest on the foundational skills, strategies, and content delivered at the middle school level, "a team responsible for writing a secondary student's IEP must conclude if what they consider to be meaningful curriculum, is in fact, more meaningful than the earning of a diploma when choosing to deviate from the general education requirements" (Benner, 1998, p. 184). The decisions made by middle school educators will be important.

Life Skills and Functional Curriculum

Life skills instruction and *real-life content* are terms often used interchangeably. This type of instruction or content refers to "specific competencies (i.e., knowledge and skills) of local and cultural relevance needed to perform everyday activities in a variety of settings typically encountered by most adults" (Patton, Cronin, & Wood, 1999, p. 2). These are the types of skills that successful adults use daily to navigate the demands of home, work, and community environments.

Patton and colleagues (1999) caution that the specific skills required in the successful demonstration of any particular life skill are highly dependent on the contextual setting for which they are used. For example, accessing or using community recreation facilities may depend on the neighborhood or town in which an individual lives. For those in large urban areas, multiple options may exist. For those in more rural settings, recreation facilities may be limited to those provided by community or church groups.

Life skills curriculum areas closely match those areas of important transition instruction recommended by professionals and researchers (Brolin, 1997; Cronin, 1996; Cronin & Patton, 1993; Wehman & Kregel, 1997). This type of instruction addresses (a) employment or career development skills; (b) postsecondary education or training; (c) domestic or home and family skills; (d) recreational or leisure skills; (e) community facilities access and use; (f) community or civic engagement and involvement; (g) physical, personal-care, and health-related skills; (h) social and emotional well-being skills; (i) personal relationships and networking skills; and (j) personal responsibility and self-determination skills.

The Life Centered Career Education (LCCE) curriculum provides another perspective on a competency framework (Brolin, 1993). The LCCE curriculum education competencies are listed in Table 4.3.

Traditionally, special educators have delivered alternate curriculum such as life skills separately from the general education curriculum. Sometimes life skills curriculum is delivered through a separate class taught by a special educator. Alternately, life skills may be embedded into other content areas and instruction provided by the special educator. In more inclusive models, some of these life skills may also be supported in the general education curriculum as required in the student's IEP.

Functional academics involves the application of basic reading, writing, communication, and mathematics skills for real-life purposes or contexts. For example, functional reading skills might be used in reading and following a recipe, selecting choices and ordering from a menu, using a telephone directory, or reading the nutritional information from food products. Skills such as making or receiving change, balancing a personal checking account, and comparing advertised discounts at competing vendors are all related to functional math skills. Table 4.4 includes a

Table 4.3
Life Centered Career Education (LCCE) Competencies

Daily Living Skills
- Managing personal finances
- Selecting and managing a household
- Caring for personal needs
- Raising children and meeting marriage responsibilities
- Buying, preparing, and consuming food
- Buying and caring for clothing
- Exhibiting responsible citizenship
- Utilizing recreational facilities and engaging in leisure
- Getting around in the community

Personal–Social Skills
- Achieving self-awareness
- Acquiring self-confidence
- Achieving socially responsible behavior in the community
- Maintaining good interpersonal skills
- Achieving independence
- Making adequate decisions
- Communicating with others

Occupational Guidance and Preparation
- Knowing and exploring occupational possibilities
- Selecting and planning occupational choices
- Exhibiting appropriate work habits and behaviors
- Seeking, securing, and maintaining employment
- Exhibiting sufficient physical–manual skills
- Obtaining specific occupational skills

Note. From *Life Centered Career Education: A Competency Based Approach* (4th ed., p. 12), by D. E. Brolin, 1993, Reston, VA: Council for Exceptional Children. Copyright 1993 by Council for Exceptional Children. Reprinted with permission.

listing of life skills, within adult domains and subdomains, that may be taught in the curriculum.

Curriculum Planning for Life and Transition Skills

Curriculum related to life skills and transition does not necessarily need to occur in a separate, special education classroom. In fact, according to Field and Hoffman (1994), "While a separate curriculum may promote the accomplishment of functional objectives, it also removes students from environments where they have the opportunity to learn one of the most important functional skills—interacting with nondisabled peers" (p. 40). Many professionals recommend and provide support for integrating this content within the general education curriculum or existing curricular options (Cronin & Patton, 1993; Cronin & Pikes, 1999; Field, LeRoy, & Rivera, 1994; Patton et al., 1999).

To make informed curricular decisions and implement effective instructional practices, educators need to be aware of and involved in the general education curriculum. In fact, life and transition skills are important not only for students with disabilities but for *all* students (Sitlington, Clark, & Kolstoe, 2000). Lehmann, Cobb, and Tochterman (2001) synthesized transition-related research; among their

Table 4.4
Sampling of Adult Domains, Subdomains, and Life Demands in a Life Skills Curriculum

Domain	Subdomain	Life Demands
Employment and education	• General job skills • General education and training considerations • Employment setting • Career refinement and reevaluation	• Seek and secure a job • Know about education and training options • Recognize job duties and responsibilities • Explore alternative career options
Home and family	• Home management • Financial management • Family life • Child rearing	• Set up household operations • Maintain a budget • Prepare for marriage and family • Understand child development
Leisure pursuits	• Indoor activities • Outdoor activities • Community and neighborhood activities • Travel • Entertainment	• Play table and electronic games • Engage in outdoor leisure pursuits • Attend special community events • Prepare to go on a trip • Engage in at-home entertainment activities
Community involvement	• Citizenship • Community awareness • Services and resources	• Understand legal rights • Know major events at the local, regional, and national levels • Access public transportation
Physical and emotional health	• Physical • Emotional	• Plan a nutritional diet • Recognize signs of emotional life needs
Personal responsibility and relationships	• Personal confidence and understanding • Goal setting • Self-improvement • Relationships • Personal expression	• Recognize personal strengths and weaknesses • Identify and achieve personal goals • Pursue personal interests • Establish and maintain friendships • Share personal feelings and experiences

Note. Adapted from *Life Skills Instruction for All Students with Special Needs: A Practical Guide for Integrating Real-Life Content into the Curriculum,* (pp.16–19), by M. E. Cronin and J. R. Patton, 1993, Austin, TX: PRO-ED. Copyright 1993 by PRO-ED, Inc. Adapted with permission.

conclusions, they reported that an integration of both academic and vocational content promotes effective school-to-career practices. They concluded that collaboration is needed to achieve such integration. "Secondary education and transition models are also needed that integrate academic, career, work-based, service learning and other learning experiences" (D. R. Johnson et al., 2002, p. 522). This type of model may include expanding and enhancing the general education curriculum with opportunities for social, functional, and self-determination skills development (Lehmann et al., 2001).

Figure 4.4 depicts a model of transition integration. At the center of the model are the core general education curriculum and individualized alternate curriculum

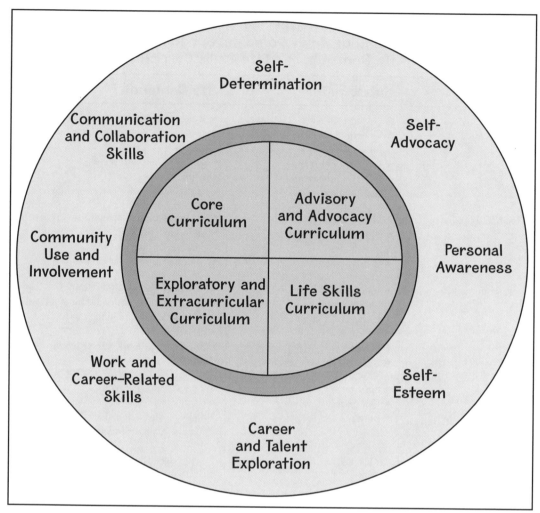

Figure 4.4. Middle school transition-supported curriculum.

needs. This grouping means that educators must explore and include the full range of curricular options for individuals with disabilities. The outer circle includes important transition skills that are important for success in school and life. We have included skills that are both developmentally appropriate and transition relevant. These skills can be addressed in all areas of general and individualized curriculum. We explore this transition-infused middle school model throughout the remainder of the chapter.

Transition-Supported Curriculum in Middle School

You may be wondering how the puzzle pieces of developmentally appropriate practices, middle school curriculum structures, individual student curriculum considerations, and transition best practices fit together to support a cohesive middle school experience for students and teachers. Perhaps you have asked yourself, "How do I navigate and address both the general education curriculum and individualized curriculum needs? Where do transition skills fit in? What is my role in addressing these important curricular areas? What supports can I access in providing these?"

Educators can use a curriculum planning and delivery framework to assist in this process. This framework merges best practice recommendations in middle school practices and curriculum, inclusive service delivery, early adolescent development needs, and transition planning. By addressing these considerations, teachers will have a powerful means of connecting transition-related skills across the curriculum. Educators will be able to provide students with multiple opportunities to engage in developmentally appropriate transition skills. Middle school programs can become naturally supportive mediums for transition skills. In other words, middle level educators and curriculum can be seen as the conduits to prepare all students for successful school and post-school transitions. The following sections include an overview of this curriculum planning and delivery framework, which we have given the acronym I-CONDUIT:

I   Identify transition needs and possibilities

C   Connect to existing middle school curriculum

O   Offer opportunities for self-determination

N   Nurture self-awareness and self-esteem

D   Develop career, interest, and talent opportunities

U   Utilize community resources

I   Implement effective instructional practices

T   Team and collaborate for success

I: Identify Transition Needs and Possibilities

Initially, you need to determine the specific transition needs of your students and identify possibilities to teach and support these transition skills. In the model presented in Figure 4.4, we include the following general areas you should consider in your curricular planning: self-determination, self-advocacy, personal awareness, self-esteem, career and talent exploration, work and career-related skills, community use and involvement, and communication and collaboration skills. You also need to include relevant life skills or functional academics in your planning and curriculum. Additionally, you must fine-tune instructional activities so that individual student needs and interests are addressed. In Chapter 6 we describe how to assess individual student's interests and abilities for transition planning so that you can further refine your planning and curriculum delivery.

A total middle school approach requires teachers to consider transition skills and career education possibilities across curriculum, content areas, environments, and students. This process will necessitate collaboration with other educators and staff members, parents, community members, and administrators. Curriculum-supporting transition skills can be taught across general and special education services and curriculum. We suggest a process of *curriculum infusion*—that is, the identification of key transition and career education competencies that can be taught, integrated, and blended into existing academic, social, exploratory, and individualized curriculum.

C: Connect to Existing Middle School Curriculum

The most powerful approach to fostering transition skills is connected, natural, and inclusive. Effective transition practices fuse career education instruction with existing middle school curricula.

Include Transition Skills in Integrated Curricula

Integrated or interdisciplinary curricula can include themes and address skills that are needed in important transition and real-life contexts. Integrated curriculum practices are not unlike "real life" in that individuals must assimilate and apply information and decision-making skills across a number of situations. These experiences provide students with opportunities to learn, practice, maintain, and generalize important transition skills in connected, contextual, and relevant environments.

Look at the transition areas identified in Figure 4.4. Take a moment and identify additional themes that lend themselves to the inclusion of skills and activities important in transition planning. A list of possible transition-related themes for interdisciplinary curriculum planning is included in Table 4.5.

Refer back to Activity 4.3, Exploration Station, earlier in the chapter. What transition-related skills and areas can you build into this interdisciplinary unit? Transition areas such as personal awareness, communication and collaboration, and

Table 4.5
Interdisciplinary Transition Themes

• Body Beautiful	• Exploration Station	• The Power of Words
• Buyer Beware	• FSI: Friend Scene Investigation	• Feelings
• Laws and Paws	• Hair Affair	• Stress
• The Muscle of Media	• Amusement: From Puns to Parks	• Transportation: Past to Future
• Community Connections	• Metamorphosis	• Risk Takers
• Heroes/Sheroes	• We Are What We Eat	• Climate
• The Games People Play	• Passage to Adventure	• Community Contributors
• Image Makers and Shakers	• Sports Savvy	• Modern Day Warriors
• The Power of Dreams	• Pollution Solutions	• Natural Disasters
• Destination Unknown	• Energy	• Brain Gain

community use can be supported in this unit. For example, one activity supporting transition might involve community interviews. Students can identify and interview a leader from a community agency to find out information about that agency. Students can use real-life skills such as directory use, telephone skills, and appropriate interviewing skills to conduct the dialogue. Perhaps students can use public transportation and conduct on-site interviews.

Infuse Transition Skills in Advisement Programs

Advisement programs offer many opportunities for transition-supported skill development and delivery. Transition content supporting social skills and networks, self-determination skills, and personal and emotional skill development and awareness occurs naturally within advisory programs. Table 4.6 (compiled from D. F. Brown, 2001; George & Bushnell, 1993; Hoversten, Doda, & Lounsbury, 1991; James & Spradling, 2002) lists several possible advisory activities that support the transition needs of middle school students.

Address Transition in Exploratory and Elective Curricula

In Chapter 2 we discussed a variety of options and content that occurs in exploratory and elective curricula. Exploratory content and curricula are critical in supporting every adolescent's budding career, interests, and talent exploration (Anafra & Brown, 2000). For students with disabilities, exploratory classes and content provide a forum to discuss, identify, and support the development of personal interests, aptitudes, and goals.

O: Offer Opportunities for Self-Determination

We defined self-determination in Chapter 3 as an individual's ability to determine goals, to acquire skills to meet those goals, to plan and take actions, and to evaluate the outcome(s) of those actions (Field, Martin, Miller, Ward, & Wehmeyer, 1998). Characteristics that contribute to self-determination are listed in Table 4.7 (compiled from L. A. Price, Wolensky, & Mulligan, 2002; Wehmeyer, Sands, Doll, & Palmer, 1997).

Schoolwide Support for Self-Determination

In a total middle school approach, supporting the self-determination of each student becomes part of the mission for all teachers, school staff, and even students. In fact, by casting a broad, schoolwide net that fosters self-determination, instructional practices and service delivery are more inclusive and normalized for adolescents with disabilities (Field, Hoffman, & Posch, 1997).

A total curriculum approach involves more than individual classrooms. Educators must look not only at direct teaching of these skills but also at schoolwide practices, environments, and decisions. This necessitates creating, identifying, implementing, and sustaining curriculum, instructional practices, and environments that model, teach, reinforce, and value students' self-determined attitudes, beliefs, actions, and behaviors.

Table 4.6
Sampling of Advisory Activities
for Transition Support in Middle School

Activity	Description	Transition Area/ Need Addressed
School Success: Personal Learning Skills Day; Study Skills Mini-Units	Instruction, discussion, and support for personal learning skills, such as metacognitive awareness of effective study habits and strategies, effective study skills, time management skills, and organizational skills	Career-related skills Self-esteem Self-advocacy Self-determination Communication and collaboration Personal awareness
Goal-Setting Day or Activities	Daily, weekly, or intermittent scheduled and supported time for activities allowing students to discuss, develop, plan, monitor, and share personal academic and career goals	Career-related skills Self-esteem Self-advocacy Self-determination Personal awareness
Career Montage	Weekly, monthly, quarterly, or annual programs such as career spotlights, guest presentations or interviews with adults in careers of advisee interest, career day exploration, job shadowing in community, and college visits	Career exploration Work- and career-related skills Communication and collaboration Community use and involvement
Student Champions	Recognition and spotlight programs that occur daily, weekly, and so on, that allow peers and adults to recognize students for positive contributions, unique talents, progress, and so forth	Self-esteem Talent exploration Communication and collaboration Personal awareness
Games and Hobbies	Daily, weekly, or regularly scheduled time to teach and engage in recreation and leisure pursuits such as board, cooperative, and collaborative games, or various hobbies (including crafts, arts, and leisure skills), demonstrated or taught by volunteers, students, or teachers	Career exploration Talent exploration Communication and collaboration

Field and Hoffman (2002) examined research and literature in self-determination curriculum and practices. Based on their analysis, they generated the following set of quality indicators for self-determination support in educational programs:

1. Knowledge, skills, and attitudes for self-determination are addressed in the curriculum, in family support, and in staff development;

Table 4.7
Self-Determined Beliefs, Dispositions, Skills, and Behaviors

Area	Description	Beliefs, Dispositions, Skills, and Behaviors
Behavioral autonomy	Movement from more dependent to more self-directed behaviors	Choice-making skills Decision-making skills Problem-solving skills Goal setting and attainment skills Independence, risk-taking, and safety skills
Self-regulated behavior	Personally mediated decisions to plan, act, and evaluate personal goals and actions	Goal-setting and attainment skills Self-observation, evaluation, and reinforcement skills Self-advocacy skills
Positive self-efficacy and beliefs	Personal beliefs and self-efficacy supporting individual empowerment	Internal locus of control (i.e., a belief system supporting personal control over critical outcomes) Positive attributions (i.e., beliefs in personal competence and abilities to bring about desired outcomes)
Self-realization (self-awareness and self-knowledge)	Ability to assess, articulate, and act based on a knowledge of personal strengths, needs, and interests	Self-awareness of personal strengths, needs, and abilities Self-evaluation and application of this knowledge

2. Students, parents, and staff are involved participants in individualized educational decision making and planning;

3. Students, families, faculty, and staff are provided with opportunities for choice;

4. Students, families, faculty, and staff are encouraged to take appropriate risks;

5. Supportive relationships are encouraged;

6. Accommodations and supports for individual needs are provided;

7. Students, families, and staff have the opportunity to express themselves and be understood;

8. Consequences for actions are predictable; and

9. Self-determination is modeled throughout the school environment. (Field & Hoffman, 2002, pp. 114–117)

Infusing Transition into Existing Curriculum

Jacobs (1989b) suggests a series of steps for planning curriculum integration. We list these steps with additional transition considerations below.

1. **Start Small.** Start small and practical when planning to infuse transition content. With colleagues, identify two or more content or discipline areas in which cross-curricular planning and integration is feasible and desired. Remember to include advisory and exploratory courses in your planning.

2. **Brainstorm.** Select and agree upon an organizing theme, issue, or event that is broad enough to span identified content areas but also includes transition-relevant skills. Brainstorm the topic across content areas. Identify possible skills and activities that address the theme. Include these supporting transition needs, skills, or areas in your list.

3. **Synthesize and Articulate.** Synthesize similar ideas and prioritize content applications. Identify activities and lessons in each content area that support the selected theme. Identify transition-supported activities within each content area or discipline. A unit planning form is provided in Appendix 4.C at the end of this chapter.

4. **Implement and Evaluate.** Compose a simple schedule and timeline for the unit. Implement the unit and provide for a collaborative evaluation of its effectiveness in addressing identified curriculum and transition objectives and skills.

Curriculum and Instruction To Support Self-Determination

Middle school core, exploratory, advisory, individualized, and interdisciplinary curricula provide a number of contexts in which self-determination can be supported on a daily basis. Skills such as making desirable choices, setting goals and designing plans to achieve goals can be addressed in a number of curricular areas and activities. Wehmeyer (2002) suggests that middle school educators:

1. teach students to examine pros and cons or advantages and disadvantages of decisions;

2. assist students in scrutinizing consequences of decisions (i.e., examine whether consequences are desirable or anticipated);

3. instruct and coach students in setting personal and academic goals, including skills in setting, achieving, and monitoring goals; and

4. provide opportunities for students to reflect on performances and personal goals.

For students with disabilities, active participation in the IEP process is critical. Students should be provided with opportunities, instruction, and supports that allow them to be actively involved in setting and monitoring relevant goals and in designing and making decisions about their educational program (Martin & Marshall, 1995; Martin, Oliphint, & Weisenstein, 1994; Thoma, 1999).

The instructional strategies implemented in the classroom also can support self-determination. Ward and Kohler (1996) reviewed federally funded self-determination demonstration projects. They identified the following instructional practices as ones that support self-determination: (a) individual and small group activities; (b) modeling; (c) role playing; (d) performance feedback; (e) case instruction and scenarios; (f) simulations; (g) self-generated activities, such as personal folios and portfolios, and (h) community-based instruction. Additionally, practices such as peer tutoring and mentoring and collaborative or teamed instruction have been identified as supportive self-determination practices (Field & Hoffman, 2002; Hoffman & Field, 1995). Clearly, it is important to use an array of active learning strategies that foster student commitment and involvement in the learning process. A summary of selected curriculum, instruction strategies, and practices that support middle school self-determination is provided in Table 4.8 (compiled from Doll, Sands, Wehmeyer, & Palmer, 1996; Field & Hoffman, 1994, 2002; Field, Martin, et al., 1998; Hoffman & Field, 1995; Serna & Lau-Smith, 1995; Wehmeyer, 1996, 2001, 2002; Wehmeyer, Agran, & Hughes, 1998; Wehmeyer & Schalock, 2001). Activity 4.5 encourages you to consider how to apply self-determination practice and curriculum in the interdisciplinary unit you brainstormed in Activity 4.3.

Activity 4.5 Self-Determination Spotlight

Think back to the interdisciplinary Traditions unit you explored in Activity 4.3. Are there opportunities to infuse self-determination curriculum and practices? List your ideas.

Perhaps you decided in Activity 4.5 that students could select from a menu of opportunities to demonstrate understanding of traditions through an oral presentation, computer-generated slide show, or creation of a poster. Maybe you decided that you would support students in their independent research of a chosen topic by

Table 4.8
Curriculum, Instruction Strategies, and Practices for Middle School Self-Determination

Social skills	• Students are taught and have occasions to provide positive feedback to peers and adults in social and academic contexts. • Students are taught and provided opportunities to use skills of providing and receiving productive criticism. • Curriculum content and schoolwide programs support the skills of resisting peer pressure and negotiation (conflict resolution, peer mediation, etc.). • Students are taught skills to effectively follow instructions and monitor their effectiveness in doing so. • Students have many opportunities to learn and apply effective conversational skills.
Choice making	• Students participate in course selection. • Students are provided choices in class assignments, selection, format, and so forth.
Risk taking	• Students are provided exploratory courses and content. • Students select course content that is new to them. • Career exploration opportunities are available.
Personal awareness and expression	• Students participate in student government activities. • A number of opportunities for relationships between and among students and staff are available. • Diverse opinions and perspectives are encouraged. • Students have the opportunity to state goals for educational programs.
Goal setting, goal attainment, and decision making	• Students are provided opportunities to participate in, plan, and develop their IEPs. • Students are provided a number of opportunities and supports to develop personal learning, academic, and career goals.
Self-management	• Students are provided instruction and support in self-monitoring and self-evaluation skills across the curriculum in content, career, and life skills.
Supportive relationships	• Peer tutoring and mentoring programs are available. • Cooperative learning and team projects are used. • Activities are designed and included to support friendship development and skills.
Individualized supports	• Universal design for learning is implemented. • Student self-advocacy is nurtured.
Reasonable and predictable consequences	• Clearly defined classroom behavior management programs are established. • Explicit schoolwide behavioral standards and a code of conduct are present. • A clearly defined system of school decision making is present. • Students are given an opportunity to state goals for educational programs.
High expectations	• Teachers and school staff communicate high expectations for students.
Effective instructional techniques	• Teachers use role-modeling techniques. • Teachers provide and support students with methods of self-reflection and performance feedback.

The Middle School Experience

scaffolding goal-setting activities and assisting students to plan a timeline to support completion of their project. You may even have selected to assist students in the self-evaluation of their written language upon completion of an expository writing assignment.

N: Nurture Self-Awareness and Self-Esteem

Middle school is an intense time of change, which frequently affects the early adolescent's self-esteem. Self-determination practices are intertwined with practices that support positive self-esteem in students. Experiences such as positive attachments, friendships, and expressions of independence and autonomy can all lead to perceptions of personal worthiness and efficacy (Powers, Singer, & Sowers, 1996). Support provided by teachers and families is necessary for students navigating the personal and social adjustments of early adolescence.

With the increased autonomy and independence that occur in the secondary school years, students have a growing need for *self-advocacy.* Self-advocacy is an important skill supporting self-awareness and positive self-esteem. It is the result of a knowledgeable, realistic, and accurate self-assessment of personal skills, interests, needs, and abilities. Self-advocacy includes the ability to recognize and communicate one's personal strengths, needs, wants, interests, and rights, and to effectively speak on one's own behalf based on this knowledge (Kling, 2000; Krebs, 2002; Martin & Marshall, 1995; Merchant & Gajar, 1997; Yuan, 1994).

It is important for middle school teachers to assist students in building accurate self-awareness. At this age, students are becoming more aware of and candid about their academic, social, and physical qualities and skills. They need to learn about personal strengths and interests to support an accurate self-appraisal. Students should also become aware of and able to articulate their own personal learning needs and the types of accommodations they require in order to succeed. Teachers can assist students in better understanding their disabilities through discussion, research, and interviews. Students should also learn how to share information about their disabilities appropriately with others.

Krebs (2002) described a portfolio approach used to support the self-advocacy of eighth-grade students with low vision. Students explored and identified what they knew and wanted to know and learn about their visual impairments. A number of lessons and instructional activities offered students opportunities to (a) research their disabilities online and through interviews; (b) role-play explaining their disabilities to peers; (c) articulate information on their disabilities in a research report; (d) create vocabulary lists of important words and definitions related to their disabilities (e.g., *peripheral vision, nystagmus, ophthalmologist*); (e) list and identify personal learning strengths and needs; and (f) write a letter to ninth-grade teachers describing their disabilities and their learning preferences and needs.

Involving students in planning, preparing, and leading conferences such as quarterly teacher–student–parent progress conferences or IEP conferences is also an effective self-awareness and self-advocacy strategy. Van Reusen, Bos, Schumaker, and Deshler's (1994) five-step Self-Advocacy Strategy is one validated strategy that can be used by special and general educators or other related service personnel to support and teach students to advocate for themselves. Original field-testing of the strategy occurred with both middle and high school students. The mnemonic I PLAN is used to help students remember the steps involved in this strategy:

I *Inventory.* To prepare for educational conferences, students are taught to identify or conduct a personal assessment and list their perceived strengths, areas to improve upon, goals, and personal choices for learning accommodations. Students record information on a personal inventory record sheet.

P *Provide your inventory information.* At the conference, students are taught to articulate the strengths, needs, and choices they listed with individuals present. Students are taught when and how to provide the information, including the use of appropriate communication and social skills.

L *Listen and respond.* Students are provided with specific rationales and skills they can use to engage in effective listening and responding throughout the conference.

Self-Determination and Self-Advocacy

1. Stress and Spotlight Self-Determination Skills

   • Create activities and instructional practices that allow students to learn and practice self-determination skills.

   • Incorporate choice making, goal setting, decision making, and self-management in daily classroom and school activities.

2. Strengthen Student Self-Esteem and Self-Advocacy

   • Use classroom activities such as personal timelines and histories, journals, and problem-solving activities.

   • Assist students in identifying and naming feelings, needs, and wants.

   • Help students build social and personal coping skills.

   • Foster friendship and social skill development.

   • Teach and provide students with opportunities to actively participate in their academic planning and IEP development.

3. Patronize Portfolios

   • Use portfolio assessment to develop self-advocacy and self-determination skills (see Chapter 6).

   • Help middle school students build individual learning profiles.

Note. List adapted from Weimer, Cappotelli, and DiCamillo (1994).

A *Ask questions.* Students learn when and how to ask questions during a conference to gain a firm understanding of the meeting content and outcomes.

N *Name your goals.* Students are taught both when and how to forward their own personally stated goals during the conference.

D: Develop Career, Interest, and Talent Opportunities

In middle school, career education provides young adolescents with an opportunity to assess and explore personal skills and interests in possible careers. Career education also helps students to acquire and practice dispositions, knowledge, and skills important in the world of work. Students have the opportunity to find out about various career fields, set career goals, and develop personal career and educational plans.

Ten- to 14-year-olds are beginning to think about their career choices. A good number of these students believe that many options are available to them; these optimistic beliefs are often a function of positive self-esteem and of supportive family practices in learning about and exploring career choices (Turner & Lapan, 2002). Other students have less encouraging and hopeful attitudes and ambitions. Also, some middle school students may have developed gender-based stereotypes of occupations or may have difficulty connecting middle school learning and curriculum with future careers (Kerka, 1994).

If a teacher asks a group of seventh or eighth graders about their career dreams, answers might include, "I want to be a lawyer because they make lots of money;" "I really like animals, so I want to be a veterinarian;" or "I'm the next Shaquille O'Neal. You'll be seeing me on the courts!" Certainly, these are wonderful, positive career aspirations. Yet, it is not uncommon for middle schoolers to suggest stereotyped career choices that show a lack of informed, realistic understanding of their personal likes and interests and of job or career requirements. To assist students in their career planning, educators should provide experiences and information that help students bridge this gap.

U: Utilize Community Resources

Effective middle school teachers use community resources. Establishing community connections requires (a) developing a personal awareness of the surrounding community, including neighborhoods, families, businesses, community agencies, and leadership structures, and (b) networking. Teachers need to make contacts within communities to seek resources, supports, and curriculum connections. Teachers can partner with businesses, community agencies, and individual community members to acquire curriculum resources and instructional support, to seek educational tutoring assistance for students, to create job shadowing opportunities, and to implement community-based learning and service activities.

Career and Interest Exploration

1. Factor in the Future

- Help students begin to think about their future through instructional activities.

- Assist students in broadening their career aspirations beyond typical stereotyped career choices through activities such as career-day events, interviewing someone in a career of interest, and providing "career spotlights" or guest speakers throughout the year.

- Provide job shadowing and service learning opportunities, as well as career guidance software (Arrington, 2000; Kerka, 1994).

2. Cultivate Career Education Throughout the Curriculum

- Integrate vocational and academic content throughout core, advisory, exploratory, and individualized curriculum.

- Support students in understanding the relationship between school and future career and life roles.

- Include learning opportunities that assist students in making connections between types of coursework and extracurricular activities available in middle and high school that support career choices.

- Teach students how to access information about careers and career requirements (McNally & Harvey, 2001; J. V. Miller, 1992).

3. Explore and Experience Options

- Provide students instruction in needed life and personal development skills that are necessary for success in careers of interest.

- Inform students and families about extracurricular activities that are available, and support student interests, aptitudes, and career goals.

- Create a classroom company or entrepreneurial endeavor that allows students to actualize important career-related skills.

Note. List compiled from Carpenter, Bloom, and Boat (1999), Gallavan and Davis (1999), Holloway (1999/2000), and McWhirter and Bloom (1994).

Service Learning

Service learning provides an excellent opportunity to address student learning and involvement in the community. It should be considered an important part of the total transition approach to middle level education. One objective of the National Education Goals is the involvement of all students in activities that promote and demonstrate good citizenship and community service (National Center for Education Statistics [NCES], 1999). The NCES (1999) reported that in 1996, approximately half of students in Grades 6 through 12 participated in community services, 26% regularly and 23% once or twice during the academic year.

"Service learning can be used to provide students with opportunities that enable them to make contributions to the community and integrate academic content into real-life situations at the same time" (Cronin & Pikes, 1999, p. 305). It is a method that integrates learning within community contexts, fosters civic responsibility, and meets actual community needs through collaboration with the school and community (Billig, 2000). Service learning is integrated with academic content and curriculum, and structured time is scheduled for learners to reflect on, discuss, write about, and share their experiences encountered in the service activity (Billig, 2000; A. M. Johnson & Notah, 1999). Researchers and proponents have identified the following benefits resulting from this type of civic engagement: (a) expanded provision of "authentic" academic content, (b) improved academic grades, (c) enhanced self-concept and self-esteem, (d) increased personal and social responsibility and problem-solving skills, (e) decreased discipline referrals, (f) increased self-knowledge, (g) improved attitudes toward adults, and (h) better student communication and social skills (S. N. Clark & Welmers, 1994; A. M. Johnson & Notah, 1999; NCES, 1999; Yoder, Retish, & Wade, 1996).

Career education is also cultivated. In service learning activities, students receive exposure to working with individuals across diverse cultures, socioeconomic groups, languages, and ages. Students must work under time constraints, experience real-life issues, and mediate collaborative solutions (B. L. Brown, 1998). Community members supporting these projects often serve as positive adult role models for students.

For students with exceptionalities, service learning provides an opportunity to become a valuable resource to others, to be recognized for talents and contributions, to be needed and wanted, and to experience the pleasures (and perhaps growing pains) associated with civic engagement. Contributions evidenced in service learning can have tremendous impact for students who have experienced repeated failure in schools or who have negative attitudes about school or themselves (McPherson, 1997).

Incorporating Service Learning in the Curriculum

Teachers may design community projects of their own, involve students in the design of projects, or connect students to school-based or community groups that sponsor existing service clubs or activities. Service learning can be incorporated within advisory programs, exploratory courses, extracurricular activities, or specific core, individualized, or interdisciplinary curricula.

Activity 4.6 promotes thinking about service learning activities that your students can do. Also, you are encouraged to suggest ideas for service learning activities as part of the Traditions unit introduced earlier in the chapter. In this unit, students might become engaged with the local museum or neighborhood senior center. They might record, document, or catalog community traditions; conduct and record oral histories with community members at the local senior center; or create a museum display of community traditions.

Activity 4.6 Community Connections

1. Brainstorm and list service learning activities that might be used at your school or in your community to successfully meet a need, and that might interest middle school students.

2. List some ideas for infusing service learning into the Traditions interdisciplinary unit introduced in Activity 4.3.

Other Community-Referenced Opportunities

Some students will have individualized needs and interests for life and community skills instruction that may not be addressed in core, exploratory, advisory, or interdisciplinary curricula, or through service learning activities. Teachers of students with disabilities who require individualized instruction or supports may need to incorporate and enhance community-based instructional opportunities. Although Beakley and Yoder (1998) recommend twice a week as an ideal for these community skills and experiences, they acknowledge that a weekly community-referenced activity is more realistic.

I: Implement Effective Instructional Practices

Teaching is rewarding, but it is hard work. It is not a job that can be performed by reading and following the directions on a checklist or even one that can be accomplished effectively within the limited 6-hour school day. Teaching requires good planning and decision making, effective instruction and assessment delivery, practiced classroom management skills, and teacher reflection.

Good teaching involves choosing appropriate structures that meet the learning objectives and the varying needs and abilities of your students. It would be wonderfully uncomplicated to believe that a single teaching approach, material, or strategy would address the needs of a group of 30 or so students in a single class period. However, teaching is not that simple. In this section we describe instructional methods and lesson-based instructional practices that have strong professional or empirical support for use with diverse groups of students at the middle school level.

Service Learning

1. Establish Partnerships and Possibilities

   - Create partnerships with community agencies, organizations, and individuals.

   - Identify specific needs of agencies or organizations within the community that can be supported through student action or support.

   - Select a project from a menu of potential projects supporting community needs.

   - Obtain parental and administrative support for the community service project.

2. Saturate Curricula with Service Learning

   - Integrate service learning within the middle school curriculum.

   - Incorporate, foster, and support relevant skills needed to complete service learning projects in instructional activities.

   - Design needed training and orientation sessions that address project site–specific setting demands.

3. Actualize and Assess

   - Devise and implement a clear schedule for the service project that includes outlined responsibilities, clear time frames, and specific logistical procedures.

   - Integrate student reflection throughout the service project.

   - Evaluate the outcomes and effectiveness of the service learning project.

Direct Instruction

Direct instruction is a systematic teaching approach that involves a series of instructional procedures, strategies, steps, and principles that are mindfully identified, organized, and articulated to promote high levels of student achievement (Rivera & Smith, 1997). Direct instruction is effective to use for all types of content and provides a foundation for other lessons that use other instructional methods to support concept learning, critical thinking, and problem solving (K. Price & Nelson, 2003).

In direct instruction, important concepts are selected and grouped for instruction around "big ideas"—those concepts that appear frequently at a grade level and are essential to student outcomes (Kame'enui, Carnine, Dixon, Simmons, & Coyne, 2002; Stein, Carnine, & Dixon, 1998). Adequate review occurs throughout the lesson and is incorporated in later instruction. Instruction occurs at a brisk pace, with material presented in manageable learning steps or "chunks." Mastery at each step is necessary prior to moving on to subsequent objectives. Teacher monitoring is provided to support, scaffold, diagnose, and correct student errors so that effective learning occurs (Polloway, Patton, & Serna, 2001; Rivera & Smith, 1997; Stein et al., 1998). In the MidEx model, direct instruction is used to support initial instruction and acquisition of important life and transition skills.

Direct instruction involves the following instructional sequence:

1. *Examination of learning targets.* The teacher identifies clear learning objectives, determines prerequisite skills needed to enter into the lesson, and reviews previously taught relevant skills and concepts (K. Price & Nelson, 2003).

2. *Explicit explanation and modeling.* The teacher presents new information and concepts through explicit explanation and modeling, checks for student understanding throughout instruction, and provides frequent positive feedback and reinforcement for correct responses. Active participation by all students is required (Rivera & Smith, 1997).

3. *Guided practice of skills.* The teacher supplies guided, scaffolded practice to all students. Students practice skills with teacher support through the use of coaching, prompting, and feedback (Stein et al., 1998). Learning supports may include visual, manual, and pictorial prompts, as well as teaching cues (Schloss, Smith, & Schloss, 2001). Scaffolds or supports are eventually reduced or faded to facilitate student independence and mastery.

4. *Independent practice.* The teacher designs individual, independent practice to provide each student adequate practice to master the skill; varies and distributes practice opportunities over time; and stresses generalization of information across contexts and settings. Teacher feedback is essential.

Strategy Instruction

In strategy instruction, teachers instruct students how to systematically use cognitive and metacognitive strategies for effective and efficient learning across content areas. Strategies refer to how someone thinks and acts when carrying out a task. Learning strategies include the steps, rules, or principles that assist in the acquisition, use, storage, and retrieval of information across situations and contexts (Deshler, Schumaker, Alley, Warner, & Clark, 1982; Lenz, Ellis, & Scanlon, 1996).

Many at-risk students and students with disabilities exhibit passive learning characteristics, have difficulties with processing and remembering information, and lack skills needed to address the setting demands of the middle school. Instruction in learning strategies can be used to enhance independence and successful learning outcomes for these students.

One well-established model, the strategies intervention model (SIM), was developed by the Center for Research on Learning at the University of Kansas. It is based on nearly 25 years of research with adolescents and at-risk students, including adolescents with learning disabilities (Tralli, Columbo, Deshler, & Schumaker, 1999; University of Kansas Center for Research on Learning [CRL], 2001). In SIM, strategy instruction is consistent, explicit, intensive, and based on mastery criteria. Students are required to make a commitment to strategy practice and use. Instruction and practice involve the use of covert models and demonstration and practice of strategy steps (Ellis & Lenz, 1996). Guided and independent practice is provided, with attention to generalization and transfer of strategy use across content materials and settings. A remembering tool or mnemonic is embedded within each strategy. A number of strategies have been developed and validated to support strategic learning, including the following (Tralli et al., 1999; University of Kansas CRL, 2001):

1. *Acquisition Strategies*—Learning strategies that support the decoding, comprehension, and recall of written material (e.g., strategies for word identification, paraphrasing, self-questioning, visual imagery, interpreting visuals)

2. *Storage Strategies*—Learning strategies that support effective storage and retrieval of information (e.g., strategies in first-letter mnemonics, paired associates, and listening and note taking)

3. *Expression and Demonstration of Competence*—Learning strategies that support student expression of knowledge, skills and understanding (e.g., strategies for sentence writing, paragraph writing, error monitoring [editing], theme writing, assignment completion, and test taking)

Many of these strategies require specialized training in appropriate application of strategy instruction. Additional SIM strategies and components include content enhancement strategies and motivation or social interaction strategies.

Educators need to know that (a) some students will need support and instruction in the use of strategies, and (b) there are materials and validated practices to support this type of instruction. General and special education teachers can collaboratively investigate options, seek training, and provide support and reinforcement for strategy instruction and use throughout the curriculum.

Study Skills Instruction

Study skills are those general and specific skills that students need in order to access, record, organize, synthesize, remember, and use information and ideas (Devine, 1987; Hudson, 1997; Polloway et al., 2001). These skills are critical to student independence (Olson & Platt, 2000). Many teachers assume that students, by the time they reach middle school, have either been taught these skills at the elementary level or have intrinsically developed these skills with their increasing maturity. Unfortunately, this is not the case for many students, including students with disabilities. For these students, study skills need to be taught directly and supported throughout middle school instructional environments. Middle level educators need to communicate common expectations and procedures for study skills and to base their decisions on accurate assessments of both student abilities and curricular demands.

Important study skills include active listening, outlining, note taking, test taking, time management, organization, adjustment of reading rates, and effective use of resources. Other study skills include presentation and report writing skills, effective textbook use, and successful homework strategies (Polloway et al., 2001; Weishar & Boyle, 1999). These study skills are important curriculum targets for middle school students. In selecting specific study skill areas for instruction, teachers should consider the following (Olson & Platt, 2000; Rivera & Smith, 1997):

1. Select those study skills that are functional and meaningful for students. Prioritize and select skills for immediate instruction that are likely to have the most significant impact for students.

2. Ensure that skills selected are those that students also believe are helpful and needed.

3. Provide instruction that includes a rationale, clear information on using the skill, and demonstration of skill use.

4. Provide opportunities for students to practice the skills and to receive teacher feedback.

5. Provide meaningful, practical opportunities to practice using the skills across the curriculum. Provide reinforcement and feedback for generalized practice.

6. Use collaborative team planning and instruction to support effective study skills instruction.

Cooperative Learning

Throughout this text we have recommended cooperative learning as a developmentally appropriate, supportive, effective technique to foster learning for middle level learners. Simply placing students together in a classroom or in small groups, however, does not constitute cooperative learning. Cooperative learning is a type of learning or instructional structure that involves small groups of students who must learn and collaborate together to achieve an instructional objective or meet a learning goal. Groups are formed heterogeneously and should represent the diversity reflected in individual classrooms. This type of learning structure capitalizes on some of the elements of early adolescence: growing autonomy, independence, peer orientation, and the need for supportive risk taking (Slavin, 1996). The following elements are necessary to construct and sustain this type of instructional arrangement (G. M. Johnson, 1999; Malmgren, 1998; Slavin, 1996):

1. *Positive Group Interdependence*—This element is fostered and achieved through the use of group goals and rewards. Rewards are achieved and available for all groups based on designated criteria. Students are recognized for their contributions to the identified group goal. By performing a needed, valued, and meaningful role, each student contributes to the success of the group task.

2. *Face-to-Face Interaction*—The classroom environment should be arranged so group members are close to one another during the

learning task. This arrangement is needed so that the critical verbal and nonverbal interactions across group members can occur.

3. *Individual Accountability*—Each student is responsible for learning the content, but the group should support each member in achieving this goal.

4. *Group Behaviors*—A number of critical social, communication, and collaboration skills are needed to accomplish the cooperative activity. These skills include listening, taking turns, perspective taking, sharing ideas, negotiating, managing conflict, providing positive feedback, and accepting feedback.

5. *Group Processing*—Reflection is a central element of cooperative learning. Group members must individually and collaboratively reflect on the effectiveness of the collaborative processes used to address the learning objectives. This might occur through discussion, dialogue, conferencing, or written evaluation and feedback.

Lesson Planning

Teachers are excited when the "teachable moment" happens and spontaneous natural opportunities present themselves, helping students to make connections. These "teaching gems," however, occur infrequently and may not lend themselves to the span of curriculum that teachers must address with students. Therefore, instruction must be intentionally and deliberately planned. To deliver instruction effectively, teachers must arrange and organize opportunities for student learning through a series of research-based practices.

Rosenshine (1983, 1987) reviewed literature and research on student achievement and found that these six planning functions lead to improved student achievement: review, presentation of new content or skills, initial student practice with checks for understanding, feedback, independent practice, and weekly and monthly reviews. Similarly, Swanson (2001) conducted an analysis of effective, empirically supported instructional interventions supporting higher order thinking and found that specific techniques, such as the use of advance organizers, specific instruction in new concepts, and the use of extended practice and daily feedback, have significant effects on student learning. These findings fit into models of instruction that include the following elements: (a) preplanning and preparation; (b) lesson introduction and initiation, including appropriate review and the use of advance organizers; (c) teacher presentation and modeling; (d) guided, scaffolded practice, including checks for student understanding; (e) synthesis or closure; (f) independent practice, including distributed practice and review; and (g) evaluation (Hunter, 1982; Rivera & Smith, 1997; Rosenberg, O'Shea, & O'Shea, 1998; Swanson, 2001).

As teachers plan, they should record their decisions on a lesson planning template or form. Using such a form is a systematic way to assist the preplanning process (Vaughn & Schumm, 1995, cited in S. P. Miller, 2002). The lesson planning form is used to assist general or special educators in formulating thoughtful preplanning decisions regarding content, accommodations, modifications, materials, and procedures. Figure 4.5 displays an example of a lesson planning template that also includes transition connections.

Middle school students respond positively to active participation strategies in any lesson. Teachers should creatively incorporate active learning strategies in each lesson. Several active learning possibilities for middle school students are listed in Table 4.9.

Lesson Planning Pyramid Decision Template

Teacher(s) _____ Class Period: _____ Date _____

Unit _____

Lesson Objective(s) _____

Transition Areas/Skills Addressed _____

Materials	Evaluation/Assessment Options
Student Grouping(s)	Setting/Environment
In-Class Assignment Options	Homework or Independent Study Options

Lesson Decision Pyramid	Lesson Agenda/Procedures
What will all, most, and some students learn?	What procedures or steps will occur in the lesson?
What some students will learn	1. _____
What most students will learn	2. _____ 3. _____ 4. _____ 5. _____
What all students will learn	6. _____ 7. _____

Figure 4.5. Lesson planning pyramid decision template. *Note.* Adapted from "Pyramid Power for Collaborative Planning," by J. S. Schumm, S. Vaughn, and J. Harris, 1997, *Teaching Exceptional Children,* 29(6), pp. 62–66. Copyright 1997 by the Council for Exceptional Children. Adapted with permission.

Table 4.9
Sampling of Middle Level Active Participation Strategies

Use a Variety of Active Responding Techniques
Incorporate a variety of active responding techniques throughout the lesson. These may include the use of individual or choral oral responses, response cards, response boards, finger signals, and physical responses.

Use Journals
Allow students to record important information or to express learning ideas and personal reactions or reflections in journals. Allow students to use words, drawings, cognitive maps, or pictures to express their ideas.

Incorporate Student-Designed Projects or Assignments
Create a menu of activity choices that allow students to acquire, practice, extend, or generalize information. Use choices that are interesting to early adolescents and ones that they can successfully complete. Possibilities include video documentaries, Web pages, Web casts, artistic creations, oral presentations, written papers, desktop publishing documents, persuasive editorials, and musical compositions.

Use Manipulatives, Materials, and Learning Games
Make manipulatives to support hands-on learning readily available for students. Create or use instructional games that give students the opportunity to practice skills individually or in pairs, small groups, or large groups.

Incorporate Role Plays
Provide opportunities for students to use role plays in learning.

Build in Simulation Activities
Create opportunities for students to learn, practice, and apply information and skills through simulations, real-life experiences, or problem-based learning.

Use Collaborative Learning Structures
Incorporate the use of collaborative learning and practice structures, such as dyads, cooperative learning groups, peer tutoring, or discussion groups.

Provide Tools that Actively Engage Students with Teacher or Text Presentations
Construct and use lecture, reading, and study guides with students. Teach students strategies for active comprehension monitoring. Incorporate the use of graphic organizers and concept maps before, during, and after learning or instruction.

Culturally Responsive Instruction

To support meaningful personal awareness, exploration, and self-determination at the middle school level, educators must implement culturally responsive instructional practices. Classrooms are wonderfully diverse communities. Over 70–80% of students in urban schools are Latino or African American (Rong & Preissle, 1998, cited in D. F. Brown, 2002). Students who are not native English speakers are quickly becoming one of the fastest growing populations (D. F. Brown, 2002). Gay underscored this in stating,

> If ethnic identify development is understood as part of the natural "coming of age" process during early adolescence, and if middle level education is to be genuinely client-centered for students of color, then ethnic sensitivity must be incorporated into school policies, programs, and practices. (cited in D. F. Brown, 2002, p. 153)

At the middle school level, students are able to understand the cultural aspects of ethnicity and extend past fashions, customs, and holidays to the exploration of perspectives, values, and nondiscriminatory practices. Teachers are encouraged to use a set of culturally sensitive strategies and to accept and realize that there are instructional practices that foster success for culturally and linguistically diverse students (D. F. Brown, 2002; Irvine & Armento, 2001). Several best practice recommendations for culturally sensitive instruction appear in Table 4.10 (compiled from D. F. Brown, 2002; Garrett, Bellon-Harn, Torres-Rivera, Garrett, & Roberts, 2003; Irvine & Armento, 2001).

T: Team and Collaborate for Success

Have you heard or seen the phrase, "There is no 'I' in 'team'"? To deliver effective curriculum—one that creates cohesive, supportive relationships between and

Table 4.10
Culturally Responsive Middle School Instruction

Principle	Classroom Practice Examples
Incorporate inductive learning and supportive instructional strategies	• Use whole-to-part teaching process. • Demonstrate and discuss the "big picture" prior to addressing individual steps or components. • Support new learning by preteaching relevant new vocabulary. • Use visual representations and graphic organizers for new concepts. • Assess and bring in students' prior background knowledge.
Provide contextual experiences	• Use stories to introduce concepts. • Incorporate culturally relevant analogies and examples. • Provide opportunities for students to share experiences on topics. • Use hands-on materials and activities to assist in understanding the concept or language. • Relate personal accounts. • Use media and activities to depict concepts. • Use culturally relevant materials.
Implement collaborative learning	• Use collaborative versus competitive learning. • Use collaborative discussions.
Use culturally responsive communication	• Use culturally sensitive and responsive communication practices. • Model standard English but recognize variations.
Support second language learners	• Demonstrate genuine interest. • Rephrase and summarize information. • Build on students' prior knowledge base. • Adapt instructional materials for comprehensibility.

among students, teachers, and families—teachers must collaborate. Collaboration ensures that middle school curriculum is created with an understanding of student needs and interests, supports success-oriented learning, nurtures beneficial interpersonal relationships, and establishes communities of learning (Kennedy & Fisher, 2001). In Chapter 2 we investigated collaborative practices involving effective parent involvement and interdisciplinary teaming. In the next section we explore another collaborative practice, co-teaching, which can also support effective learning and transition skills for middle school students.

Collaborative Teaching

In collaborative teaching, or co-teaching, the special educator provides direct services to students with disabilities within the general education classroom (Bauwens & Hourcade, 1995; Elliot & McKenney, 1998; Nowacek, 1992; Salend, Gordon, & Lopez-Vona, 2002; Weiss & Lloyd, 2003; White & White, 1992; Zigmond & Magiera, 2001). One definition of cooperative or co-teaching is

> an educational approach in which general and special educators work in a co-active and coordinated fashion to jointly teach heterogeneous groups of students in educationally integrated settings (i.e., general classrooms). In cooperative teaching both general and special education teachers are simultaneously present in the general classroom, maintaining joint responsibilities for specified education instruction that is to occur within that setting. (Bauwens, Hourcade, & Friend, 1989, p. 18)

In a co-teaching model, students may experience benefits such as (a) an additional level of service provided in an inclusive environment, (b) higher academic or behavioral expectations, (c) availability of peer role models, and (d) increased peer acceptance (Dieker, 2001; Nowacek, 1992; Zigmond & Magiera, 2001). For educators, advantages include enhanced opportunities to observe individual students and tailor instruction, provision of a forum for the professional exchange of ideas, improved satisfaction with teaching, and decreased feelings of isolation (Hourcade & Bauwens, 2001; Nowacek, 1992).

Several co-teaching models have been proposed in the literature (see Table 4.11, compiled from Dieker, 2001; Weiss & Lloyd, 2003; Zigmond & Magiera, 2001). Teachers should select a model based on the needs of a unique group of students, as well as the expertise, background, and experience of the educators involved.

Barriers that impede effective co-teaching include lack of time for adequate planning, ill-defined or vague educator roles and responsibilities, conflicting teaching styles or philosophies, forced co-teaching assignments, scheduling concerns, tracking of students, and a decrease in services to students not involved in co-teaching models of service delivery (Gerber & Popp, 2000; Zigmond & Magiera, 2001). Best practice recommendations for implementing co-teaching address these barriers. For co-teaching to be effective, researchers have identified the need to (a) schedule co-teaching classes appropriately in the master schedule, (b) plan for considerate class composition, (c) establish a common planning time for co-teachers, (d) provide adequate physical space and symbols of status or authority for both teachers,

Table 4.11
Models of Co-Teaching

Model	Description
One teach, one assist	Both team members are present in one classroom. One team member leads the instruction for a lesson or unit. The other team member assists by clarifying directions or activities for students, monitoring student performance, observing students, or providing specialized tutoring.
Station teaching	Both team members are present in one classroom. The classroom is structured physically to allow two small group areas of instruction and a third area for independent work. Each team member leads a different lesson supporting curriculum content at a separate station. Students rotate through the stations in small groups and complete assigned independent work with minimal supervision.
Parallel teaching	Both team members are present in one classroom. The class is equally split into two heterogeneous groups. Each teacher provides instruction (i.e., the same lesson content) to one group of students using an instructional delivery method that best suits his or her teaching style and the needs of group members. Each group's composition should be representative of the diverse interests, abilities, languages, and cultures of the entire class.
Alternative teaching	Two unequal groups of students are created. One team teacher engages in large group activities centered on review and extension of a previously taught concept or skill. The other teacher works with a small group of students in reteaching, preteaching, or supplemental instruction.
Team teaching	Both teachers are present in the same classroom and are equally responsible for instructional delivery to the whole class. At any particular time during the lesson, one teacher may take a lead; however, the other teacher heads instruction in a different part of the lesson or unit. In this model teachers jointly present at times with one teacher elaborating on the directions and the other teacher providing explanations or examples.

(e) maintain multiple service delivery models, (f) provide needed resources and training, and (g) establish program evaluation procedures (Austin, 2001; Bauwens & Hourcade, 1991; Gerber & Popp, 2000; Walther-Thomas, Korinek, McLaughlin, & Williams, 2000; Weiss & Lloyd, 2003). Professionals recommend that approximately one fifth (Walther-Thomas, Korinek, & McLaughlin, 1999) to one third (Zigmond & Magiera, 2001) of any one co-taught class be composed of students with identified disabilities to ensure a heterogeneous mix of students.

In the MidEx model, co-teaching practices allow educators to augment instructional practices. The expertise of each educator (a content specialist and a learning specialist) can provide greater learning opportunities for students and teachers. Access to appropriate curriculum, including important transition skills, can be improved for all students.

Bringing It All Together

Make Connections

As a middle level educator, you play a critical role in creating and sustaining a rich learning environment for early adolescents. You are the conduit through which a valuable curriculum that is steeped in interesting content, motivating practices, and transition-relevant skills can be constructed.

Engage in Reflection

In Figure 4.6, key concepts and practices presented throughout this chapter are incorporated into the MidEx model. A total transition approach provides appropriate curriculum with supportive instructional practices within the context of the most naturally occurring environments possible. This endeavor is most effective with collaborative input, involvement, and support.

Summary

The middle school curriculum establishes a cornerstone for the future transition successes of students. A sound, cohesive foundation for the effective transition of all students is established by using a systematic framework to identify transition needs, connect to existing middle school curriculum, offer opportunities for self-determination, nurture self-awareness and self-esteem, deliver career exploration and education, use community resources, and team for success.

One mark of a great educator is the ability to lead students out to new places where even the educator has never been.

—Thomas Groome

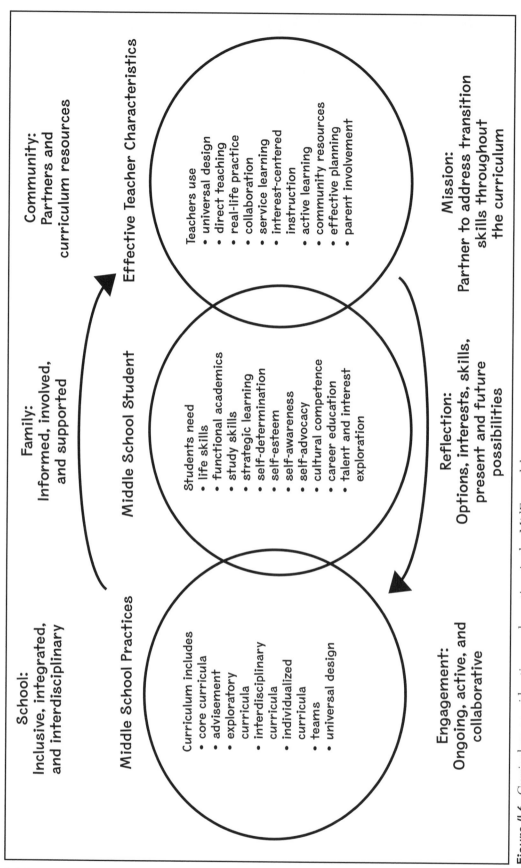

Figure 4.6. Curriculum considerations and practices in the MidEx model.

The Middle School Experience

Impact of Information on Your Mission

1. List your mission keywords (feel free to change your keywords as you progress).

2. Describe a story from your teaching or experience that relates to providing appropriate curriculum and transition instruction for middle schoolers. What was your own experience as a middle school student? What types of more or less positive teaching experiences or practices have you witnessed?

3. What influenced your actions or the actions of others (e.g., students, teachers, or parents) in the story?

4. What information did you learn in this chapter that influences this story?

5. What teaching practices might you change based on this new information?

APPENDIX 4.A

Objectives and Activities for a Sample Interdisciplinary Unit on Traditions

Language Arts	Social Studies	Science
• Compare and contrast folk sayings and proverbs. • Discuss past and present traditions, mores, or values in selected cultures or groups depicted in fiction. • Evaluate the accuracy of fictional portrayal of traditions and cultural customs. • Compare and contrast traditional stories or fairy tales from two or more cultures or countries. • Research a tradition of choice and write an expository piece on the tradition. • Create a persuasive print or electronic advertisement that markets a new "tradition." • Discuss and provide examples of the importance of storytelling in sustaining cultural traditions and customs. • Conduct interviews in the community to research local and familial customs and traditions.	• Define and provide examples of and rationale for familial, community, and cultural traditions. • Provide examples of types of traditions: clothing, ceremonies, celebrations, leisure activities, and so on. • Identify artifacts that reveal past and present traditions. • Discuss how traditions of the past impact current society. • Debate traditional historical perspectives versus nontraditional historical perspectives of state history. • Identify the impact of state geography, climate, culture, and economy on local traditions.	• Delineate and discuss traditional and nontraditional fields of science. • Identify traditional methods of scientific observation and inquiry. • Discuss the impact of new scientific theories, practices, and fields of study on traditional practices, beliefs, and knowledge.

APPENDIX 4.B
UDL Planning Example: How a Bill Becomes a Law

Options for Instructional Presentation[a]	Options for Student Expression	Options for Student Engagement
• Provide social studies text and other reference materials for students to chart how the bicameral (two-house) legislation system emerged. • Provide access to a text reader program for social studies readings describing how a bill becomes a law. • Make available government reference materials in the first languages of students. • Provide and post a flowchart or graphic organizer outlining the process of how a bill becomes a law. • Arrange a field trip for the class to visit the state legislature. Have students interview a legislator to explain how a piece of legislation was passed. • Provide newspapers and magazines (print and electronic versions) for students to generate a listing of current legislative issues. • Use television (with closed captions) to examine recent broadcasts of local and national issues.	• Create a diagram of the process by which a bill becomes a law using a graphic organizer program. • Design an oral or digital presentation that depicts a history of the two-house legislation system. • Write a report that describes the legislation process using word processors or voice recognition software. • Interview a special-interest group representative and present findings in an oral report. • Create a mock radio, television, or Webcast on one or more current issues, with varied perspectives and solutions to the issue. • Produce a letter to a newspaper or magazine editor on a selected issue, outlining issue, impacts, and a proposed solution.	• Use assistive technology supports to access information or produce individual projects. • Provide options in activities to complete projects individually, with partners or with small groups. • Provide a checklist and conferencing to support completion of long-term projects such as a mock television program. • Allow selection of project demonstration formats from a menu of possible choices.

[a]Lesson presentation ideas adapted from *How a Bill Becomes a Law: An AskERIC Lesson Plan* (Lesson plan No. AELP-GOV0015), by D. A. Roja, 1994, retrieved May 10, 2003, from http://www.eduref.org/cgi-bin/printlessons.cgi/Virtual/Lessons/Social_Studies/US_Government/GOV0015.html

APPENDIX 4.C
Middle School Interdisciplinary Content Unit Planning Form

Theme _____

Subject(s) _____

Content Standards _____

Teachers _____ Projected Dates for Unit _____

Supporting Materials _____

Unit Outcomes	
Unit Outcomes	Modifications to Outcomes for Students (Who/What)
Transition Areas Addressed	

Learning Objectives and Activities		
Specific Objectives	Assignments/Activities/Projects	Accommodations/Modifications (Who/What)
Transition Objectives	Transition-Related Activities	

Assessment		
Specific Objectives	Assignments/Activities	Accommodations/Modifications
Transition Assessment Needs		

CHAPTER 5

Behavioral, Social, and Emotional Growth in Middle School

Kathryn Krudwig

Free advice from middle school students you may want to disregard:

"Let them chew gum."

"Try to act like the class."

"Have parties every Friday."

"Bring a lunch from home so you don't have to eat cafeteria food."

"Keep a whistle (just in case)."

"Watch R-rated movies."

"Don't set your expectations for us too high."

"If the class starts talking, don't tell them to be quiet, just sit there."

"It's going to be noisy. I recommend earplugs."

"Bring some aspirin."

"There's no 'perfect' class, so always expect the worst."

"Act cool."

"Figure out their real names."

"Don't get nervous."

Learning Objectives

1. To describe the behavioral and social developmental tasks of students in middle school.

2. To explain how your beliefs and practices related to classroom management and student achievement align with research-based principles.

3. To demonstrate how you can physically arrange your classroom to facilitate learning.

4. To select behavior management strategies that can support all your students.

5. To explain how you can best support the social and affective growth of all your students.

6. To describe how you can join with families and community to enhance your combined capacity to support positive student outcomes.

Introduction

The middle school years and adolescence are exciting periods of development and preparation for adulthood. Just when parents and teachers think they have finally trained elementary school–age children to act appropriately in public, the adults watch anxiously as the youngsters molt into something akin to creatures from outer space. Rather than approaching adolescence as an alien war zone, significant adults need to adopt practices that effectively support the growth of young people into responsible, contributing citizens.

The purpose of this chapter is to help teachers think about and plan for successful ways to support the behavioral, social, and emotional growth of students in middle school. For the purposes of this book, *behavioral* refers to the responses of an individual to the rules and procedures in school and community, and *social* and *emotional* refer to interpersonal and intrapersonal relationships, respectively. All students, regardless of language, economic, physical, racial, geographic, gender, cultural, or ability differences, strive to make sense of their world by applying what they learn behaviorally, socially, and emotionally. Teachers can support students' efforts to understand with strategies designed to meet the needs of all students—that is, through universal design. With the goal to support universal design, I include these topics in this chapter: (a) developmental tasks for middle school students related to social and emotional growth; (b) teacher beliefs and practices essential for successful classroom management and student achievement; (c) options for organizing a productive learning environment; (d) universal behavior management strategies; (e) universal strategies for supporting social and emotional growth; and (f) strategies for collaborating effectively with families and community in support of educational goals.

What Are the Social and Emotional Developmental Tasks of Students in Middle School?

Physical maturation, cognitive growth, emotional development, and a widening social arena converge, sometimes intensely, in the lives of young adolescents. They strive to answer new questions as they journey through the next few years:

> *How do I view myself and my future? Where do I fit into things? What will I become? How can I nurture and build positive relationships with peers and adults? How can I handle life's challenges, problems, decisions, and choices? How can I develop as a moral, ethical, active, committed human being? How can I get involved in the world of work? My school? My neighborhood? How can I develop a positive answer to the question, Who am I?* (Elias & Butler, 1999, p. 75)

Students in middle school undertake several developmental tasks as they experience adolescence. They begin to develop a sense of self separate from the adults in their lives, as well as explore, take risks, and practice problem solving. They do not arrive on the adolescent scene totally unprepared. Typical cognitive development equips preteens with increasing abilities to analyze information and think logically, form opinions, and express a range of ideas and preferences. Hopefully, by the time they become adults, they are well equipped to make responsible decisions in life. Individuals who successfully meet the challenges and opportunities of adolescence become more independent, autonomous, and self-reliant (Solodow, 1999).

The goal for all adolescents, including students with disabilities, is to become empowered and self-determined adults. During their journey toward adulthood, students in middle school need fair limits, diverse experiences, positive interpersonal relationships with both peers and adults, feelings of competence, and opportunities to show responsibility (Elias, 1993). Although perhaps unnerving for parents who do not want their child to make harmful choices, opportunities for independent thinking and choice making are critical to the young person's development of self-determination. According to Wehmeyer (1992), "Self-determination refers to the attitudes and abilities necessary to act as the primary causal agent in one's life, and to make choices and decisions regarding one's quality of life free from undue external influence or interference" (p. 16).

Challenges inherent in growing up can appear daunting to young teens. They must adjust to physiological changes over which they have no control. This can be very stressful for the 11-year-old girl who suddenly finds herself 2 inches taller than the tallest boy in the class, or for the 13-year-old boy whose voice still sounds like his 6-year-old sister's. Trying to "look good" to the rest of the teen world can become quite problematic for some students. Inevitably, some young teens find themselves ostracized in and out of school by their peers for the way they look or dress.

Other challenges originate in family and community situations. Balancing time and loyalty between family and friends can lead to ongoing stress for students in middle school and their families, particularly when parents do not approve of new friends. Preteens may have the desire to exercise their independence without sufficient insight into their parents' concerns for safety or adequate communication skills to discuss family issues. Their efforts to express independence may look like rebellion to parents (Crudelle & Erickson, 1995). Stress may be lower when preteen behavior remains close to the family norm. For instance, a daughter whose family is heavily involved in sports may stay in the family's "comfort zone" if going out with friends involves sports-related activities.

Exposure to violence through television and other media may negatively impact students' perceptions of personal safety in the world at large and their responses during conflict. Results from studies of the relationship between media violence and behavior suggested that viewing violence on television increased both insensitivity to violence and aggressive behavior, particularly among children who were already aggressive (H. M. Walker, Colvin, & Ramsey, 1995; Widom, 1989).

Activity 5.1 encourages you to think about your positive and negative experiences during adolescence, as well as your feeling about them. Reflecting on your memories can help you as a middle school teacher.

Activity 5.1 Your Own Teenage Years

Reflect on your own years as a young teenager. In recording your thoughts, try to recapture not only memories but also how you felt in different situations.

1. List what you remember as positive elements of your adolescent experience.

2. List the parts of your adolescence you wish had been different.

3. What insights into your adolescence do you have now that you did not have at the time?

4. What implications do these insights have for your practice as a middle school teacher?

The Middle School Experience

How Do My Beliefs and Practices Support Classroom Management and Student Achievement?

Given the rich diversity of students in middle school, bringing several hundred of them together in a school can test even the most experienced administrators and teachers. Understandably, one of the greatest challenges teachers face is how to create and manage a productive learning environment. You have choices as an educator about how you structure your thinking about the broad issue of classroom management and the more specific issues that derive from student behavior. Your beliefs constitute your philosophy of teaching and guide your behavior. Before reading further, complete Activity 5.2, which helps you reflect on your teaching philosophy.

The practices described later in this chapter are grounded in a learner-centered philosophy. The current construct of learner centeredness was defined by McCombs and Whisler (1997) as

> *the perspective that couples a focus on individual learners (their heredity, experiences, perspectives, backgrounds, talents, interests, capacities, and needs) with a focus on learning (the best available knowledge about learning and how it occurs and about teaching practices that are most effective in promoting the highest levels of motivation, learning, and achievement for all learners). This dual focus, then, informs and drives educational decision making.* (p. 9)

The American Psychological Association (APA) Presidential Task Force on Psychology in Education and the Mid-continent Regional Education Laboratory worked collaboratively to extract underlying principles of best practice from the cumulative body of educational and psychological research (APA Task Force on Psychology in Education, 1993). In their entirety, these principles address both the process of learning and a holistic view of the learner. The learner-centered principles are derived from both educational and psychological research and, if followed,

> *can ensure that educational decisions will be responsive to the student, thereby avoiding issues of alienation, boredom, perceptions of irrelevancy, and other current issues students express with the traditional educational system and reform efforts that do not consider the individual student.* (p. 7)

A listing of the principles, categorized under four psychological factors that differentiate learners and impact both learners and the learning process, is found in Table 5.1.

Learner centeredness is applied in the classroom through a variety of practices. Teachers create a warm environment by respecting and attending to students' points of view. They hold high expectations for student performance and encourage students always to put forth their best efforts. Students participate in the selection of academic goals and learning tasks. In turn, teachers support autonomy in students, who become intrinsically motivated to do high-quality work. Collaborative work

Activity 5.2 Your Philosophy of Teaching

To help you articulate your philosophy of teaching, write an ending for each of the following sentence starters. You may add other beliefs you hold about learning, students, families, and yourself as a teacher. When finished, reread the sentences. You have just framed your philosophy of teaching. You can extend the list and streamline your statements as you continue to read this chapter.

1. Students need

2. Most parents

3. Students with disabilities

4. To learn well

5. Disruptive students

6. The room arrangement

7. I expect

8. I should

9. The classroom environment

Table 5.1
Principles of Best Practice for Teaching Middle School Students

Cognitive and Metacognitive Factors

1. The learning of complex subject matter is most effective when it is an intentional process of constructing meaning from information and experience.

2. The successful learner, over time and with support and instructional guidance, can create meaningful coherent representations of knowledge.

3. The successful learner can link new information with existing knowledge in meaningful ways.

4. The successful learner can create and use a repertoire of thinking and reasoning strategies to achieve complex learning goals.

5. Higher order strategies for selecting and monitoring mental operations facilitate creative and critical thinking.

6. Learning is influenced by environmental factors, including culture, technology, and instructional practices.

Motivational and Affective Factors

7. What and how much is learned is influenced by the learner's motivation. Motivation to learn, in turn, is influenced by the individual's emotional states, beliefs, interests and goals, and habits of thinking.

8. The learner's creativity, higher order thinking, and natural curiosity all contribute to motivation to learn. Intrinsic motivation is stimulated by tasks of optimal novelty and difficulty, relevant to personal interests, and providing for personal choice and control.

9. Acquisition of complex knowledge and skills requires extended learner effort and guided practice. Without learners' motivation to learn, the willingness to exert this effort is unlikely without coercion.

Developmental and Social Factors

10. As individuals develop, they encounter different opportunities and experience different constraints for learning. Learning is most effective when differential development within and across physical, intellectual, emotional, and social domains is taken into account.

11. Learning is influenced by social interactions, interpersonal relations, and communication with others.

Individual Differences Factors

12. Learners have different strategies, approaches, and capabilities for learning that are a function of prior experience and heredity.

13. Learning is most effective when differences in learners' linguistic, cultural, and social backgrounds are taken into account.

14. Setting appropriately high and challenging standards and assessing the learner and learning progress—including diagnostic, process, and outcome assessment—are integral parts of the learning process.

among students encourages respect for diversity, reflective thinking, and broadening of perspectives. Students evaluate their own work and use self-assessments to improve. Finally, students perceive assignments to be relevant. In sum, learner centeredness facilitates motivated students who achieve through active engagement in a learning process they perceive as meaningful. McCombs and Whisler (1997) maintained that underlying everything that learner-centered teachers do is the assumption that all students want to learn.

The current body of research on learner centeredness provides a conceptual frame that aligns well with the MidEx model presented in Chapter 1. Pause now to review and reflect on how the parts of the model relate to one another in the context of what you have just read about effective teaching. Figure 5.1 offers one way to visualize and appreciate the dynamic nature of the model and the value of what research has to offer classroom practice. Then do Activity 5.3 to assess how learner centered your teaching is.

How Do I Organize a Productive Learning Environment?

I am so tired of students disrespecting me and trying to get away with everything! Over the Thanksgiving break, I'm coming up here and decorating the room the way I like it. I'm going to put blue curtains on the window and family pictures on my desk. When they come back, they're going to know that this is my classroom!

Unfortunately, the exhausted, frustrated middle school teacher who made this comment failed to understand that her plan may alienate her students even more. She thinks that decorating the classroom to reflect her personal preferences and interests will somehow legitimize and enhance her authority and lead to increased student compliance. If this teacher were more learner centered, she would create a classroom environment responsive to her students' identities and interests, one in which they could feel invited to belong, learn, and behave responsibly. What do you think her students would have advised, had she asked them? Following are typical responses obtained from a sampling of 177 students in two large, urban middle schools who answered the question, "If a brand new teacher came to you for advice on how to best manage a middle school classroom, what advice could you give?" (Krudwig, 2003b).

"Have really good classroom rules." (11-year-old male)

"Be nice but reasonable." (12-year-old male)

"Let everyone participate." (13-year-old female)

"Plan ahead." (13-year-old female)

"Do some hands-on projects, because it helps." (14-year-old male)

"Have a good sense of humor." (14-year-old female)

"Try to teach something we don't know about." (11-year-old female)

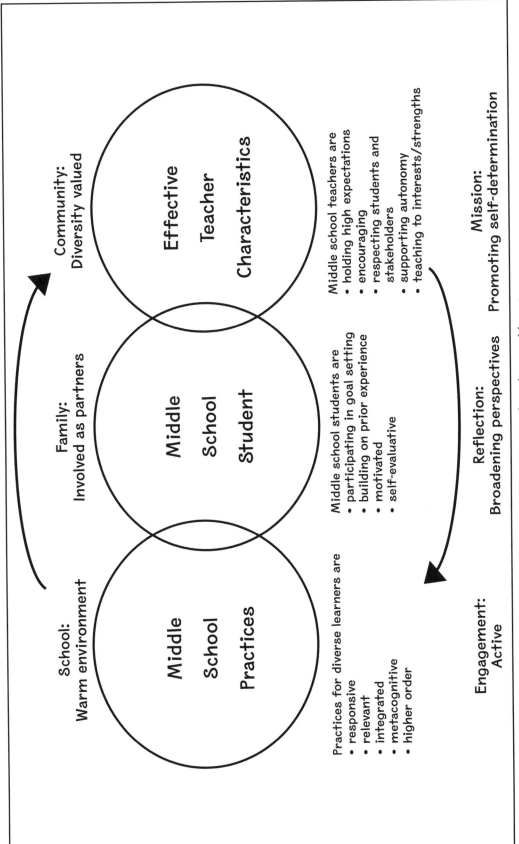

Figure 5.1. How the MidEx model relates to critical features of learner-centered teaching and learning.

Activity 5.3 Your Professional Practices

How learner centered is your teaching? Use the Professional Practices Checkup to rate your teaching practices. For each item, check the response that best describes how often you do each behavior in the list: never, seldom, sometimes, or consistently. The more "consistently" boxes you check, the more you are using a learner-centered approach in teaching. When finished, compare your practices with your teaching philosophy (see Activity 5.2) to see how they align.

Professional Practices Checkup				
Am I:	Never	Seldom	Sometimes	Consistently
1. Linking new information to what my students already know in ways that make sense to them?	☐	☐	☐	☐
2. Providing practice in logical problem solving applied to a variety of social and behavioral concerns?	☐	☐	☐	☐
3. Creating a caring learning environment that is responsive and inviting to all my students?	☐	☐	☐	☐
4. Helping students identify their interests and goals?	☐	☐	☐	☐
5. Offering a degree of personal choice and control to students?	☐	☐	☐	☐
6. Tapping the natural curiosity of my students by including novelty and challenge in learning activities?	☐	☐	☐	☐
7. Providing guided practice and support for student effort in social and behavioral learning, as I would do with academic learning?	☐	☐	☐	☐
8. Offering structured opportunities for students to develop and practice positive communication and interpersonal skills?	☐	☐	☐	☐
9. Providing informal opportunities for students to strengthen communication, social, and interpersonal skills in the context of academic assignments?	☐	☐	☐	☐
10. Utilizing my students' differences in life experience, heredity, physical ability, language, and culture as strengths in learning activities?	☐	☐	☐	☐
11. Setting appropriately high standards and expectations for my students and myself?	☐	☐	☐	☐
12. Assessing student growth and communicating social and behavioral achievements with students and their families?	☐	☐	☐	☐

The Middle School Experience

Physical Arrangement

Organizing a productive learning environment requires attention to both the physical arrangement and the classroom's interactive expectations as described in rules and routines. When students walk into a classroom for the first time, they can infer some things about the teacher simply by looking at the physical arrangement. A well-organized room reflects that the teacher is well prepared and looking forward to teaching them. A room that looks cluttered and carelessly arranged may suggest to students, accurately or not, that the teacher is distractible, underprepared, or disinterested in teaching. The way the desks are arranged will tell students whether the teacher expects them to compete or cooperate with one another. Interesting materials on the walls, some of it reflecting the diversity of the student population in the school, can help students feel that this is where they belong and can learn. Something in the room that makes the students smile may tell them that the teacher has a sense of humor, is self-confident, and likes them. Given the power of the classroom environment to influence students' initial perceptions and expectations, the room arrangement needs to be thoughtfully planned.

Two major considerations should determine how you arrange your classroom. First, what kinds of interactions will you need during instruction? Will students sometimes need to work together on projects? Will you need their attention focused at times to the front of the room for instruction? Second, what kind of arrangement will help all students feel included and supported in the learning community? The following are strategies that take both considerations into account.

1. Arranging desks or tables so three or four students are routinely sitting together will eliminate the need to pull desks together for group projects. This arrangement will also allow peer tutoring to happen naturally, as students will be able to check their work against a neighbor's during academic practice sessions. Peer tutoring benefits students with disabilities by supporting their development of communication and prosocial skills, and benefits peer tutors by strengthening their communication and helping skills (Staub & Hunt, 1993).

2. If you prefer seating students in rows, consider eliminating every other aisle so students are sitting in pairs. This arrangement allows some of the advantages mentioned above.

3. If space allows, you could have a traditional seating arrangement with single rows, supplemented by group tables across the back of the room. This will permit students to move between individual and group assignments as needed.

4. Avoid isolating students who struggle socially or academically. Seating a student against a back wall will likely increase social isolation. Rather, pull these students toward the front of the room. Consider seating them next to high-achieving students, who may be willing and able to contribute peer support.

5. The walls in your classroom can serve as a vehicle to assure all students that they are equally valued members of the class. Consider including the following types of items on walls: pictures or words reflecting all cultural backgrounds in the class, words of inspiration, unposed pictures of students at work and positively interacting with you and other students, and samples of students' work.

Rules and Routines

Underlying every smooth-running classroom is a set of clearly stated and understood rules and routines. Rules express your core classroom standards related to student effort and behavior. You should have three to five rules posted prominently on a wall where all students can easily view them. Rules should be short and written in positive language. Writing rules in first person language can promote student ownership of their messages. Examples include:

I will come prepared to class

I will treat property and people with respect

I will demonstrate positive effort during lessons

I will support my and others' academic success

You will know you have enough rules when every infraction you might expect from a middle school student can be addressed by one of your rules. For instance, a student who is distracting during a small group assignment can be reminded that supporting his and his friends' academic success requires maintaining an academic focus. Another approach for generating rules, recommended by Elias and Tobias (1996), is to engage the class in creating a classroom constitution, including both rights and rules. Whether you create rules for your class or use a more democratic approach, you should post them prominently in the room.

Routines are procedural steps for maintaining daily classroom operations. For instance, how do you want students to submit homework, turn in daily class work, request your help, conduct themselves in small group assignments, and access restroom and library privileges? You can prevent confusion and misbehavior by carefully planning procedures and giving written copies of them to students on the first day of school. Include universal, schoolwide routines that are already in place for some operations, such as how students are to obtain hall passes, and your own in-class routines. Following are descriptions of six routines that may help you get started in planning the smooth operation of your classroom.

@ **1. Setting up class jobs.** Create a Job Pocket Chart (see Figure 5.2) and fasten it to a wall. Label each pocket with a different class job. Label four pockets as "On Vacation" ("V" in Figure 5.2) and position them evenly among the pockets. Jobs can be the myriad short but important tasks that contribute to an efficiently run class system, such as keeping the classroom pencils sharpened or closing the blinds when the sun becomes too intense. Set up as many jobs as possible. Write each student's name on a

Figure 5.2. Job pocket chart. As name cards move to the right, students change jobs and periodically earn a "vacation."

different 3×5 card so that the student's name shows when the card is put into a pocket. Put one name card into each pocket and divide all leftover name cards among the four vacation pockets. Each Monday, shift the cards one pocket to the right, assigning each student to a different job or to go on vacation. The student in the last pocket on the chart will move to the first pocket for the next shift. Consider involving the class in identifying helpful jobs they can do and, for fun, deciding where they will take their vacations. The vacation pockets can then say "Bahamas," "a Trip to the Moon," "Australia," or other exciting destinations your students dream about visiting.

Establishing a routine that engages students in taking care of their classroom can benefit both you and your students. Jobs provide opportunities to develop organizational skills. Working together toward a common goal, such as a well-maintained learning environment, can contribute to students' social responsibility, sense of belonging, and commitment to community. Finally, these positive outcomes can help prepare students to transition successfully into high school and beyond.

2. Submitting homework. Obtain four narrow crates, all the same color. Make a pocket folder with a large-letter name label on it for each student. Put one fourth of the folders in each crate, based on alphabetical order. Set the crates up in four different locations in the room. As students enter the room, they are to file their completed homework in the appropriate drop box and then sit down. Placing the crates in different locations prevents having all students trying to file their homework in one box at the beginning of class. Another advantage of using a drop box system is that you can easily peruse the crates for empty folders when you have a minute, perhaps when the class is engaged in independent work, and then visit (privately) with students about their missing homework.

3. Self-grading homework. For some types of classes, it may be useful for learning outcomes to have students grade their own homework or review it as you guide the class through the assignment on the day it is due. For these types of assignments, teach your students to keep their homework at their desks so they will have it for review and self-grading.

4. Submitting in-class work. When students complete independent work or tests at their desks, teach them to pass their papers to the person on their left (or right). When the papers get to the last row, have each person in that row pass the sets of papers forward, or have one person in the row get up and gather the sets. Either you or a student should immediately file the stack in a pocket folder and then put the folder in a crate marked "To Be Graded." You can streamline this system by having different colored pocket folders for different periods in the day.

5. Establishing a grading rubric. Keep in mind that not all work products need to be in the traditional paper-and-pencil format. Students can demonstrate that they can comprehend, solve, create, design, improvise, apply, synthesize, and form judgments in many different ways. Whatever the nature of the product, decide how you will evaluate performance before you make the assignment. For performance-based products, set up an assessment rubric and explain it to your students before they begin the project. The rubric will set the standard for mastery and will help guide student effort. This type of preplanning and organization will help your students maintain an academic focus as well as provide you with data you need to assess progress and plan for future academic activities.

6. Collecting assignments for absent students. In addition to a drop box system for incoming homework, you can set up a pick-up station for students to get the assignments they missed while absent. A pick-up station consists of one crate that contains a named folder for each student. One of the class jobs can be to stock the pick-up station. The student who holds this job will make sure that a copy of everything you pass out during the day goes into each absent student's pocket folder in the pick-up station. You need only one crate because few students are typically absent on any given day. The pick-up station should be away from the drop boxes and differently colored to assist students who rely on these extra cues.

7. Requesting your attention. Asking students to raise hands to initiate or answer questions is a reasonable routine. However, some teachers have problems because they do not teach students to use the procedure consistently. Allowing students to call out without raising their hands reinforces and encourages everyone in the class to call out without raising their hands (Skinner, 1984).

Provide each student with a visual "I Need You as Soon as You Can Get to Me" tag to hang on the side of his or her desktop. The tag should be made of a durable material, such as cloth or plastic, and have one brightly colored side, such as red, to let you know you are needed. Students can flip the tag so the request shows when they want help. When you are finished helping them, flip the tag back to the "I'm Fine" side. Letting your students make their own tags may help them invest in using the procedure.

There are two advantages to having a supplementary system for getting your attention during independent or small group assignments. First, you can minimize distractions from students whose arms are wearing out from frantically waving at you. Second, this system gives you the option of quietly asking a student who understands the academic material to help one student while you head for the student whom you need to help.

Activity 5.4 includes a chart for planning your classroom rules and routines. It also provides instructions for creating a student handout with the information.

What Behavior Management Strategies Will Support All My Students?

After a long day filled with persistent resistance from Jeremy, a middle school teacher vented her frustrations to a colleague: "Jeremy just won't focus and talks out constantly. What should I do?" This educator wants a "magic bullet." It is understandable to want to know exactly what to do when encountering disruptive or challenging behaviors from students; however, there is no magic bullet that will universally and permanently "fix" student misbehavior. Social and emotional learning needs to be as carefully planned as academic learning (Cohen, 1999; Sternberg, 1997). Learner-centered behavior management plans are responsive to student needs on two levels: prevention and intervention. They prevent the bulk of potential behavioral problems and include strategies that guide students to increase their interpersonal and intrapersonal skills.

In Activity 5.5, reflect on your middle school teachers' behavior management and disciplinary practices. Think about whether or not they were effective and why.

Students in middle school still depend on the adults in their lives for structure, even as they strive for personal independence. An important role of middle school teachers is to promote cooperative classroom behavior and the development of students' self-regulation and motivation to learn. What can you do to motivate your students to cooperate with their academic program? Muir (2001) interviewed six underachieving middle school students in an effort to learn what they believed would increase their motivation to learn. The students' responses suggested that they were more likely to be motivated when teachers are caring, actively engage students in learning activities, make learning interesting and fun, and help students build new understandings based on previous learning. Not surprisingly, these students' insightful recommendations are included in the principles of best practice listed in Table 5.1.

Activity 5.4 Your Classroom Rules and Routines

Write a draft of your classroom rules and routines on the following chart. Then type your rules and routines, limiting the length to two pages. Create an interesting title for your procedures, and include your name and room number. Copy the document on colorful card stock, laminate it, and hole-punch each card. Give students copies to keep in their school binders.

Classroom Rules
1.
2.
3.
4.
5.

Topic	Classroom Routines

The following are guidelines and strategies for promoting behavioral growth in all students.

@ 1. Communicate to your students that you care about them.

Students are more likely to cooperate with and work for teachers whom they perceive as caring (Noddings, 1992; Wentzel, 1997). Maintain a calm manner and voice tone when correcting misbehavior. Convey respect and warmth for the student even as you redirect behavior.

@ 2. Teach replacement skills.

Students need to learn what to do instead of the behavior you want them to stop. For instance, rather than telling students to stop losing things, help them develop a system for organizing and managing their belongings.

Activity 5.5 Behavior Management and Disciplinary Practices

List five of the most common behavior management and disciplinary practices you remember teachers using when you were an adolescent. Based on your memory, indicate whether these practices worked well by checking a box.

Strategy	Did it work?	
	Yes	No
1.	❏	❏
2.	❏	❏
3.	❏	❏
4.	❏	❏
5.	❏	❏

Did you list any strategies that were ineffective? Why do you think they did not work?

3. Praise students.

Providing praise immediately following a positive behavior will increase the likelihood that the behavior will occur again (Skinner, 1970). Lack of positive reinforcement for a behavior will eventually lead to extinction of the behavior. Englemann and Carnine (1991) suggest that teachers give three praise statements for every disapproving statement. Thomas, Becker, and Armstrong (1968) found that positive behavior increased in classrooms where teachers praised appropriate classroom behavior. Likewise, negative student behaviors increased when teachers ignored positive behavior and criticized students. Praise student effort, which is something students can control, rather than personal attributes, such as intelligence, over which they have no control. Effective praise is immediate, has a positive tone, offers corrective information, and is specific. For instance, say, "Roy, you stayed with that problem until you solved it!" rather than, "Roy, you are so smart! That's perfect!" Schunk (1987) found that when students believed their achievements were due to effort, it contributed to student self-efficacy, academic achievement, and motivation to learn.

4. Group students in ways that allow positive role models in the class to influence students who need to increase behavioral or academic skills.

According to Bandura (1986), students are most likely to model after someone they perceive as similar to themselves and as coping successfully. You can also model procedures to promote student use. For instance, raise your own hand immediately after asking an academic question, saying, "If you would like to offer an answer, please raise your hand."

5. Use proximity control and nonverbal cues to redirect misbehavior.

Proximity control refers to walking toward or standing near a student who is getting off task while maintaining the momentum of the activity at hand. Nonverbal cues can be agreed upon, privately, with a student and used when needed to change a persistent habit. For instance, you might agree to casually cross your arms or clasp your hands together, while continuing the lesson, as the agreed-upon signal for a particular student to lower her voice level.

6. Avoid power struggles.

You can calmly offer a misbehaving student a choice to do the right thing or accept a logical consequence. Understanding the possible motives underlying student misbehavior may help you to avoid taking a situation personally. According to Dreikurs, Grunwold, and Pepper (1971), behavior is goal directed. Students who misbehave are attempting to gain attention, seek power, compensate for emotional hurt through revenge, or express discouragement. Deci, Hodges, Pierson, and Tomassone (1992) found that, for students with emotional and learning disabilities, motivation to stay on task depended on feeling accepted, competent, and autonomous. According to Glasser's (1997) choice theory, student misbehavior is driven by one or more of these unmet needs: power, belonging, freedom, and fun. An assumption underlying Glasser's theory is that each person has control over his or her own behavior. You can guide a student to gain insight and exercise self-control for the right reasons by asking a few focused questions: What are you doing? What do you need? Is this behavior helping you get what you need? What can you do that will work better?

7. Involve students in academic task planning.

Self-determination contracts can help students develop self-regulation by involving them in ongoing cycles of planning the day's work, working, evaluating success in completing the plan, and making needed adjustments to the plan for the next day (Martin et al., 2003). Martin and colleagues found significant improvements in academic progress over the school year in 10 preteens with severe behavioral disorders.

© **8. Teach academic and behavioral goal setting.**

Schunk (1985) found that encouraging students with learning disabilities to set goals facilitated goal achievement, self-efficacy, and commitment to working toward their goals. Self-efficacy, according to Bandura (1977, 1997), is self-judgment regarding one's capability to accomplish a goal. A positive correlation exists between self-efficacy and student academic effort, persistence, and willingness to choose difficult tasks (Bandura, 1997). Multon, Brown, and Lent (1991) found that self-efficacy contributed to academic achievement.

How Can I Promote Social and Emotional Growth in Students?

Students in middle school are on the threshold of their futures. Over the next few years, they will engage in a great deal of exploration and problem solving as they seek to find out how they can fit into and contribute to their larger worlds. A diversity of social and emotional development is reflected in the answers from middle school students who were asked, "What was one of the best decisions you've ever made?" (Krudwig, 2003b).

"One of the best decisions I've made is to be responsible." (12-year-old female)

"To get a pet rabbit." (11-year-old male)

"Making sure I pick the right friends, not to go wild, and not to be stupid enough to smoke." (11-year-old female)

"Got meat on my nachos." (12-year-old male)

"Being a good student in class." (11-year-old male)

"Tell people to quit making fun of me." (11-year-old female)

"Who cares?" (12-year-old male)

"Not being mean or violent." (12-year-old male)

"To not be afraid to try things." (12-year-old male)

"Not stealing the car." (13-year-old female)

Developing social ease is much more difficult for some students than others. Sabornie (1994) found that students with identified learning disabilities reported feeling more lonely and participated less in class than their nondisabled peers. In addition, teachers rated them less socially competent than their nondisabled peers.

Many middle schools incorporate an advisory period into the school day. In some classrooms, the advisory period serves merely as a study period or a time when students "hang out" while the teacher gets ready for the day. In other classrooms, it is designed to serve as an "anchor" for students. Teachers review daily announcements and address a variety of topics, such as how to get organized and resolve student concerns.

CARE Meetings

Academic progress depends on development of both intrapersonal and interpersonal skills (Richardson, 2000). The acquisition of social, emotional, and problem-solving skills facilitates general social adjustment in young adolescents (Caplan et al., 1992). With careful planning and implementation, the traditional advisory period can be expanded into a CARE meeting to help students grow socially and emotionally (Krudwig, 2000). The letters in "CARE" stand for the four major goals of the process: Community, Autonomy, Resilience, and Empowerment.

Utilizing the power of the peer group to influence attitudes and social behavior, the CARE meeting is a group-based instructional tool for promoting skills in critical thinking, responsibility, problem solving, and decision making in the context of real-life issues. Unlike a general group discussion, as you may expect from the term "meeting," CARE meetings engage a structured process, developed through action research by the author. They can be scheduled weekly or even daily, depending on the needs of the class and what is allowed in the schedule. The following are steps involved in setting up and implementing a variety of CARE meeting activities. You may incorporate other activities to meet the social and affective growth needs of your students.

@ **Step 1.** Have the group sit in a circle if possible. This will facilitate eye contact, communication, and a sense of belonging.

@ **Step 2.** Establish a rule that desks must be cleared off. If you permit students to have books or other materials in front of them, some students may distracted. Another option is to use chairs rather than desks.

@ **Step 3.** Reserve a part of a blackboard for an agenda and ask students to list their names if they would like to discuss an issue. One of the valuable skills that impulsive students can learn through the use of the agenda is to delay their need for immediate gratification until an appropriate time. Impulse control is commonly addressed in programs for students with disabilities. The following is a sample agenda:

  Agenda
  1. Relaxation
  2. Goals
  3. Compliments
  4. Developmental lesson
  5. Issues:
      a. Tom
      b. Shirley
      c. William

Step 4. Begin each CARE meeting with a brief relaxation exercise. This activity helps students transition from their previous assignment and focus on the upcoming activities. Although commercial relaxation materials are available, you may want to try a simple exercise I have used successfully for over 20 years. First, show the students how to find a pulse on either the wrist or neck. Students seem to have a high interest in feeling their own heart rhythms and find this activity relaxing. Next, with one student volunteering to keep time, invite everyone to count his or her pulse for 1 minute while relaxing. You should do the same. When time is up, share your pulse rate and then pass a soft ball or other "it's my turn to talk" item around the circle, allowing but not forcing students to share their pulse rates.

Step 5. If the class has established a group goal, such as staying on task or maintaining a calm, low-volume sound level, then pass the soft ball around, allowing each student to share an opinion about how the group has performed since the last CARE meeting. Students can reserve the right to pass without comment. Record the outcome of the group's self-assessment on a graph posted on a wall. This process will gradually build positive peer pressure within the group. Encouraging comments (e.g., "Keep trying; this goal seems to be getting easier for you all the time") can help the class tolerate frustration and continue working toward the goal. Also, being nonjudgmental and direct will keep the responsibility for change focused on the students.

Step 6. You may choose to have the students share compliments. Each student, in turn, may offer a compliment to a peer or to the whole group. A rule of thumb for giving compliments is that they must refer to a person's behavior, attitude, or accomplishment(s). This rule prevents surface comments such as, "I like your shoes." Through practice, your students will become skilled in sharing positive opinions of one another. Sharing compliments will encourage your students to nurture a considerate community. As a variation, you can invite students to compliment themselves. This may be a much harder task for many students.

Step 7. Send a question around the group, inviting students to answer but allowing them to pass if they wish. With a relatively new group, ask low-risk questions (e.g.,"Do you have a pet?" or "What's your favorite ice cream flavor?"). As the group grows in experience, add questions that invite more sharing (e.g., "How many siblings do you have, and where are you in the birth order?" or "How many schools have you attended so far in your life, and which one did you like the best? Why?"). Eventually, add questions that invite students to share opinions about significant community events or life issues (e.g., "If you had the power to cure just one problem in the world, what would you fix?" or "Have you ever thought about living in another state or country when you grow up, and if so, where would that be?"). According to Cohen (1999), understanding others' viewpoints and being able to self-reflect are critical skills for managing life situations. Establish a rule that no one can criticize or comment on anyone else's response to the questions you pose. This will help provide a safe environment for the shyest members of the class to join the discussion. The structured format of this activity provides important advantages for the development of communication skills. First, the questions help class members get to know one another in the many dimensions that friends become acquainted. Second, shy students have equal access to the discussion without risk of rejection. Third, students get practice in simply listening and accepting others' ideas and opinions without comment. For students who love to dominate and speak the last word in conversations, this is an important communication skill to develop. Finally, students have the opportunity, over time, to understand that students they thought were quite different from themselves actually share some of the same preferences, life circumstances, goals, and aspirations. A carefully planned question or two at each CARE meeting can contribute to the development of a strong, mutually supportive classroom community.

@ **Step 8.** Introduce topics that you believe will help meet the social and affective needs of your class. Invite school and community resources to the CARE meeting as well. For instance, when students complain about a particular school policy, consider inviting an administrator to your next meeting. Given that you have properly prepared the administrator regarding the issue, you can help the group better understand the policy while practicing how to express feelings constructively to a person in authority. You may also want to bring structured lessons to CARE meetings to support the development of interactive communication and problem-solving skills. The following is a sampling of curricula for your consideration:

- *Skillstreaming the Adolescent: New Strategies and Perspectives for Teaching Prosocial Skills* (Goldstein & McGinnis, 1997)

- *The EQUIP Program: Teaching Youth To Think and Act Responsibly Through a Peer-Helping Approach* (Gibbs, Potter, & Goldstein, 1995)

- *Aggression Replacement Training: A Comprehensive Intervention for Aggressive Youth* (Goldstein & Glick, 1987)

- *Anger Management for Youth: Stemming Aggression and Violence* (Eggert, 1994)

- *The PREPARE Curriculum: Teaching Prosocial Competencies* (Goldstein, 1999)

Over time, students will have many opportunities to express opinions, listen to one another respectfully, practice prosocial skills, make objections constructively, speak assertively, problem solve, and make responsible decisions. The positive peer pressure that develops will support your high expectations.

@ **Step 9.** When students have conflicts with other students, it is tempting for teachers to spend their energy on figuring out who is at fault and how to punish. This type of focus is reactive rather than proactive. Blame and punishment may conclude an existing situation but accomplish nothing relative to preventing the next situation. Furthermore, some students enjoy the sheer excitement of a crisis and, as participants or observers, would rather see the problem continue than end.

CARE meetings offer ongoing opportunities to turn conflict situations into positive, meaningful learning experiences in problem solving and conflict resolution. Imagine that Tom and William are students in your class and the following scenario occurs: Both Tom and William have been suspended from the bus and have received other referrals for near-fights with each other in the cafeteria and other less structured campus settings. Their mutual animosity spills into the classroom as an undercurrent of negativity and verbal sniping. Each blames the other, and traditional consequences have not improved the situation. You can teach students to skip blame and high drama and move toward solutions with a four-part conflict-resolution strategy. For each part of the strategy, called a "round," pass a soft ball around the circle, allowing but not requiring each student to add information and insights as a solution is constructed. Each round, described below, introduces a different question to the class.

1. Ask, "What can you briefly tell us about the situation?" Send this question around the circle, begining with the person who raised the issue. The other student(s) in the conflict are then given a turn, followed by the rest of the class members. Name calling, sarcasm, blaming, and other put-downs are off limits. What you want are nonjudgmental, straightforward observations.

2. Ask, "What do you see as a reasonable solution? In other words, let's assume that we want this situation to get better. What could help?" As you did in Round 1, begin with the person who raised the issue. If someone suggests something illegal or simply unrealistic, such as "let everyone hit him," either ignore the suggestion or simply point out that the solution is not viable and move on to the next student. Over time, students will become increasingly skilled at suggesting realistic and peaceful solutions.

3. Turning to the second party in the conflict, ask, "You have heard a variety of solutions. Which one would work best for you, given that we are seeking a true solution to this issue?" When the student has selected a solution, turn to first party in the conflict and ask if this solution would also work for him or her. At this point in the process, the rest of the class shifts from participants to witnesses as you guide the conflicting parties to agreement on a solution. When the conflicting students reach consensus on a solution, proceed to Round 4.

4. Set a timeline for trying out the new solution, typically until the next CARE meeting. At the end of that time, have an agenda item to check the social contract by sending the soft ball around the class, inviting students to comment on whether the contract is working. For instance, you can ask, "As

we recall, Tom and William made a verbal contract to let each other alone in the cafeteria and bus. How is your plan working so far, Tom? William?" If the contract is working, set a longer timeline for another follow up. If the contract is not working, use the four-round process again, this time streamlining the contract or adopting a different solution.

Well-structured, regularly held CARE meetings can support several positive student outcomes, including (a) a sense of community, (b) effective communication, (c) peaceful conflict resolution, (d) increased interpersonal skills, (e) increased decision-making skills, and (f) increased self-determination for students. As you see solutions working, encourage your students to take this solution-focused strategy beyond the classroom. Never cancel a CARE meeting unless the whole school is dismissed. It is important to value this time and to use it productively.

Educationally Supporting Students with Trauma

Given today's level of risk for violent incidents in our nation's schools and society, it is important for teachers to understand the impact that trauma can have on student performance in school (Kinchin & Brown, 2001; Richards & Bates, 1997). Trauma can happen dramatically, as with a tornado, sudden abandonment, incest, death of a loved one, or a serious accident. It can also quietly accumulate over years, creating mounting fear, isolation, depression, and anxiety in individuals. Examples of cumulative traumas include living in a dangerous neighborhood, having parents who fight continuously, being constantly ridiculed, and being homeless. Living with violence or the threat of violence not only threatens social well-being, but can also diminish students' ability to focus academically (Dreyfoos, 1990; Kinchin & Brown, 2001; Motta, 1994).

With or without a diagnosis of post-traumatic stress disorder (PTSD) or therapeutic intervention, most traumatized students will continue attending school. Following is a brief discussion of PTSD, the ways it can manifest in school, and how CARE meetings can provide educational support to struggling students.

PTSD is a coping response to an extraordinary life stress. The following four conditions define PTSD: (a) history of trauma; (b) reexperiencing the trauma; (c) emotional numbing; and (d) at least two of the following: memory problems, concentration problems, sleep disturbances, hyperalertness, and avoidance of people and situations that trigger memories of the trauma (American Psychiatric Association, 1994). The history of the trauma refers to its origin. It includes such events as war, incest, long-term psychological abuse, physical abuse, rape, violent death of a parent or other family member, or natural disasters, such as earthquakes, hurricanes, plane crashes, and fires. PTSD is an equal-opportunity condition, developing in otherwise psychologically healthy individuals.

An individual affected by PTSD may experience the following behavioral symptoms in a variety of combinations: depression; extreme isolation; rage; emotional numbing; alienation; sleep disturbances, physical exhaustion, lethargy, or difficulty concentrating; feelings of worthlessness; problems with intimacy; memory impairment; suicidal ideation or attempts; unrelieved grief; anxiety or panic attacks; survival guilt; flashbacks; and substance abuse (Armsworth & Holaday, 1993; Kinchin & Brown, 2001). How might these symptoms manifest themselves in the school environment? A traumatized student may

1. Tire quickly and exhibit moodiness, as though everything requires too much effort

2. Overreact, become defensive quickly, react physically to express frustration, and exhibit flash anger as though ordinary situations pose danger

3. Become perfectionistic, quitting if things do not turn out perfectly, and wanting to be in control

4. Lack trust in adults, and be secretive about family information

5. Crave attention and seek action

6. Underachieve, describe self as worthless, and think about suicide or hurting self as a way to solve problems

Such patterns put students at risk for consistently violating school rules, which in turn traditionally leads to in-school consequences or out-of-school suspension.

Using the CARE meeting as an instructional tool for helping students learn how to constructively communicate and behave with peers and teachers can provide ongoing learning opportunities in place of short-term consequences. Specifically, the CARE meeting process can help struggling and traumatized students master the following goals: (a) controlling anger, (b) developing prosocial skills, (c) decreasing social isolation, (d) developing a sense of community, (e) developing verbal problem-solving skills, and (f) building interpersonal trust.

Implementing a CARE meeting for the first time may raise two issues for teachers. First, the subject matter addressed in CARE meetings may not appear to fit into the standard course curriculum, such as language arts or math. However, all academic areas include skill building in critical thinking and problem solving. According to Elias (2001), facilitating students' abilities to appreciate, belong, and contribute will positively impact their academic effort and concentration. A second issue teachers may find problematic initially is teaching students to function as

Activity 5.6 School Mission Statement and CARE Meetings

1. What is your school's mission statement?

2. How could holding regular CARE meetings support the goals of your school's mission?

a group, a fairly sophisticated skill in itself. Teachers need to be patient with the process. With guidance and practice, the class can become more trusting, cohesive, and skilled at discussing and solving issues. Students will develop skills they can use for the rest of their lives.

Activity 5.6 provides an opportunity for you to consider how CARE meetings can support the goals of your school's mission. Think about how holding regular meetings affects the implementation of the school's mission.

How Can I Collaborate Effectively with Families and Community?

Families as Partners

A focus group consisting of parents of children with disabilities responded to the following question: "If you could share one positive message with teachers about what you, your child, and your family need from them, what would it be?" (Krudwig, 2003a).

"See my child before you see his disability."

"I depend upon you to keep my family informed."

"You can open my child's world by touching her heart."

"Understand the power of collaboration and communication for building my child's strengths."

"Be part of my child's success: You can plant miracles."

"Don't ever forget that you became a teacher because you wanted to make a difference."

"Facilitate my child's future."

"Look for the abilities in my child's disability."

"Embrace the potential of my child."

These messages reflect the passion of parents' hopes and expectations for their children as they progress through school. These messages also suggest that parents generally are committed to working toward positive school outcomes for their children. According to Snodgrass (1991), children continue to value the expectations and approval of their parents throughout adolescence. Because of their critical role in the lives of their children, parents need to be recognized as essential and invaluable educational partners.

Unfortunately, teachers often describe parents as uncaring and uncooperative. Some parents only hear from teachers when there is a problem. Some parents do not even know the names of their child's teachers. Parents from the dominant culture tend to be better informed about school operations and are more involved in school than parents from minority cultures (Kalyanpur & Harry, 1999; Lynch & Stein, 1987).

Once the blaming begins, family–school relationships can erode to almost irretrievable levels. Poor relationships, however, are not inevitable. Positive partnerships between teachers and parents can be nurtured and strengthened. The place to start is to examine your underlying assumptions about parents. Look back at the philosophy of teaching you framed in Activity 5.2. What did you write about parents? These are the assumptions that will drive your actions. If you want positive outcomes for your students, it is critical that you hold positive, rather than negative, assumptions about their families. Some positive assumptions about parents follow:

Parents want their children to do well in school.

Parents love their children and do their best with what they know.

Parents have good insights and ideas.

In contrast, some negative assumptions about parents are as follows:

Parents don't care.

Parents don't know enough to help with school issues.

If parents were any good, their children wouldn't be acting like this.

These are only a few examples of positive and negative assumptions. The following is a menu of specific strategies for building and maintaining positive, collaborative relationships with all of your students' parents and families.

1. In the first week of school, send home a brief classroom handbook for parents, including your philosophy of teaching, classroom rules and routines, and a statement of your commitment to work collaboratively with parents. Use reader-friendly language.

2. Learn whether families are patriarchal, matriarchal, or a blend, and respect each family's decision-making structure. For example, if the father makes major family decisions, conversations and meetings about programmatic changes need to include him.

3. Keep a three-ring binder containing a Contact Log for each student. Figure 5.3 illustrates the top portion of a Contact Log. Record the relevant information from all home and community contacts, as well as student conferences, in the log. Reviewing the log before each family communication will help you to follow up on previous conversations. It will also show you whether the content of your communications is consistently positive, negative, or a mixture. In phone calls and meetings, be sure to mention student strengths and accomplishments even when you have issues to resolve. Parents will appreciate evidence that you are not "out to get" their children.

4. Embed invitational language in your conversations with parents. Examples include the following: "What do you think? Have you noticed this,

too? How are you feeling about it? What has worked for you before? Is there anything I can do to help? What is your child saying at home that might help me understand what I can do to help? When would be the best time in your schedule for us to meet? Would you like to bring anyone with you? Can we work something out that won't put a hardship on you? What do you think your daughter could do to help the situation?"

5. Invite parents to help in the classroom or share information about their cultures with your class.

6. Invite parents to bring relatives or friends to Individualized Education Program (IEP) meetings and parent conferences. Preplan IEP meetings with parents so they will be able to contribute in a meaningful way.

7. Make personal phone calls to all parents, inviting them to your school's open house and other school-related events. If a parent does not have a phone or is living in a community shelter, mail a written invitation. Make every effort to reach every family. Videotape class activities, capturing images of every student in successful interactions and activities. At open house, run the videotape so parents can see their children in a positive light.

8. There may be times when a parent or guardian simply cannot provide additional supervision, time, attention, or support for a student. Some parents work more than one job. Some have serious health issues. Parents may not have the understanding or skills to change family patterns. Some are simply exhausted from years of struggling with unresolved school issues. Nonetheless, keep your positive assumption in place. When a parent cannot actively partner with you, plan in-school structures and interventions that will not

Contact Log		
Student _____		
Grade _____ Guardian(s) _____		
E-mail _____		
Home phone _____ Work phone _____ Other _____		
Address _____		
Date	Contact(s)	Relevant Information

Figure 5.3. Contact Log for communication with families, students, and community resources.

require an active contribution from the family, but keep the family in the plan. You can do this by sharing your intervention ideas, explaining that you hope it will not burden the family, and asking the parent for verbal support. Follow up by sending weekly postcards home with positive messages about student effort and information about progress. The goal is to help the parent understand that you are committed to a positive relationship and to nurture a gradually increasing level of parental support and participation in educational decisions.

Service Learning

Krudwig (2003b) asked middle school students, "What is one of the most important things you've ever done for someone else?" Here are some responses:

> "I helped build something in a park as a community service." (12-year-old male)

> "I gave a homeless lady $30 and a McDonald hamburger and sat there and talked with her until my mom came back." (12-year-old female)

> "I mowed a lawn for free." (12-year-old male)

> "I helped an old lady in a nursing home. Me and my mom drove her to the grocery store, sewing store, and even the pet store. I opened and closed the car doors for her, opened store doors, helped her with groceries, etc." (11-year-old male)

> "I have helped this shelter make food and get ready for homeless people." (14-year-old female)

Service learning offers experiential opportunities for students to increase their social and academic competence through participation in community service projects (Billig, 2002b). Nonprofit community agencies, organizations, and events offer many ongoing opportunities and resources for service learning. Bohnenberger and Terry (2002) extended the concept of service learning to include student-initiated solutions for community needs they identified. Research has established a relationship between social competence and success in postsecondary employment and independent living (Rutherford, Chipman, Digangi, & Anderson, 1992).

If your school does not already have a service learning program in place, the following steps may help you begin bringing service learning into your curricula:

1. Survey your students to determine their current level of community service involvement.

2. Brainstorm with your students about ways they can improve their community.

3. Send a letter home to parents, asking them to suggest ideas and to indicate ways they would allow their children to participate in service learning projects in the community.

4. Visit community businesses, agencies, and organizations to explore service learning opportunities. Ask for letters of support from those who are willing to partner with the school.

5. If you plan on incorporating a service learning assignment into your curriculum, be sure to gain both administrative and parental approval before proceeding. If you are not in a position to establish a formal service learning component in your program, you can still raise your students' awareness about community-based opportunities, encourage them to serve, and invite them to share their experiences in CARE meetings.

Summary

Educators should work together to create a learning community in which every student feels accepted, valued, and invited to academically succeed. Schools can help middle school students develop behaviorally, socially and emotionally. We encourage educators to reflect on how their own beliefs and practices related to classroom management and student achievement, arrange classroom to facilitate learning, use behavior management strategies that support all students, and collaborate with families and community stakeholders to ensure positive student outcomes.

Care.
Build relationships with your students.
Learn everything you can about how to teach well.
Hold high expectations.
Don't get stuck.
Look for the lessons when you struggle.
Take care of yourself.
Teach passionately.

—*Kathryn Krudwig*

Impact of Information on Your Mission

1. List your mission keywords (feel free to change your keywords as you progress).

2. Describe a challenging classroom situation you have experienced or observed.

3. What assumptions or beliefs about learning or students do you think underlay the decisions made by you or other adults in the situation?

4. What, if anything, could your understandings gained from this chapter have contributed to the situation, either to validate the good decision making that occurred or to improve the way the situation turned out?

5. What idea or concept did you like most from this chapter?

6. What practice(s) can you embrace from this chapter to enhance the effectiveness of your teaching and the quality of outcomes for your students?

CHAPTER 6

Transition Assessment

What is your hardest class and favorite class in middle school?

Joe: Math is my hardest class. When I was younger, I was in an advanced math class in second grade and I couldn't get multiplication—everyone else knew. I didn't get it for a while and it was hard. In sixth grade I was afraid to ask questions in math and I didn't have a good teacher. In seventh grade I had a great math teacher who went over all the homework in class and always offered help during recess and study time. I don't know what math will be like for me next year. Art and English are my favorite classes. I like writing, and recently I've been drawing—I used to draw when I was younger and now I entered some drawings in an art fair.

Zoey: Science is my hardest class because it's complicated. In seventh grade my teacher helped me by letting me come back to class after school and recheck my answers. I like reading best and English was fun in seventh grade. My English teacher was fun and we learned stuff in fun ways—like we learned about drama by putting on a play. I also like band because my teacher is fun and he gets us to play better—we won awards.

What classes do you want to take in high school?

Joe: I don't have any idea what classes they have in high school. I'd like to learn more cooking so I can cook for my parents. I'd like to take more art classes and maybe a free writing class with poetry.

Zoey: What classes are there? Photography if they have it. I'd like to participate in the foreign exchange program and host a student from Japan at my house when I'm in high school this year.

Learning Objectives

1. To describe current issues regarding assessment in middle schools.

2. To identify IDEA 2004's mandate related to transition assessment.

3. To describe transition assessment methods for middle school students.

4. To describe how to use the results of transition assessment to plan a course of study and postsecondary goals for middle school students.

Introduction

Assessment is an integral part of education. Teachers routinely assess students' knowledge of subject matter. Teachers may use the results of assessment, both standardized and informal, to group students for instructional purposes. School psychologists may assess students' academic aptitudes and behaviors to determine eligibility for special education services. Guidance counselors may assess how well a student interacts with peers. Administrators in school systems often assess principals, teachers, and other instructional staff according to how well students perform on local, state, and national assessments.

The No Child Left Behind (NCLB) Act of 2001 (P.L. 107–110) requires documentation of all students' achievement through assessments and accountability measures. The NCLB Act requires states to have content standards, reading and math assessments in third through eighth grades (and once in high school), and report cards that document adequate yearly progress of all students on assessments. Some states have also adopted high-stakes assessment programs, which are linked to diploma options. Students with disabilities must participate in these high-stakes assessments as required under the Individuals with Disabilities Education Act (IDEA) Amendments of 1997 and the IDEA Improvement Act of 2004 (IDEA 2004), and are entitled to appropriate accommodations on the tests (Thurlow, House, Scott, & Ysseldyke, 2000; Thurlow, Lazarus, Thompson, & Robey, 2002). Accommodations that students may need in order to participate in state assessments are described in Chapter 7.

Students with disabilities participate in assessment activities with special educators for various purposes throughout their school years. These can include assessments to determine eligibility for special education services or the need for accommodations in the classroom and on assessments (Pierangelo & Giuliani, 2002; D. D. Smith, 2006; T. E. C. Smith, 2001):

- to develop Individualized Education Programs (IEPs), plan effective instruction, monitor student progress, and reevaluate the need for special education services on a periodic basis (R. L. Taylor, 2000; Vaughn, Bos, & Schumm, 2003)

- to develop functional behavioral support plans (Hartwig & Ruesch, 2000)

- for facilitating transition planning (G. M. Clark, 1998; Sitlington, Neubert, & Leconte, 1997)

Why Do Transition Assessment in Middle School?

The IDEA 2004 (§ 614) requires that students' postsecondary goals be based on age-appropriate transition assessments related to training, education, employment, and independent living skills. The focus of this chapter is on transition assessment practices during the middle school years, an area that has received little attention. During the middle school years, students with disabilities can explore their interests and preferences, advocate for accommodations, and explore options in high school and the community.

Transition assessment is an ongoing process that helps students with disabilities to gain an understanding of their strengths, interests, and needs. Transition assessment has the following purposes (Sitlington, Neubert, Begun, Lombard, & Leconte, 1996):

- To identify the student's level of career development so that appropriate career education and coordinated transition activities can be planned

- To identify the student's needs, preferences, interests, and abilities in relation to postsecondary goals such as employment, postsecondary education and training, independent living, and community involvement

- To determine an appropriate focus of study and appropriate placements within educational, vocational, and community settings that will facilitate the attainment of these goals

- To determine self-determination skills needed to participate in regular education and to pursue postsecondary goals

- To identify accommodations, supports, services, and interagency linkages that the student will need to attain and maintain his or her postsecondary goals

Think about your own middle or junior high school experience. Answering the questions in Activity 6.1 can help you focus on how you can assess students for transition planning.

Transition Planning and Assessment

Transition planning for students with disabilities has received increased attention over the past 20 years for varied reasons. IDEA 1990 mandated that each student must have a statement of transition services in his or her IEP by age 16, that transition include a broad range of postschool outcomes, and that interagency linkages be identified if necessary. The IDEA Amendments of 1997 mandated that students' IEPs include a statement of transition service needs by age 14. As described in Chapter 3, the IDEA 2004 now requires that students' IEPs address transition by the age of 16 and include measurable postsecondary goals based on transition assessments. Because transition services must still address a student's course of study needed to reach postsecondary goals, transition planning and career education activities are necessary during the middle school years.

Students with disabilities continue to experience poor postsecondary education and employment outcomes (Murray, Goldstein, Nourse, & Edgar, 2000; Sitlington & Frank, 1999; Wagner & Blackorby, 1996); because of this fact, transition assessment must be an ongoing process. Obviously, planning for postsecondary education or skilled employment opportunities takes concentrated effort on the part of middle and high school personnel to help students identify relevant courses and training. In an analysis of research on postsecondary education and employment outcomes for youth with disabilities, the National Council on Disability (2000, p. 15) identified "assessment of needs before developing a student centered transition plan" as a necessary component to enhance better postschool outcomes. Finally, students and their families are often bewildered with the complexity of services and supports after they exit high school (Neubert & Moon, 1999). Therefore, identifying interagency linkages and exploring community resources must begin in middle school for some students with disabilities.

Students are to be invited to the IEP meeting when transition service needs are discussed ("Assistance to States," 1999). Clearly, students with disabilities need to participate in transition assessment activities as early as possible.

Transition Assessment Framework

The methods and personnel involved in transition assessment vary depending on the student's age and his or her career development needs in middle school. The transition assessment process must be ongoing and individualized for each student; it is best accomplished through a team approach. Teams may include general and special educators, guidance counselors, school psychologists, and related personnel such as speech and language specialists, occupational and physical therapists, assistive technology specialists, and social workers (S. K. Fisher, 1999; Harvell, 1999; Levinson & Murphy, 1999; Shepherd & Inge, 1999). For some students, educators or transition specialists need to be invited from the high school so that academic and work-based planning can take place as the student gets ready to exit middle school.

During middle school, teachers should focus on assisting students to

- identify and explore interests, preferences, and strengths;
- increase awareness of jobs in the community;
- increase awareness of high school options including academic courses, vocational–technical courses, and work-based learning opportunities;
- determine needs, accommodations, and supports; and
- develop tentative postsecondary goals.

The transition assessment framework outlined in Figure 6.1 will assist teachers and students in this exploration and assessment process. This framework allows teachers to choose from a variety of methods for assessing a student and for assessing potential environments (Neubert, 2003). The lower box in Figure 6.1 depicts the process of making the match between the student and the environment(s). Refer to this framework as you read the following sections; the section headings are questions teachers can ask themselves when they assess students.

Methods for Assessing Students

Review and Analyze Background Information
Interviews (Student and Family)
Commercial Tests, Inventories, Rating Scales
- Achievement, Aptitude
- Adaptive Behavior
- Interests
- Learning Styles
- Life Skills
- Self-Determination, Social Skills
- Transition Planning Needs
Curriculum-Based Assessment
Informal Assessments
Work Samples
Situation Assessments (Behavior Observation)
Functional Behavior Assessments
Person-Centered Planning Approaches

Methods for Analyzing Environments

Job and Task Analysis in Employment Sites
Analysis of Secondary Courses and Programs
- Regular Education (Advanced Placement Courses)
- Career and Technical Education
- Work-based Experiences
- Community-based Life Skills
- Youth Employment Programs
- ROTC
Analysis of Postsecondary Courses and Programs
- Admission, Financial Aid, Majors
- Support Services
Community Analysis
- Independent Living Options
- Community Agencies and Services
- Transportation
- Social and Recreational Programs

Is There a Match? Compare Data on Student and Environment

Yes Make placement and monitor progress
Include information in student's IEP

Possibly Identify supports, accommodations, instruction needed
Identify assistive technology needed
Include information in student's IEP

No Continue to collect data on other environments, supports
Continue to collect data on the student
Initiate the matching process again

Figure 6.1. Transition assessment framework. *Note.* From "The Role of Assessment in the Transition to Adult Life Process for Students with Disabilities," by D. A. Neubert, 2003, *Exceptionality, 11,* pp. 63–71. Copyright 2003 by Erlbaum. Reprinted with permission. Adapted from *Assess for Success: Handbook on Transition Assessment* (p. 99), by P. L. Sitlington, D. A. Neubert, W. Begun, R. C. Lombard, & P. J. Leconte, 1996, Reston, VA: The Council for Exceptional Children. Copyright 1996 by the Council for Exceptional Children. Adapted with permission.

How Do I Assess Students' Needs, Interests, and Preferences?

Middle school provides a time for students to explore their unique interests and strengths in academic courses, extracurricular activities, and community experiences. Many students with disabilities are well aware of their needs and limitations in academic areas by the time they reach middle school. The challenge for middle school personnel is to nurture students' strengths, interests, and preferences. This challenge includes helping students answer questions such as the following:

- What do I like to do in school? What do I like to do at home?
- What am I good at?
- What would I like to do after high school?
- What kind of courses can I choose from in high school?
- What kind of jobs are interesting to me in the community?

Students can keep track of answers to these questions in a portfolio and ultimately share this information at IEP meetings when transition service needs are discussed. Figure 6.2 depicts one student's answers to these questions.

There are many methods for assisting students as they explore their preferences, interests, and needs. The Methods for Assessing Students in Figure 6.1 draw from practices in special education, career education, self-determination, rehabilitation, and vocational education. There are also several handbooks and resources that describe transition assessment practices in more detail (G. M. Clark, 1998; G. M. Clark, Patton, & Moulton, 2000; Hughes & Carter, 2000; Mount, 2000; Sax & Thoma, 2002; Sitlington & Clark, 2006; Sitlington et al., 1996; Sitlington, et al., 2000).

How Do I Review and Analyze Background Information?

As students with disabilities enter middle school, it is important that special education teachers review their previous assessment information. This information can be summarized in a portfolio, along with ideas for further assessment and exploration activities that need to take place. The portfolio should contain the following student information:

- Interests and preferences
- Medical information
- IEP goals and services
- Strengths (what the student does well)
- Needs (amount of support and accommodations necessary in academic classrooms)
- Social skills
- Self-determination skills

Figure 6.2. Things that I like.

- Family support and input
- Behavior support plans

How Do I Conduct Interviews with Students and Families?

Students entering middle school are likely to have very little information in their records about their interests and preferences. Interviewing is the first step in gaining information on what students like to do and how they see themselves at school and at home. Talking with students about their strengths and what they like is a quick and inexpensive way to collect data on interests and preferences. Ask students what they like to do at school, after school, and at home. Ask about hobbies, sports activities, and dreams for the future. Table 6.1 provides an example of a middle schooler's interests, needs, and dreams for the future when she was in sixth

Table 6.1
All About Me

My Interests and Preferences in Sixth Grade	My Interests and Preferences in Eighth Grade
Things I'm good at or like • Science—I'm good at it! • Reading—I like to read stories • Animals—Watching birds, riding horses • Gymnastics—I'm flexible • Doing Power Point presentations • Playing trombone in the band	**Things I'm good at or like** • Biology • Reading class and reading books • Animals • Dance • Fashion • Music—playing guitar • Horseback riding
Things I need help with—People who help • Homework—I don't like it • Math—sometimes it's hard • Writing tires me • My mom and teachers help	**Things I need help with—People who help** • Homework • Math and science • Note taking • My mom and dad, tutor, resource teacher help
Things I'd like to do when I grow up • Own a day care for animals • Go to college • Be a lawyer for animals	**Things I'd like to do when I grow up** • Model • Go to college • Actress or singer • Design clothes • Work with rats

and eighth grades. As students go through middle school, this information should be updated and expanded so that a holistic view is gained. This information can be summarized and placed in a student's portfolio.

Although middle school is a time for students with disabilities to gain independence and self-determination skills, it is also a time when special educators must work with families to identify relevant courses, diploma options, postsecondary goals, and interagency linkages for their children during high school and beyond. Talking with families about their hopes and dreams for their children's future can provide special educators with important information for transition planning. It can also provide an avenue to discuss the importance of having students attend their IEP meetings and participating actively in transition planning.

In addition to using interview forms, educators can use person-centered planning approaches that allow students, along with their families, teachers, and significant others, to map out a plan for school and the future (Mount, 2000; Pearpoint, Forest, & O'Brien, 1996; Sax & Thoma, 2002). Person-centered planning assists individuals with disabilities to develop goals and dreams for the future and to identify supports that are needed to achieve these goals. Person-centered planning, a long-term approach to assessment, is known alternatively as personal futures planning, lifestyle planning, Making Action Plans, and Planning Alternative Tomorrows with Hope (Sax, 2002).

Commercial transition materials are also available for students and families to provide input on transition assessment needs in a systematic format. The *Transition*

Planning Inventory (G. M. Clark & Patton, 1997), for example, includes separate forms to be completed by the student, at home by family members, and in the school by teachers. The data collected on these forms are then recorded on a Profile and Further Assessment Recommendation Form. This form can become part of the student's portfolio and be used at IEP meetings when transition service needs are discussed.

What Commercial and Informal Inventories and Instruments Are Available?

Teachers can choose from a variety of informal checklists and questionnaires that help to identify students' needs, preferences, and interests in terms of transition planning and self-determination skills (e.g., G. M. Clark, 1998; G. M. Clark et al., 2000; Hughes & Carter, 2000; Sitlington et al., 1996). There are also career education materials, which provide structure through competencies, lesson plans, and activities to identify students' interests and explore the school and the community (e.g., Brolin, 1997; Brolin & Lloyd, 2004). Some students may need to participate in career exploration activities before they can truly identify their interests and preferences.

Interest inventories provide a structured format to collect information on students' interests. In choosing from the many commercial interest inventories available, teachers should consider the reading level and appropriateness of each assessment for middle school students. Information on interest inventories and other assessments can be found in the *Mental Measurements Yearbook,* which is available at most local libraries or can be accessed online for a fee (http://www.unl.edu/buros). Many interest inventories provide suggestions on exploring areas of interest using occupational resources. These materials provide information on jobs, salaries, training needs, and demand for specific jobs. Online resources such as the *Occupational Outlook Handbook* (http://www.bls.gov) [go to Occupations] and O*Net (http://online.onetcenter.org) also provide occupational information, and school libraries or career centers have additional information on jobs, colleges, and career exploration.

How Can I Incorporate Situational Assessment and Behavior Observation?

Observing students in a variety of environments also provides data that can be used to identify needs, strengths, interests, and preferences in transition planning. By varying the observations (e.g., during extracurricular activities, academic classes, and projects in the community), one can see how the student responds to different environments, teachers, and peer groups.

In informal observations, a teacher or other observer periodically records the student's behavior and performance in the natural environment and keeps the information in the student's portfolio. This record can be used to identify behaviors and skills that require intervention or support, as well as behaviors and skills in which the student shows a strength and interest. Teachers can also use formal or structured observation systems, which have coding and scoring systems (R. L. Taylor, 2000). Rating scales can also be used to assess the environment in which a student may participate in the future.

Situational assessment—the systematic observation process for evaluating behaviors in controlled and semicontrolled environments—is often used in vocational or employment settings (Dowd, 1993). The demands of the environment (e.g., work tasks, independent living tasks, community functioning skills) can be varied while behaviors, such as interests, skill levels, and social interactions are recorded (Sitlington et al., 1996). For students in middle school, this type of assessment is useful during "tryouts" in the school, such as working in the library, front office, or technology lab; while students are engaged in community service projects; and while students explore the demands and work environments of jobs in the community. At the conclusion of community service or "tryouts," students should always be questioned about what they liked at these sites, their interests in specific tasks, and their desire to explore similar jobs further. Guidelines have been developed by the U.S. Departments of Labor and Education for teachers to use in developing unpaid job experiences for assessment, exploration, or training purposes (see Inge, Simon, Halloran, & Moon, 1993; Simon, Cobb, Norman, & Bourexis, 1994).

If students with disabilities are truly accessing the general education curriculum, it may be necessary for some to participate in community-based exploration during the summer to further identify their interests and abilities. This exploration could be accomplished through volunteer experiences, summer exploration courses of career and technical programs in the local school system, or summer youth employment programs through the Workforce Investment Act of 1998 (http://www.onestops.info).

How Do I Assess Potential Environments?

During the middle school years, analyses of environments should focus on the types of secondary courses, programs, and diploma options that are available to students in the local school system. The main idea is to collect information on potential environments through interviews with school or community personnel or by condensing information available through written descriptions or Web sites that describe school system courses and community programs. Information from these analyses helps students and teachers to understand the content and prerequisites of courses and programs, the requirements of jobs, and the types of services and programs offered through community agencies. This information will then be used to determine a student's focus of study during transition planning.

How Do I Analyze Secondary Courses and Programs?

Students with disabilities and their families are asked to make difficult decisions regarding their academic and vocational preparation, and in some cases diploma options, during the middle school years. IDEA 2004 mandates that students with disabilities must be included in general education curriculum to the maximum extent possible. If students are not included in general education, their IEPs must include an explanation of why they are not participating in these classes.

National reports have highlighted the urgent need for students with disabilities to participate in the general education curriculum to increase access to postsecondary education (American Youth Policy Forum and Center on Education Policy, 2002; National Council on Disability, 2000). The implications for the middle school years are that students with disabilities need challenging courses in content areas so they have the option of participating in advanced placement or career and technical courses in high school. Ellis (n.d.) has cautioned against "watered-down" content courses for students with disabilities that may serve as general education courses but do not truly prepare students for college or more challenging courses as they journey through high school. Therefore, it is important to determine what the requirements of specific courses are and, most important, how students can be supported and succeed in these classes and receive appropriate accommodations (Nolet & McLaughlin, 2000).

Advanced placement courses offer students the opportunity for challenging instruction and preparation for college. Students, their families, and middle school teachers should explore the options available at the high school level and make sure that courses taken during middle school will prepare students for challenging content. It is important for middle school teachers to explore how assistive technology (software, computers, and calculators) can assist students to participate in challenging content courses (Maccini, Gagnon, & Hughes, 2002). Assistive technology is discussed in more detail in Chapter 7. It is also important for students, teachers, and families to begin exploring requirements for majors at selected colleges to understand what courses are needed prior to college, what is involved in getting into college, and what support services are available in postsecondary settings (Brinckerhoff, McGuire, & Shaw, 2002).

Career and technical education courses are general education courses that can provide students with disability-specific vocational training while integrating academic content (Cobb & Neubert, 1998). Most high schools offer at least one vocational technical education course and many offer multiple courses or planned programs. Teachers, parents, and students can start by looking at their school system's Web site for vocational technical courses and work-based learning opportunities; the names of courses and types of programs vary widely among systems. Although many options exist in career and technical education, we provide brief descriptions of only a few programs.

- **Tech Prep Programs.** In tech prep programs, students take a sequence of vocational courses (e.g., drafting) for 2 years in high school and then can articulate to a community college to finish another 2 years of planned academic and vocational courses (e.g., drafting courses). Tech prep programs may be referred to as 2 + 2 programs and provide an opportunity for students to link skilled training with postsecondary education.

- **Career Academies.** A career academy is a school within a school that focuses on a career theme in a field for which there are employment opportunities in the local area. The curriculum combines training, academic content, and often work experience in the summer or during the last years of high school.

- **Career Pathways.** Career pathways are broad clusters of occupations that revolve around a theme shared by the occupations (e.g., health occupations). Students generally explore occupations and training requirements before choosing a cluster or area of concentration.

@ **School-Based Enterprises.** In school-based enterprises, students produce goods or services for sale or use by other people. Examples include school restaurants, construction projects, childcare centers, and auto shops.

@ **Work-Based Experiences or Cooperative Education.** Most high schools offer some form of cooperative education or work–study programs. Students work in the community for a portion of their day, typically during the junior and senior years. Job placements are generally arranged by the work coordinator or the student, and support and follow up are periodic. Cooperative education is a general education offering and differs from special education work–study or transition programs. Special education work–study programs often provide unpaid vocational training, functional skill development, and work experience with more extensive support to students with disabilities.

Students with disabilities and middle school teachers should also explore whether the school system offers a summer exploration program with career and technical education courses. In this program students can sample courses (e.g., automotive, drafting, culinary arts, and nursing) and explore their interests and preferences in a vocational training environment. Finally, students and their teachers may want to explore whether summer programs offered through Workforce Development Programs are provided in the local school system. These programs receive funds from the U.S. Department of Labor and offer youth opportunities to explore and prepare for employment (Hoff, 2000).

Using Transition Assessment Data: Is There a Match?

The transition assessment framework (Figure 6.1) provides middle school teachers with a structure to assess students in different environments, such as in the regular classroom, during extracurricular activities, and in the community. Teachers also have the opportunity to talk with students about their interests, administer interest inventories, and assist students in their use of occupational resources to explore areas of interest. In addition, students and teachers can collect information and determine which courses and programs in middle and high school will assist the students in meeting their postsecondary goals.

As teachers collect this assessment data they should compile it in the student's portfolio and then use it to plan a course of study in the student's IEP. The match process involves comparing information on the student's characteristics (abilities, interests, need for accommodations) with specific information obtained about courses, programs, and community opportunities (see the lower box in Figure 6.1). The IEP team identifies academic courses, vocational training opportunities, and community service opportunities that best match a student's needs, preferences, interests, and tentative postsecondary goals and dreams. The IEP team also considers reasonable accommodations, supports, and assistive technology that may enhance the student's ability to participate in inclusive environments, such as advanced placement courses, career and technical education courses, and the community. For some students, additional career exploration or assessment activities are needed to determine this match. Some school systems have vocational assessment specialists who can help students further identify their interests and continue exploration activities. Other school systems may use a guidance counselor, special educator, or transition specialist to help with this process. As additional assessment data are collected, this information should be added to the student's portfolio, along with additional recommendations, so that the assessment process is systematic and ongoing.

As students with disabilities near the end of middle school, assessment activities should focus on documenting and compiling assessment data. Each student, his or her family, and high school personnel can then use this information. As a student with a disability exits middle school, he or she should understand what type of courses, programs, or experiences are needed to reach postsecondary goals. When students attend their IEP meetings to discuss needed transition services, they should be prepared to share information about their needs, preferences, and interests with the team.

Summary

Transition assessment is an ongoing process that needs to be coordinated and conducted by various people in the school system. Transition assessment provides students and their families with information on a range of options available in the school system and community. The transition assessment process supports student choice and provides school personnel with data to develop a statement of needed transition services at the IEP meeting. It also provides students and their families with information on a range of options available in the school system and community. Additional information on using transition assessment data and developing IEPs can be found in Chapter 7.

Knowledge must come through action: you can have no test which is not fanciful, save by trial.

—Sophocles

Impact of Information on Your Mission

1. List your mission keywords (feel free to change your keywords as you proceed).

2. Describe a story from your teaching or experience that relates to this chapter. Perhaps an event came to mind while you were reading this chapter.

3. What influenced your actions or the actions of others (e.g., students) in the story?

4. What information did you learn in this chapter that influences this story?

5. What transition assessment practices might you change or start based on this new information?

CHAPTER 7

IEPs and Transition Planning

What are your goals for the future?

Joe: I want to become a writer. I like to write. I'm good at poetry. it's a good way to express yourself and stuff. I'm not sure where I would work as a writer—I'd probably find out from relatives or friends to figure out like where I could find a place to publish my work and stuff.

Zoey: I want to be a vet. I like animals and I like science. I don't know where I'd work.

How do you use computers for school?

Joe: I like using computers because of the Internet—I like chat rooms where you can role-play an animated character from a cartoon or something. For schoolwork I use Microsoft Word whenever I have to do a report. I usually use PowerPoint to do projects so it can be creative and get the point across. One of my teachers found an Internet site called Quia—I got to study for quizzes and tests at this site—it used games. matching. word search to study and it really helped me to get good grades in this class.

Zoey: I like to use computers for the Internet and doing research on animals. Computers helped me in school because I learned to type and use different software programs. In seventh and eighth grade we had a computer class during rotations.

Learning Objectives

1. To explain the process of developing an IEP.

2. To describe who is invited to an IEP meeting.

3. To describe your role as a middle school special educator at the IEP meeting.

4. To list the major components of an IEP.

5. To describe how to use transition assessment information in students' IEPs.

6. To explain the student's role in the IEP process.

7. To identify the steps in developing a Section 504 Plan for a student with a disability.

Introduction

Shawna has been struggling with reading and writing since elementary school. The school system has intervened in a number of ways by providing support through a reading specialist and providing structure for writing assignments through her elementary classroom teachers. When Shawna transitioned to middle school, her workload increased and her grades in English, reading, and social studies fell noticeably during the sixth grade. During seventh grade, her parents and a guidance counselor decided it was time to collect more assessment information to determine whether Shawna would qualify for special education services. Shawna was evaluated by the school psychologist and a special educator, who collected information about her abilities, needs, and present levels of performance. Based on this information, the Individualized Education Program (IEP) team at her school determined she was eligible for special education services as a student with a learning disability.

The next step is for the IEP team to write Shawna's IEP. Imagine that you are the special educator at the IEP meeting. Your role is to discuss the results of observations conducted in Shawna's content courses and review the results of assessments you administered for reading, writing, and interests. The IEP team will need to collect additional transition assessment data on Shawna this year so she can plan her postsecondary goals and transition service needs by the time she leaves eighth grade. She wants to go to college and is interested in becoming a veterinarian. She likes to play volleyball and wants to bike across the state at some point. As you read this chapter, think about how to help with Shawna's IEP and transition planning.

What Is an IEP?

Students with disabilities who are eligible for special education services must have an IEP. It might be easiest to think about an IEP as a blueprint that allows a student to reach his or her goals and dreams. For Shawna, some of her IEP goals will relate to teachers' providing direct instruction in reading and providing instructional support for writing activities in her content courses. Another goal may relate to Shawna's use of assistive technology (notebook computer and software) in the writing process. Shawna's goal to go to college needs to be addressed by making sure she is in challenging content courses and passes state and local assessments. In addition, Shawna will need career exploration to investigate her interests and continue to identify her dreams. Another goal might be to find a local bike race for the summer.

The IEP process is governed by the Individuals with Disabilities Education Act (IDEA; 1990, 1997, 2004), and the final regulations for these laws. Because states and local school systems have flexibility in how they design their IEPs (Office of Special Education and Rehabilitative Services [OSERS], 2000), IEP forms vary widely. Some students with disabilities who are not eligible for special education services may have a Section 504 Plan (regulated by Section 504 of the Rehabilitation Act of 1973), which allows them to receive accommodations in the classroom and on state and local assessments. This chapter provides a brief overview of the IEP process, key definitions and legal mandates regarding the IEP, suggestions for integrating transition planning in the IEP process for middle school students, and suggestions and resources for incorporating supports, accommodations, and assistive technology in students' IEPs or 504 Plans.

How Is an IEP Developed?

To be eligible for special education services, a student must have participated in an evaluation process to determine the presence of a disability and the potential educational impact of the disability on the student's progress in general education (OSERS, 2000). The results of the evaluation are reviewed by a team of professionals and the student's parents to determine whether the student is eligible for special education. The team membership depends on the student's needs but generally includes an administrator, a special educator, a school psychologist, a guidance counselor, regular educators, and related service personnel such as a speech therapist or an assistive technology specialist.

Parents must give permission for their child to be evaluated and for any tests that are administered as part of a reevaluation later; they must also be invited to all meetings for the discussion of eligibility or writing of the IEP. If the IEP team determines that the student is not eligible for special education, the process stops and the student's records will include documentation of why he or she was not eligible. At this point parents have the right to disagree with the results of the evaluation and request an Independent Educational Evaluation, which is conducted outside of the school system (Wright & Wright, 2002). In some cases, a teacher or counselor might suggest that the team develop a 504 Plan, which entitles the student to accommodations in the classroom and on assessments rather than special education services. The differences between an IEP and a 504 Plan are explained later in this chapter.

If the student is found eligible for special education services (i.e., has a disability and needs special education and related services), the team designates the student's disability according to the categories identified in IDEA: Autism, Deaf–Blind, Blind, Emotional Disturbance, Hearing Impairment, Mental Retardation, Multiple Disabilities, Orthopedic Impairment, Specific Learning Disability, Speech or Language Impairment, Traumatic Brain Injury, Visual Impairment including blindness, or Other Health Impairment. The majority of students receiving special education services have learning disabilities, and some students with attention-deficit disorders receive special education services under the category Other Health Impairment. In the last decade, the categories of Other Health Impairment, Orthopedic Impairment, and Specific Learning Disability experienced the largest increases in numbers of students identified for services under IDEA (President's Commission on Excellence in Special Education, 2002).

Once a student has been found eligible for special education services, the next step for the team, along with the parent and student, is to develop an IEP. Each school has someone who is familiar with federal, state, and local policies regarding the development and implementation of the IEP. Because the IEP is a legal document, it is important that each teacher understand the content required in the IEP and his or her specific responsibilities in implementing the IEP. Once the IEP is written, the parents must receive a copy and sign it before special education services can begin. The IEP must be reviewed annually, although a meeting can be called at any time by parents or teachers to revise the IEP. Students are reevaluated every 3 years to determine if they continue to be eligible for special education services.

Who Must Attend the IEP Meeting?

Everyone who attends the IEP meeting must sign documents indicating that they attended and participated in the meeting. The following people generally attend the IEP meeting (Rebhorn, 2002; Storms, O'Leary, & Williams, 2000):

- **Parent or Guardian.** Parents (or guardians) should provide information on the student's interests, strengths, and needs, as well as their vision of postsecondary goals. Parents should be viewed as equal partners in the IEP planning and decision-making process.

- **Student.** If the IEP team will be discussing transition needs, the student must be invited to the meeting. Otherwise, it is up to the school staff and family to decide when to invite the student. We recommend that students in middle school be invited to and participate in their IEP meetings to encourage self-determination skills. Students should communicate their strengths, interests, needs, and postsecondary goals or dreams to the IEP team.

@ **Local Educational Agency (LEA) Representative.** An example of an LEA representative is a school administrator who knows the general curriculum and resources in the school system. This person should support the teachers and be able to address allocation of resources to make sure the IEP is implemented.

@ **General Education Teacher.** The general education teacher should know the general education curriculum and be able to explain what students are typically expected to do in these classes. In addition, this person should be able to give input into appropriate positive behavioral interventions, supplementary aids and services, program modifications, and supports for school personnel consistent with the IEP content requirements. General educators may attend only the part of the IEP meeting that requires their participation.

@ **Special Education Teacher.** At least one special educator who works with or will work with the student and is familiar with special education practices at the school must be invited. The middle school special educator should be able to address the student's needs, interests, and preferences and postsecondary goals or dreams if the student chooses not to talk about these. In addition, this teacher should provide information on the student's progress in the general education curriculum, propose strategies and accommodations that address the student's needs, suggest courses of study that match the student's interests, and link the student to appropriate related services and agencies outside the school.

@ **Person to Interpret Evaluation Results.** A school psychologist or other professional must be able to speak about the student's evaluation in terms of results and their implications for special education services and for instructional practices and supports.

@ **Other Personnel.** A variety of other personnel who have knowledge or expertise related to the student can be invited to the IEP meeting. These professionals could include related services personnel, such as an occupational therapist, speech–language therapist, or assistive technology specialist; a translator or interpreter for the family; an advocate, tutor, or educational consultant that the parent identifies; or personnel from community agencies (e.g., social services, mental health) if interagency linkages are necessary.

IDEA 2004 adds a number of new provisions related to attendance at IEP meetings, including the provision that a member of the IEP team does not have to attend all or part of the IEP meeting if the parent and local school personnel (a) agree that the member's attendance is not necessary because the member's curriculum or related service is not being discussed at the meeting and (b) agree to excuse the member provided he or she submits written input into the development of the IEP prior to the meeting.

What Is My Role as a Middle School Special Educator?

You will be asked to introduce yourself and review any appropriate assessment data. Depending on the age of the student, your responsibilities will vary. Here are some typical duties:

1. Review the assessment data you collected, including observations in general education classrooms and formal and informal assessments. Identify strategies and supports that have been or may be successful in addressing the student's needs.

2. Review any transition assessment data collected. These data could include the results of an interest inventory, information gathered through student and parent interviews, observations made in situational assessments, and information the student gathered from exploring occupations and courses or training available in the local school system.

3. If a student has not identified his or her needs, strengths, interests, preferences, or tentative postsecondary dreams, advocate for an IEP goal that addresses this need (e.g., "By the end of eighth grade, the student will have identified an area of interest and relate this interest to a postsecondary goal and a course of study for high school").

4. Review any information related to the student's self-determination skills. Encourage and prepare the student to participate in the IEP process. For example, have the student consider his or her strengths, interests, needs, and tentative postsecondary goals.

What Needs To Be Included in an IEP?

Table 7.1 lists the components to include in the IEP; each is explained briefly in this section. Although special education students have always been entitled to receive services in the least restrictive environment, IDEA 2004 requires access to the general education curriculum and to state and local assessments for all students with disabilities. IEP teams must also review special factors when developing IEPs, including the student's strengths, parents' input, language needs of students with limited English proficiency, assistive technology needs, and strategies and supports when behavior is an issue (Huefner, 2000; Yell & Shriner, 1997). To learn more about the IEP process, complete Activity 7.1.

Current Educational Performance

The IEP includes a statement of the student's current educational performance or present levels of education performance, including how the student's disability affects his or her involvement and progress in the general education curriculum

Table 7.1
Contents of the IEP

- Current educational performance

- Measurable annual goals

- Special education and related services

- Participation in general education

- Participation in state and local assessments

- Student progress

- Transition services

(IDEA, 1997; OSERS, 2000). When developing an IEP, team members should also include the following information:

- Student's strengths, interests, preferences
- Student's academic, developmental, and functional needs
- Student's postsecondary goals and dreams
- Student's desired focus of study during high school
- Initial evaluation results
- Parents' concerns

Activity 7.1 Understanding IEPs in Your School System

1. Arrange to interview a guidance counselor, special educator, or administrator at a middle school. Write the types of responsibilities they have at IEP meetings. Ask for a copy of a blank IEP form so you can examine the format and content. Also, ask for a blank copy of a 504 Plan.

2. Go to your school system's Web site. What type of information is available to teachers and parents regarding the special education process in this system? List all titles of the documents you find.

© 2006 by PRO-ED, Inc.

Measurable Annual Goals

The main purpose of the IEP is to identify measurable goals, including academic and functional goals. Short-term objectives and benchmarks must be written only for those students who take alternate assessments that are aligned to varied achievement standards (Council for Exceptional Children, 2004). For a student in middle school, the IEP team should first consider the student's overall goals for life after school before developing annuals goals (G. Greene & Kochhar-Bryant, 2003; Storms et al., 2000). A discussion of postsecondary goals should include postsecondary education, employment, vocational education, independent living, community participation, and adult services. This information should then be linked to a course of study in high school. For example, Shawna is interested in attending a postsecondary education program after graduation, so her course of study in high school should include advanced placement and foreign language courses to prepare for college. Related services and accommodations would revolve around her accessing and succeeding in general education classes and passing state assessments. By considering the student's postsecondary goals first, transition planning becomes the force that drives the IEP process.

In designing measurable annual goals, the team should think of these as the outcomes the team would like to see the student achieve for the year; these goals are directly related to the student's present levels of performance and transition assessment data. Activity 7.2 gives you practice in writing a goal based on information about Shawna.

Special Education and Related Services

Special education is defined as "specially designated instruction, at no cost to the parents, to meet the unique needs of a child with disability" (Wright & Wright, 2002, p. 29). This can include instruction in the classroom, home, hospital, and institutions; instructional areas include physical education, vocational education, travel training, and speech–language services or other related services.

For the IEP the team must determine how the student will receive special education services while participating to the maximum extent possible in general education curricula. Specially designated instruction must address how the student will access the general curriculum so that he or she can meet the educational standards within the public school agency that apply to all students. It will be important for the IEP team to consider how general and special educators will deliver instruction, provide accommodations, and monitor progress for the student.

Related Services
Related services include transportation, and developmental, corrective, and other supportive services that assist a student with a disability to benefit from special education. These can include the following:

- Speech–language pathology and audiology services

- Psychological services

Activity 7.2 Shawna's IEP Discussion for Eighth Grade

Read the following information that Shawna's IEP team discussed at her meeting and come up with an additional goal.

SHAWNA'S POSTSECONDARY GOAL/VISION

To obtain a high school diploma and attend a 4-year college; to live independently

PRESENT LEVEL OF PERFORMANCE

Shawna requires accommodations to participate in regular education content courses and to take state assessments. Her evaluation grade-level results are as follows: Reading 5.9; Mathematics 9.1; Written Language 5.9. She gets along well with peers and teachers, participates in the school science club and volleyball team, and expresses interest in working with animals, science and math courses, and becoming a veterinarian.

GOAL

Shawna will participate in regular education courses that emphasize preparation for college and meet the requirements for obtaining a diploma with support from the special educator.

- By the end of October 2005, Shawna will keep track of all assignments in her daily planner with 100% accuracy.

- By the end of January 2006, Shawna will have obtained a grade of B or better in her regular education courses.

- By the end of January 2006, Shawna will have demonstrated note-taking and test-taking strategies in English, social studies, and science.

Develop Another Goal for Shawna:

- Physical and occupational therapy

- Recreation, including therapeutic recreation

- Early identification and assessment of disabilities in children

- Counseling services, including rehabilitation counseling

- Orientation and mobility services

- Medical services for diagnostic or evaluation purposes

- School health services and social work services in schools

- Parent counseling and training

Supplementary Aids and Services

Supplementary aids, services, and supports are to be provided in regular education classes or other education-related settings to enable students with disabilities to be educated with peers without disabilities (Wright & Wright, 2002). These aids and services are meant to facilitate the inclusion of students with disabilities in general education by going beyond the services that benefit the student in special education (Huefner, 2000).

Participation in General Education

IDEA 1997 mandates that statements about the student's present levels of performance, annual goals, and special education and related services are based on how the student participates in the general education curriculum. If an IEP team determines that the student will not participate in regular education for some part of the school day, an explanation of this decision needs to be included in the IEP document. OSERS (2000) pointed out that students with disabilities are to be placed in special classes or separate schools only if the severity of the disability impacts the student's ability to participate in general education with the use of supplemental aids or services. IDEA 2004 further mandates that the statement of measurable annual goals must be designed to meet the student's needs to be involved in and *make progress* in the general education curriculum.

Participation in State and Local Assessments

Some states use high-stakes assessments in making decisions about student promotion or high school graduation (deFur, 2002; D. R. Johnson & Thurlow, 2003; Quenemoen, Lehr, Thurlow, Thompson, & Bolt, 2000). The impact of high-stakes assessment on students with disabilities has received increased attention, especially in terms of how to merge educational reform efforts with transition service needs and promote optimal postsecondary outcomes (D. R. Johnson, Stodden, Emanuel, Luecking, & Mack, 2002). Because high-stakes assessments are often tied to graduation requirements, it is important not only to address how middle school students will be prepared to participate in these assessments through challenging course content, but also to identify the accommodations they need to be able to participate in content courses and to pass state assessments.

The IDEA Amendments of 1997 require that students with disabilities be included in state and local assessments with appropriate accommodations when needed. IDEA 2004 contains similar provisions and requires a statement of any individual appropriate accommodations that are necessary to measure the academic achievement and functional performance of a student on state and district assessments. If the IEP team determines that the student will participate in an alternate assessment, the team must document the reason for this decision in the IEP document. The No Child Left Behind (NCLB) Act of 2001 (P.L. 107-110) also mandated that all students participate in state assessments and further reinforced the need for accommodations for students with disabilities (as defined under IDEA) to measure academic achievement relative to state content standards (Thurlow, Lazarus, Thompson, & Robey, 2002).

In response to IDEA and NCLB, many states have established a list of accommodations that can be listed on students' IEPs or 504 Plans or provided to students with limited English proficiency. Listed accommodations generally reflect the changes that will be made to standard testing materials or procedures (Lignugaris/Kraft, Marchand-Martella, & Martella, 2001). An accommodation is not intended to change the standard of learning or to lower the expectations for performance that have been set for all students. For a student to receive accommodations on national, state, or local assessments, the accommodations must be listed on the student's IEP or 504 Plan. Students generally receive accommodations on state assessments under the following categories (Thurlow et al., 2002):

- *Presentation Accommodations:* These alter the way in which a test is presented to the student. Possibilities include large print, Braille, read aloud, sign language, visual cues, and rereading or clarifying directions.

- *Equipment and Material Modifications:* Students are allowed to use equipment or materials that are not typically permitted. Examples include use of calculators, magnification equipment, light or acoustic modifications, and use of audio- or videocassette.

- *Response Accommodations:* These alter the way a student responds to the assessment. Examples include the use of a proctor or scribe to write in the test booklet; tape recording of the student's verbal responses (rather than writing); and use of a communication device, spell checker, brailler, or computer.

- *Scheduling and Timing Accommodations:* These changes include extended time breaks, testing over multiple sessions or days, or testing at a time that is most beneficial to the student.

- *Setting Accommodations:* These involve where the test is administered. For example, the student might take a test in a room by him- or herself or be seated in the front of the room in a corner desk.

Once accommodations for assessments are identified for students with disabilities, it is important that the students understand the accommodations they are entitled to and learn how to advocate for themselves in testing situations. Additional information on accommodations and the impact assessments may have on diploma options for students with disabilities can be found at the National Center on Educational Outcomes (http://education.umn.edu/NCEO).

Student Progress

An IEP has a projected date for the beginning of the services and modifications and the anticipated frequency, location, and duration of those services and modifications (OSERS, 2000). Once annual goals are written for the IEP, it is up to school staff to monitor the individual's progress in meeting these indicators, revise the IEP as needed to be consistent with the student's instructional needs, and make decisions about curriculum changes. The IEP must include a description of the student's progress toward meeting annual goals, as well as statements about how progress is measured and when periodic progress reports are provided to parents.

The IEP is generally reviewed once a year by the IEP team to determine if the student is making progress toward achieving the goals. OSERS (2000) suggests that IEP teams consider the following during the annual review:

- The student's progress or lack of progress toward annual goals and in the general education curriculum

- Information gathered through any reevaluation of the student, by the parents, or from teachers and other school staff

- Any anticipated needs

For younger middle school students, the IEP team should consider what transition assessment data are needed to address postsecondary goals and transition service needs that have to be included in the IEP by age 16.

Transition Services

In the past some school systems used attachments or individual transition plans to address transition needs and postsecondary goals for students with disabilities. We recommend, however, that transition service statements be part of the IEP to comply with IDEA 2004 and to encourage the IEP team to address transition needs as part of the IEP process on an annual basis. As discussed in Chapters 3 and 6, beginning no later than when the student is 16 (and updated annually), the IEP needs to specify (a) appropriate measurable postsecondary goals based on age-appropriate transition assessments related to training, education, employment, and independent living skills and (b) transition services including a course of study to meet the goals.

Transition services are to be based on the student's needs, strengths, interests, and preferences, as well as dreams for postsecondary goals (McAffee & Greenawalt, 2001). Therefore, the student has choices regarding his or her postsecondary goals, course options in middle and high school, and opportunities to explore interests and preferences. If you involve students in transition assessment activities described in Chapter 6, you will meet these requirements. Researchers have begun documenting the positive effects of providing direct instruction on students' involvement in IEP meetings and transition planning (S. K. Allen, Smith, Test, Flowers, & Wood, 2001; Powers et al., 2001; Zhang, 2001).

How Does Assistive Technology Fit in the IEP Process?

Assistive technology can be an important tool in helping students with disabilities to access and succeed in general education classes and to meet their IEP goals. In 1997 the IDEA Amendments required that assistive technology be considered by the IEP team (S. K. Fisher & Gardner, 1999), and IDEA 2004 continues to address this need. Examples of technology that might assist students with reading and writing difficulties in the general education classroom include voice recognition software (which changes spoken words into type on the computer screen), word prediction software, software for organizing, spell checkers, personal computers, and Kurzweil readers.

Assistive technology is discussed in terms of devices and services. Assistive technology devices are items, equipment, or product systems that can be acquired commercially off the shelf, modified, or customized to increase, maintain, or improve students' functional capacities. Assistive technology services are those that help the student and the IEP team to select, acquire, or use an assistive technology device. Examples of these services include the following:

- Evaluating the student in his or her customary environment (e.g., the classroom)

- Purchasing, leasing, or providing assistive technology devices

- Selecting, designing, fitting, maintaining, or replacing assistive technology devices

- Coordinating and use of other therapies and interventions, or services with assistive technology devices (e.g., existing education and rehabilitation plans)

- Providing training or technical assistance to the student, family, or teachers

Assistive technology devices may also be discussed in terms of no-, low-, mid-, or high-tech options (Educational Resources Information Center, 2002; Houchins, 2001). Lo-tech solutions include software programs (e.g., webbing, flow-charting, task analysis) and simple devices (e.g., keyguards, book holders, nonskid matting). High-tech options include notebook computers, personal digital assistants, or portable word processing keyboards to help students with the mechanics of note taking.

In addition to understanding the terms associated with assistive technology, teachers should know who to contact in the school system about student referrals for assistive technology evaluations or requests for assistive technology devices. To evaluate the assistive technology needs of students, school systems may use occupational therapists or designate specific personnel (e.g., assistive technology specialists). The only way to know if assistive technology will benefit the student is to try it in the environment in which he or she would use it. Two common reasons that students do not use assistive technology are that use of the devices makes them look different from other students and that insufficient training was provided to the student, teachers, or parents.

The following Web sites have more information about assessment and assistive technology.

http://www.cec.sped.org

From the Council for Exceptional Children homepage, go to Publications and Products, then CEC Online Catalog, then Assistive technology and request a copy of the Assistive Technology Consideration Quick Wheel.

http://www.jan.wvu.edu

The Job Accommodations Network (JAN) is a free service from the Office of Disability Employment Policy, U.S. Department of Labor. Access JAN's Searchable Online Accommodation Resources (SOAR) to explore various accommodations for students with disabilities in educational and work settings.

http://www.abledata.com

Go to Products for a database of 29,000 assistive technology products, including descriptions, prices, and ordering information.

http://www.ataccess.org

This site, operated by a network of community-based resource centers, developers, and vendors, provides information and support services to individuals with disabilities to increase the use of assistive and information technologies.

What Is a 504 Plan?

Section 504 Plans are regulated by the Rehabilitation Act of 1973, a federal law that prohibits discrimination of individuals with disabilities in programs and activities (including public schools) that receive federal funds (Office of Civil Rights, 2002). Section 504 and the Americans with Disabilities Act of 1990 are antidiscrimination laws and do not provide funding to schools based on the number of students with 504 Plans. IDEA differs from these laws in that it is a grant statute and schools must meet specific conditions to receive funds available through IDEA.

Some students with disabilities have a Section 504 Plan rather an IEP. A Section 504 Plan allows students to receive accommodations on assessments and in the classroom. Accommodations for assessments might include extended time on tests, use of assistive technology for writing tasks, or testing at certain times of the day. Accommodations in the classroom might include fewer tasks per assignment, highlighting of key points, presentation of information or directions in multiple formats, or changing a student's seat.

Students with attention-deficit disorder, other health impairments, vision impairments, and hearing impairments are increasingly receiving accommodations under Section 504 even if they do not qualify for special services under IDEA (Blazer, 1999; T. E. C. Smith, 2001). At the beginning of this chapter, the process for determining an individual eligible for special education was discussed. Remember, the student must have a documented disability (e.g., autism, mental retardation) and need special education and related services to participate in educational activities. Some students may have documented disability but only need accommodations to participate in the general education classroom (i.e., extended time on tests, magnification equipment to read the text). These students may qualify for a 504 plan but not for an IEP. A number of excellent resources explain the differences between Section 504 and IDEA in terms of serving students with disabilities in public schools (deBettencourt, 2002; T. E. C. Smith, 2001) and provide help for teachers who are developing and implementing 504 Plans (Blazer, 1999; T. E. C. Smith & Patton, 1999).

A major difference between Section 504 and IDEA is in how the term *disability* is defined. Section 504 defines qualified students as those who have a physical or mental impairment that substantially limits one or more major life activities (e.g., walking, hearing, seeing, learning), have a documented record of the limitation or disability, and are regarded as having an impairment by teachers, parents, and other professionals (T. E. C. Smith & Patton, 1999). The key is to determine whether the disability has a substantial limitation on the student's ability to learn or participate in school activities (T. E. C. Smith, 2001) and to determine what reasonable accommodations will assist the student in a school setting.

To receive accommodations under Section 504, students must participate in an assessment process to determine their educational needs, aptitudes, or achievement. Assessment data must come from a variety of sources and be collected through multiple methods. Periodic reevaluation of the student is required to determine whether the student continues to need accommodations or requires a significant change in placement at school. Students with an IEP or a 504 Plan must be provided with a free and appropriate public education.

All schools have someone who is responsible for Section 504 procedures. Some school systems use IEP team members, whereas others designate guidance counselors, school psychologists, or administrators to be the contact point for initiating and writing 504 Plans. Most schools also have written material about the process for teachers and parents along with specific forms for developing 504 Plans. As with IEPs, the formats of 504 Plans vary from one school district to another.

Students with 504 Plans generally have a case manager assigned to them. School districts also assign this job to different professionals (e.g., guidance counselor, special educator). Once a 504 Plan is written, it is the responsibility of the student's teachers to implement the plan and provide any accommodations that the student is entitled to receive. If teachers fail to implement a plan, the school district can be held in noncompliance with Section 504. Students with 504 Plans are not required by law to have statements of transition service needs and postsecondary goals, as are students with IEPs. Middle school teachers should encourage students to request accommodations that are listed on their 504 Plans. These self-determination skills are crucial because students with disabilities who have 504 Plans or IEPs will receive accommodations in postsecondary education and in the workplace only under Section 504 once they exit the school system.

Summary

This chapter has provided an overview of the IEP process, with an emphasis on integrating transition assessment information in students' IEPs. In addition, the importance of including appropriate accommodations, related services, assistive technology, and other support services in the IEP process is highlighted. This is necessary so students are able to meet IEP goals, participate in general education classes and state assessments, and meet diploma requirements, which ultimately impact postsecondary goals for students with disabilities.

The IEP process requires collaboration with the student, school staff, community agency personnel, and family members. It is a process that must be learned through direct experience; however, understanding the requirements of IDEA is the first step. There are many excellent resources to help teachers with writing IEPs or 504 Plans, including the following:

http://www.ed.gov (search for IEP)

http://www.cec.sped.org

http://www.ericec.org

http://www.ldonline.org

http://www.nichcy.org

http://www.wrightslaw.com

Middle school provides a perfect opportunity for special educators to help students with disabilities understand their strengths and needs and develop self-advocacy skills. This effort will lay the foundation for transition planning in high school and help students realize their dreams and goals in the future.

Only those who risk going too far can possibly find out how far one can go.

—*T. S. Eliot*

Impact of Information on Your Mission

1. List your mission keywords (feel free to change your keywords as you proceed).

2. Describe a story from your teaching or experience that relates to this chapter. Perhaps an event came to mind while you were reading this chapter.

3. What influenced your actions or the actions of others (e.g., students) in the story?

4. What information did you learn in this chapter that influences this story?

5. What practices might you change based on this new information?

CHAPTER 8

Progressive Reflection

What do you like about your teachers?

"Our teachers are nice and cool, they have personality, they help us after school on schoolwork, and we have parties."

"They are nice, funny, all men, let us do everything, give us candy, and they don't give us a lot of homework."

"We do activities, they greet us at the door, they are funny, they help us if we have problems, they have faith, and they are all women."

"They tell jokes, they give us free time, we can eat in class, they give us candy, they teach us things we don't know a lot about, and they do not give any homework."

Learning Objectives

1. To explain how you take the time for personal and professional reflection.

2. To describe why you like teaching middle school, or to describe how you like your education coursework.

3. To explain what you like about the way you teach, or to explain what you think are potential teaching strengths as a preservice teacher.

4. To describe how you will ensure that you have ongoing professional growth.

What Is Professional Development?

Take a minute to think about what you do to recharge your professional battery. Do you go to in-service trainings? Talk to your colleagues? Watch an educational video? Take a walk? Listen to music? Attend a professional conference? Read a textbook? Most likely you do a combination of these things. Even though your school district does not give in-service credits for taking a walk or listening to music, these are crucial downtimes for self-reflection and learning. Most working educators can remember at least one time in their lives when they were so tired of their work that they thought about quitting the profession. Then after taking a break, relaxing during a weekend at the beach, going to a movie with friends, or reading a good book, they felt renewed and ready to face students once again.

Professional development is the "means by which educators acquire or enhance the knowledge, skills, attitudes, and beliefs necessary to create high levels of learning for all students" (National Staff Development Council, 2001, p. 2). After reviewing professional development research, Guskey (2003) concluded that promising practices in professional development can best be described using "yes, but ..." statements. For example, teachers need to display effective leadership qualities, but they also need to follow administrative directives. Based on the multiple and highly complex characteristics (e.g., school location, quality of the teachers, administrative support) that influence professional development, it may be unrealistic to put together one set of guidelines that works in all situations. Realizing this limitation, the National Staff Development Council (NSDC; 2001) developed standards that provide a framework or vision for making staff development more responsive to the needs of students and educators. Through the standards, the NSDC not only provides content (e.g., quality teaching, family involvement) guidelines but also addresses the conditions (e.g., data-driven, collaboration) and the context (e.g., leadership, learning communities) in which staff development occurs.

Applying NSDC's (2001) guidelines to professional development makes the learning experience more personal and tailored to meet the needs of both students and teachers. Kelleher's (2003) six stages of professional development utilize this tailored approach. These stages begin with teachers setting the learning goals and end with the evaluation of how these goals are met. Between the setting and achieving of the goals is the professional development intervention. Aspects of the professional development that are important are content knowledge, instructional demonstrations by colleagues, teacher collaboration and dialogue, professional developers that work collaboratively with teachers, self-reflection, and a safe environment (Morris, Chrispeels, & Burke, 2003; Paez, 2003).

Professional development is a dichotomy between what educators learn and the responsiveness of the learning environment. This dichotomy is important for educators to recognize because, as they learn and grow professionally, they must also foster growth within the system in which they work. Has a colleague ever expressed that he does fine with the students and believes he is an effective teacher but he has great difficulty functioning with the administration? Your colleague's frustration may be due to a conflict between his professional growth and the lack of growth in the system in which he works. Uneven growth in the teacher–environment dichotomy will lead to frustration and ineffective teaching unless an understanding is reached between the two. Therefore, as you spend time reflecting on your growth as an educator, you must also reflect on the broader system and community in which you work. Understanding growth or the need for growth in both arenas will help you better understand your role as an educator and better define your mission.

Why Is Self-Reflection Important?

Are you familiar with the child's game Truth or Dare? In this game the first child asks the second child a question. The second child answers the question either with the truth or dares the first child to catch her in her mistruth. We suggest that you play this game with yourself as a self-reflection activity. Basically, ask yourself some direct questions about your life, your work, or any other issues you want to explore. Then answer the question either in a truthful manner or in a manner that you think may be truthful but requires more thought. Through this type of self-exploration, individuals often can improve their work and their lives.

Self-reflection is crucial to a teacher's ability to improve his or her instruction and teaching (Jay & Johnson, 2002; Ukpokodu, 2002). Teachers become better at their profession by regularly evaluating their students' needs, examining their current role in meeting those needs, and considering how they can better help meet the students' needs (Darling-Hammond, 1998). Teachers' self-reflection can be extended to include their perceptions of what education should be and what role they want to play in their own concept of education—in other words, their life's mission. M. Greene (1991) talks about people needing life projects or forms of purposeful work. Early in the century Dewey (1916) wrote, "Self and interest are two names for the same fact; the kind and amount of interest actively taken in things reveals and measures the quality of selfhood which exists" (p. 408). Dewey went on to write, "The self is not ready-made, but something in continuous formation through choice of action" (p. 408). If one's life project is teaching, then according to Dewey this interest is part of who one is. Additionally, individuals are works in progress who need self-reflection and continual analyses to grow.

Reflecting on Your Mission and the MidEx Model

Activity 8.1 is meant to guide you as you self-reflect about your work in middle schools. Completing the activity, which is based on the MidEx model (see Figure 8.1), will give you an opportunity to explore your thoughts, strengths, and areas of need related to teaching middle school. This activity is designed as a culmination to this text. It is a means of reflecting on your professional and personal growth and learning. After you have completed the activity, think back to the professional development discussion in this chapter to discover how you can continue on a path that will allow you not only to survive but to thrive. Remember to use the Internet to further expand your ideas and practices (see the Web sites listed in the previous chapters and Appendix A).

Summary

This chapter has offered you the opportunity to think about your own professional growth and development and to ponder your potential and current skills as a leader in your school and community. After reading this book and completing the exercises, you may discover that your teaching has become more purposeful and insightful. Many educators, when faced with new teaching approaches or philosophies, may consider the new ideas to be additional burdens on their already overburdened work lives. We hope that you can easily embed the concepts included in the MidEx

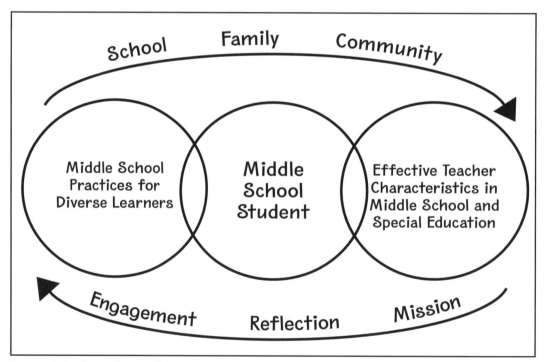

Figure 8.1. The MidEx model.

Activity 8.1 The MidEx Model: Your Personal Reflection

To complete the following activity, review the Impact of Information on Your Mission sheets that you completed at the end of each chapter. Reflect on what you have learned. The components of the MidEx model serve as the topic headings (see Figure 8.1). Under each heading write your current thinking (e.g., new ideas, revisited ideas, revised ideas) in sentence or bullet format. At the end of the exercise, revise your mission statement. Save this sheet and revise it periodically to reflect changes in your professional and personal growth. Note any Web sites that you find helpful under these topics.

- Middle School Student

- Effective Practices in Middle School

- Effective Practices in Middle School for Diverse Learners

- Teacher Characteristics in Middle School

- Teacher Characteristics in Special Education

- School

- Family

- Community

- Engagement

- Reflection

- Your Mission Statement

model in your teaching without feeling that they are burdensome. MidEx ideas are more about the way in which you teach rather than additional information you have to teach. As you begin and continue your own professional growth using this model, you may begin to notice that your students have also become more engaged, reflective, and self-determined, and that your consistent and targeted teaching efforts have resulted in significant progress and growth among your students. As the esteemed teacher, Aloysius, told his student, Josephus, nearly 300 years ago,

> Drops wear down the stone not by strength but by constant falling. If you will work thus, you will be delighted to see the way in which light gradually illuminates what had been obscure and how in some manner the curtain of darkness seems to be drawn away. (Fux, 2004, p. 27)

With these ancient and wise words in mind, teachers of middle school students with diverse needs will most certainly facilitate learning, growth, and living.

> People often say that this or that person has not yet found himself. But the self is not something one finds, it is something one creates.
>
> —Thomas Szasz

APPENDIX A

Internet Resources

Jeanne Repetto, Meridith Taylor, and Michael Palmer

The Internet can enhance your professional development and curriculum. Web sites provide a quick resource for educators, parents, and students to locate information about a new topic, find new resources and activities for the classroom, and locate new lesson plans. The following Web sites are listed under these topics: (a) middle school; (b) transition; (c) special education; (d) families and information on disabilities; (e) curriculum, instruction, and lesson plans; (f) content areas; and (g) other sites for teachers. Many of the Web sites have information on multiple topics and lead to additional links and resources.

Middle School

http://www.nmsa.org
> The National Middle School Association (NMSA), with over 30,000 members, is dedicated to the growth of middle level education. This site includes information on No Child Left Behind Act of 2002, middle school services, research, and professional development activities.

http://www.middleschool.net
> Designed for teachers by teachers, this Web site provides information on lesson plans, tutorials, and information on state standards across the curriculum; information for administrators, support staff, and parents who homeschool their children; and professional development opportunities.

http://www.middleweb.com
> This site contains articles and links about middle school curriculum, teaching strategies, professional development, parent involvement, and classroom assessment.

http://www.emtech.net

From the Emerging Technologies homepage, go to Middle Grades Resources for information and articles on behavior management, curriculum, and developmental issues for students in middle school. This web page has information for teachers, parents, and students.

http://www.serc.org

The Satellite Educational Resources Consortium (SERC) is the only distance learning organization in the United States that combines the resources of state departments of education and public television licensees. The site provides information about foreign languages, math, and science and has a link for professional development for math and science teachers at the middle school level.

http://www.education-world.com

Designed for teachers, parents, and students, this site has links to other middle schools around the country and provides informational articles about middle school issues. Once on the homepage, go to the advanced search and type in "Middle School."

http://www.TPRonline.org

The Prevention Researcher (TPR) is a journal designed to help at-risk youth. It provides articles and books for teachers and parents to prevent youth from at-risk behavior. Once on the homepage, search for "Middle School," and a number of related articles will appear.

http://mathforum.org

From the homepage, click on Teachers' Place, then Middle School Teachers. This site is designed for math teachers at the middle school level. There is information on teaching abstract skills such as problem solving and prealgebra. The site also offers resources for teachers interested in professional development.

Transition

http://www.ncset.org

The National Center on Secondary Education and Transition (NCSET) provides resources, technical assistance, information on secondary education and transition topics for students with disabilities, and links to other Web sites that may be beneficial to teachers, students, and their families. From the homepage, go to the bottom of the page to search for specific items.

http://www.vesid.nysed.gov

Once you get the page for the New York State Education Department's Vocational and Educational Services for Individuals with Disabilities, click on Special Education, then Transition, and then Student and Family Resources. This site provides information for parents, students, and teachers on how to implement transition processes in schools or communities. It includes a timeline for transition planning and questionnaires to assess students' and parents' satisfaction with transition services.

http://www.careeradvantage.org

This site provides information and links on continuing education, professional, trade, and vocational schools. Occupation headings include technology, graphic design, animation, business, culinary, fashion design, and interior design.

Special Education

http://www.cec.sped.org

The Council for Exceptional Children (CEC) is a professional organization that seeks to improve educational outcomes for individuals with exceptionalities, students with disabilities, and students who are gifted. This site provides resources, links, and professional conferences for teachers and transition specialists. Once on the homepage, go to the search icon to locate specific topics.

http://specialed.freeyellow.com

The Special Education Home Page provides information on different disabilities and legal information relating to special education.

http://www.rfbd.org

The Recording for the Blind and Dyslexic (RFBD) is an educational resource enabling those with print disabilities to complete their education. The organization provides materials and resources for people who cannot read standard print because of visual, perceptional, or other physical disabilities.

http://www.iser.com

Go to Directory Search by State. Internet Special Education Resources (ISER) provides resource information on the following subjects: advocacy services (including nationwide, statewide, regional, and local), special education products, learning centers, attention-deficit disorders, learning disabilities assessments, and IEPs and Section 504 Plans.

http://www.specialedconnection.com

Special Ed Connection provides references on state-specific information, best practices, case decisions, and judicial and administrative decisions. It also provides an e-mail newsletter, which provides parents with information on developments in special education.

http://www.specialednews.com

The Special Education News Web site provides special education information and general resources for families and educators. Educators use this site to share views. The site provides information on the following subjects: transition, specific disabilities, state information, early intervention, conflict resolution, behavior management, Internet and assistive technology, and recreation and sports.

http://www.ericec.org

The Council for Exceptional Children's Information Center on Disabilities and Gifted Education gathers and disseminates professional literature, information, and resources on the education and development of individuals of all ages who have disabilities and/or who are gifted.

http://seriweb.com

Special Education Resources on the Internet (SERI) provides information for all areas related to special education. It provides links for a number of topics, such as inclusion, law resources, autism, transition resources, and behavior disorders.

http://chadd.org

Children and Adults with Attention-Deficit/Hyperactivity Disorder (CHADD) is a nationwide, nonprofit organization serving individuals with attention-deficit/hyper-activity disorders (ADHD). CHADD provides advocacy, research, education, and supports to parents, educators, professionals, and the general population. You can download specific Fact sheets, such as parenting a child with ADHD, medical management of children and adults with ADHD, and educational rights of children with ADHD. Also available in Spanish.

http://nichcy.org

The National Dissemination Center for Children with Disabilities (NICHCY) is a national information center that provides information on disabilities and disability-related issues to families, educators, administrators, journalists, students, and the population at large. Information is available on specific disabilities, special education and related services for children in school, educational rights, early intervention services, and transition to adult life. The site also includes parent materials and information and publications from disability and professional associations. Also available in Spanish.

http://www.nami.org

The National Alliance for the Mentally Ill (NAMI) is an advocacy organization dedicated to improving the lives of persons with severe mental illnesses, including schizophrenia, bipolar disorder (manic–depressive illness), major depression, obsessive–compulsive disorder, and severe anxiety disorders. Options include information on illnesses and treatments, NAMI help line, education and training programs, outreach, children and adolescents, current publications, event and convention information, and Web links.

http://ldonline.org

LD OnLine focuses on learning disabilities, dyslexia, ADD, and ADHD, but also includes many topics related to special education, learning differences, and related issues for parents, teachers, and professionals. Topics include assessment, accommodations, assistive technology, IEPs and 504 Plans. Also available in Spanish.

Families and Information on Disabilities

http://www.nwrel.org

The Northwest Regional Educational Laboratory (NWREL) provides reviews of literature that examine issues including parent involvement in education (e.g., what works for parent involvement, and what grades are most important for parents to be involved).

http://www.bssnp.com

The Bart Stevens Special Needs Planning (BSSNP) site provides resources for parents on financial and estate planning for families with a child who has special needs, including information on guardianship and advocacy with government agencies.

http://www.kidsource.com

Easy to navigate for both parents and teachers, this site explains the laws that mandate transition services and collaborative consultation for problem solving. Once on the homepage, go to the bottom and click on the Search icon.

http://www.advocacycenter.org

The Advocacy Center for Persons with Disabilities, a nonprofit organization, promotes human and legal rights of individuals through the provision of information and advocacy in the state of Florida. Program topics include protection and advocacy for individuals with mental illness and developmental disabilities, client assistance, and technical assistance.

http://www.eparent.com

The *Exceptional Parent Magazine* Web site contains internal links to resources, education, healthcare, life planning, technology, mobility, sports, and toys, with timely information for families and professionals.

http://www.schwablearning.org

Schwab Learning is dedicated to parents of children with special needs. This site provides information on learning disabilities, related resources, and ways for families to communicate.

http://www.parentingkids.com

This site has a number of products for parents (e.g., *Parents, Kids, and Tobacco; What About Gangs?*)

Curriculum, Instruction, and Lesson Plans

http://www.teachersfirst.com

Educators and parents can join a mailing list and receive weekly information about current issues related to special education and links for classroom and professional resources (including daily teaching tips).

http://www.pbs.org

This site is for teachers, parents, and students. Click on PBS TeacherSource for information on all content areas for Grades K–12 and links to lesson plans and professional development activities.

http://www.funbrain.com

> This site provides games that can be adjusted for ability level. It has resources for teachers, parents, and students; a link to design a grade book; and a homework helper.

http://www.education-world.com

> Education World provides information for parents, teachers, students, administrators, and specialists on professional development, lesson plans, and recent research related to education.

http://www.kimskorner4teachertalk.com

> Go to Classroom Management. This site offers information on classroom management and behavioral interventions. It also provides information on teaching grammar and writing.

http://wizard.4teachers.org

> Web Worksheet Wizard allows teachers to create unique web documents and personalize articles and page contents. Teachers can download worksheets across content areas.

Content Areas

Reading, Writing, Language Arts

http://www.teachers.net
http://www.kimskorner4teachertalk.com

Math

http://mathforum.com
http://math.rice.edu/~lanius/Lessons/index.html
http://www.winternet.com/~mchristi/piday.html

Science

http://www.learner.org
http://www.nationalgeographic.com
http://www.enchantedlearning.com

Social Studies

http://www.civics-online.org
http://www.familyeducation.com
http://www.teachervision.fen.com
http://www.gameskidsplay.net
http://www.enchantedlearning.com
http://www.nationalgeographic.com
http://www.teachwithmovies.org

http://www.storyarts.org
http://www.vocabulary.com
http://www.teachers.net
http://www.eduplace.com
http://www.geocities.com/crgoudie/ourland.html
http://www.hfmgv.org
http://www.siue.edu/~jandris/north/questn.html
http://www.nps.gov
http://lcweb2.loc.gov/ammem

Other Sites for Teachers

http://www.honolulu.hawaii.edu/intranet
    Go to Faculty Development, then Faculty Guidebook

http://www.kimskorner4teachertalk.com

http://www.teachnet.com
    Go to Power Tools, then Classroom Decor

http://www.teachers.net

http://bbyo.org

http://www.childfun.com/themes/school.shtml
    Go to Activity Themes

References

Agran, M., Alper, S., & Wehmeyer, M. (2002). Access to the general curriculum for students with significant disabilities: What it means to teachers. *Education and Training in Mental Retardation and Developmental Disabilities, 37,* 123–133.

Allen, H. A. (1992). Middle grade education: A one hundred year perspective. *Education Report, 32*(2), 1–2, 4.

Allen, S. K., Smith, A. C., Test, D. W., Flowers, C., & Wood, W. M. (2001). The effects of "Self-Directed IEP" on student participation in IEP meetings. *Career Development for Exceptional Individuals, 24,* 107–120.

Alspaugh, J. W., & Harting, R. D. (1997). The effects of team teaching on the transition to middle school. *ERS Spectrum, 15*(1), 9–14.

Alspaugh, J. W., & Harting, R. D. (1998). Interdisciplinary team teaching versus departmentalization in middle schools. *Research in Middle Level Education Quarterly, 21*(4), 31–42.

American Psychiatric Association. (1994). *Diagnostic and statistical manual of mental disorders* (4th ed.). Washington, DC: Author.

American Youth Policy Forum and Center on Education Policy. (2002). *Twenty-five years of educating children with disabilities: The good news and the work ahead.* Washington, DC: Author.

Ames, L. B., Ilg, F. L., & Baker, S. M. (1988). *Your ten- to fourteen-year-old.* New York: Delacorte Press.

Anafra, V. A., Jr., & Brown, K. M. (2000). Exploratory programs in middle schools [Electronic Version]. *NASSP Bulletin, 84*(617), 58–67.

Anafra, V. A., Jr., & Waks, L. J. (2002). Developmental appropriateness versus academic rigor: An untenable dualism in middle level education. In V. A. Anafara, Jr. (Series Ed.) & V. A. Anafra, Jr. & S. L. Stack (Vol. Eds.), *The handbook of research in middle level education series: Middle school curriculum, instruction and assessment* (pp. 41–55). Westerville, OH: National Middle School Association.

Anderman, L. H., & Midgley, C. (1998). *Motivation and middle school students.* Champaign, IL: ERIC Clearinghouse on Elementary and Early Childhood Education. (ERIC Document Reproduction Service No. ED 421281)

APA Task Force on Psychology in Education. (1993). *The learner-centered psychological principles: Guidelines for school redesign and reform.* Washington, DC: American Psychological Association and the Mid-continent Regional Educational Laboratory.

Armsworth, M. W., & Holaday, J. (1993). The effects of psychological trauma on children and adolescents. *Journal of Counseling and Development, 71*(4), 49–56.

Arrington, K. (2000). Middle grades career planning programs. *Journal of Career Development, 27*(2), 103–109.

Arth, A., Lounsbury, J., McEwin, C. K., & Swain, J. (1995). *Middle level teachers: Portraits of excellence.* Westerville, OH: National Middle School Association and National Association of Secondary School Principals.

Assistance to states for the Education of Children with Disabilities and the Early Intervention Program for Infants and Toddlers with Disabilities, Fed. Reg. 34 C.F.R. Parts 300 and 303 et al. *Final Regulations, 64*(48), 12420–12670.

Assistive Technology Act of 1998, 29 U.S.C. § 3002.

Austin, V. L. (2001). Teachers' beliefs about co-teaching. *Remedial and Special Education, 22,* 245–255.

Bandura, A. (1977). Self-efficacy: Toward a unifying theory of behavioral change. *Psychological Review, 84,* 181–215.

Bandura, A. (1986). *Social foundations for thought and action: A social-cognitive theory.* Englewood Cliffs, NJ: Prentice Hall.

Bandura, A. (1997). *Self-efficacy: The exercise of control.* New York: Freeman.

Barresi, A. L. (2000). The successful middle school choral teacher. *Music Educators Journal, 86*(4), 23–28.

Bartels, S. M., & Mortenson, B. (2002). Instructional consultation in middle schools: Description of an approach to training teachers to facilitate middle school teams. *Special Services in the Schools, 18*(1), 1–21.

Bauwens, J., & Hourcade, J. J. (1991). Making co-teaching a mainstreaming strategy. *Preventing School Failure, 35*(4), 19–28.

Bauwens, J., & Hourcade, J. J. (1995). *Cooperative teaching: Rebuilding the schoolhouse for all students.* Austin, TX: PRO-ED.

Bauwens, J., Hourcade, J. J., & Friend, M. (1989). Collaborative teaching: A model for general and special education integration. *Remedial and Special Education, 10*(2), 17–22.

Beakley, B. A., & Yoder, S. L. (1998). Middle schoolers learn community skills. *Teaching Exceptional Children, 30*(3), 16–21.

Belenardo, S. J. (2001). Practices and conditions that lead to a sense of community in middle schools. *NASSP Bulletin, 85*(2), 33–45.

Benner, S. M. (1998). Curriculum development and instructional approaches. In *Special education issues within the context of American society* (pp. 175–202). Belmont, CA: Wadsworth.

Benz, M., & Lindstrom, L. (1997). *Building school-to-work programs: Strategies for youth with special needs.* Austin, TX: PRO-ED.

Bigge, J. L., & Stump, C. S. (1999). *Curriculum, assessment, and instruction for students with disabilities.* Belmont, CA: Wadsworth.

Billig, S. H. (2000). Research on K–12 school-based service learning. *Phi Delta Kappan, 81,* 658–664.

Billig, S. H. (2002a). Involving middle-grader's parents. *The Education Digest, 67*(7), 42–45.

Billig, S. H. (2002b). Service learning. *Research Roundup, 19*(1), 1–6.

Blackorby, J., & Wagner, M. (1996). Longitudinal postschool outcomes of youth with disabilities: Findings from the National Longitudinal Transition Study. *Exceptional Children, 62,* 399–413.

Blalock, G., & Benz, M. (1999). *Using community transition teams to improve transition services.* Austin, TX: PRO-ED.

Blazer, B. (1999). Developing 504 classroom accommodation plans: A collaborative systematic parent–student–teacher approach. *Teaching Exceptional Children, 32*(2), 28–33.

Bohnenberger, J. E., & Terry, A. W. (2002). Community problem solving works for middle level students. *Middle School Journal, 34*(1), 5–12.

Bradford, D. J. (1999). Exemplary urban middle school teachers' use of the five standards of effective teaching. *Teaching and Change, 7*(1), 53–78.

Bremer, C. D., Clapper, A. T., Hitchcock, C., Hall, T., & Kachgal, M. (2002). Universal design: A strategy to support students' access to the general education curriculum. *Information Brief: Addressing Trends and Developments in Secondary Education and Transition, 1*(3) 1–5.

Brinckerhoff, L. C., McGuire, J. M., & Shaw, S. F. (2002). *Postsecondary education and transition for students with learning disabilities* (2nd ed.). Austin, TX: PRO-ED.

Brolin, D. E. (1989). *Life centered career education.* Arlington, VA: Council for Exceptional Children.

Brolin, D. E. (1993). *Life centered career education: A competency based approach* (4th ed.). Reston, VA: Council for Exceptional Children.

Brolin, D. E. (1996). Reflections on the beginning … and future directions. *Career Development for Exceptional Individuals, 19*(2), 93–100.

Brolin, D. E. (1997). Life-centered career education: A competency based approach (5th ed.). Reston, VA: Council for Exceptional Children.

Brolin, D. E., & Lloyd, R. J. (2004). *Career development and transition services: A functional life skills approach.* Columbus, OH: Merrill Education/Prentice Hall.

Brown, B. L. (1998). *Service learning: More than community service* (ERIC Digest No. 198). Columbus, OH: ERIC Clearinghouse on Adult Career and Vocational Education. (ERIC Document Reproduction Service No. ED 421640)

Brown, D. F. (2001). The value of advisory sessions for urban young adolescents. *Middle School Journal, 32*(4), 14–22.

Brown, D. F. (2002). Culturally responsive instructional processes. In V. A. Anafara, Jr. (Series Ed.) & V. A. Anafra, Jr., & S. L. Stack (Vol. Eds.), *The handbook of research in middle level education series. Middle school curriculum, instruction and assessment* (pp. 57–73). Westerville, OH: National Middle School Association.

Caplan, M., Weissberg, R. P., Grober, J. S., Sivo, P. J., Grady, D., & Jacoby, C. (1992). Social competence promotion with inner city and suburban young adolescents: Effects on social adjustment and alcohol use. *Journal of Clinical and Counseling Psychology, 60*(1), 56–63.

Caprio, M. W., & Borgeson, D. S. (2001). Teaching to learn: Why should teachers have all the fun? *Journal of College Science Teaching, 30,* 408–411.

Carnegie Council on Adolescent Development, Task Force on Education of Young Adolescents. (1989). *Turning points: Preparing American youth for the 21st century.* Washington, DC: Author.

Carpenter, C. D., Bloom, L. A., & Boat, M. B. (1999). Guidelines for special educators: Achieving socially valid outcomes. *Intervention in School and Clinic, 24*(3), 143–149.

Castle, D. R., & Castle, W. D. (1999). A middle grades teacher advisory system for at-risk students. In C. W. Walley & W. G. Gerrick (Eds.), *Affirming middle grades education* (pp. 17–25). Needham Heights, MA: Allyn & Bacon.

Center for Disease Control. (1999a). *Facts on adolescent injury.* Retrieved June 8, 2005, from http://www.cdc.gov/nccdphp/sgr/adoles.htm

Center for Disease Control. (1999b). Physical activity and health: A report of the Surgeon General: Adolescents and young adolescents fact sheet. Retrieved from http://www.cdc.gov/nccdphp/sgr/adoles.htm

Center for Disease Control. (2000). Tobacco use among middle and high school students: National Youth Tobacco Survey 1999 [Electronic version]. *MMWR Highlights, 49*(3). Retrieved June 8, 2005 from http://www.cdc.gov/tobacco/research_data/survey/mmwr4903fs.htm

Clark, D. C., & Clark, S. N. (2000). Developmentally responsive curriculum and standards-based reform: Implications for middle level principals. *NASSP Bulletin, 85*(615), 1–13.

Clark, G. M. (1998). *Assessment for transition planning.* Austin, TX: PRO-ED.

Clark, G. M., Patton, J. R., & Moulton, L. R. (2000). *Informal assessments for transition planning.* Austin, TX: PRO-ED.

Clark, G. M., & Patton, J. R. (1997). *Transition Planning Inventory.* Austin, TX: PRO-ED.

Clark, S. N., & Welmers, M. J. (1994). Service learning: A natural link to interdisciplinary studies. *Schools in the Middle, 4*(1), 11–15.

Cobb, R. B., & Neubert, D. A. (1998). Vocational education: Emerging vocationalism. In F. R. Rusch & J. G. Chadsey (Eds.), *Beyond high school: Transition from school to work* (pp. 101–126). Belmont, CA: Wadsworth.

Cohen, J. (1999). *Educating minds and hearts: Social emotional learning and the passage into adolescence.* New York: Teachers College Press.

Coleman, J. C., & Hendry, L. B. (1999). *The nature of adolescence* (3rd ed.). London: Routledge.

Collins, W. A., & Repinski, D. J. (1994). Relationships during adolescence: Continuity and change in interpersonal relationships. In R. Montemayor, G. R. Adams, & T. P. Gullotta (Eds.), *Personal relationships during adolescence: Advances in adolescent development.* (Vol. 6, pp. 7–36). Thousand Oaks, CA: Sage.

Cook, I. D., & Thurman-Urbanic, M. (1990). *Transition manual: TRIAD telecommunications project.* Institute: West Virginia Graduate College.

Cooke, G. J. (1995). Choice not chance: Strengthening school transitions. *Schools in the Middle, 4*(3), 8–12.

Council for Exceptional Children. (1999). *IDEA 1997: Let's make it work.* Reston, VA: Author.

Council for Exceptional Children. (2002). *What every special educator must know: The standards for the preparation and licensure of special educators.* Reston, VA: Author.

Council for Exceptional Children. (2004). *The new IDEA: CEC's summary of significant issues.* Reston, VA: Author.

Cronin, M. E. (1996). Life skills curricula for students with learning disabilities: A review of the literature. *Journal of Learning Disabilities, 29*(1), 53–68.

Cronin, M. E., & Patton, J. R. (1993). *Life skills instruction for all students with special needs: A practical guide for integrating real-life content into the curriculum.* Austin, TX: PRO-ED.

Cronin, M. E., & Pikes, T. (1999). Life skills instruction. In L. F. Masters, B. A. Mori, & A. A. Mori (Eds.), *Teaching secondary students with mild learning and behavior problems* (3rd ed., pp. 287–309). Austin, TX: PRO-ED.

Crudelle, J., & Erickson, R. (1995). *Making sense of adolescence: How to parent from the heart.* Ligouri, MO: Triumph Books.

Darling-Hammond, L. (1998). Strengthening the teacher profession: Teacher learning that supports student learning. *Educational Leadership, 55*(5), 6–12.

deBettencourt, L. U. (2002). Understanding the differences between IDEA and Section 504. *Teaching Exceptional Children, 34*(3), 16–23.

Deci, E. L., Hodges, R., Pierson, L., & Tomassone, J. (1992). Autonomy and competence as motivational factors in students with learning disabilities and emotional handicaps. *Journal of Learning Disabilities, 25,* 457–471.

deFur, S. H. (2002). Education reform, high-stakes assessment, and students with disabilities: One state's approach. *Remedial and Special Education, 23,* 203–211.

deFur, S., & Taymans, J. (1995). Competencies needed for transition specialists in vocational rehabilitation, vocational education, and special education. *Exceptional Children, 62,* 39–51.

Deshler, D. D., & Putnam, M. (1996). Learning disabilities in adolescents: A perspective. In D. D. Deshler, E. S. Ellis, & B. K. Lenz (Eds.), *Teaching adolescents with learning disabilities: Strategies and methods* (2nd ed., pp. 1–8). Denver, CO: Love.

Deshler, D. D., Schumaker, J. B., Alley, G. R., Warner, M. M., & Clark, F. L. (1982). Learning disabilities in adolescent populations: Research implications. *Focus on Exceptional Children, 15*(1), 1–12.

Deshler, D. D., Schumaker, J. B., Harris, K. R., & Graham, S. (1999). Meeting the challenge of diversity in secondary schools. In S. Graham, K. R. Harris, & M. Pressley (Series Eds.) & D. D. Deshler, J. Schumaker, K. R. Harris, & S. Graham (Vol. Eds.), *Advances in teaching and learning: Vol. 2. Teaching every adolescent every day: Learning in diverse middle and high school classrooms* (pp. vii–xii). Cambridge, MA: Brookline Books.

Devine, T. G. (1987). *Teaching study skills* (2nd ed.). Boston: Allyn & Bacon.

Dewey, J. (1916). *Democracy and education.* New York: Macmillan.

Dewey, J. (1938). *Experience and education.* New York: Macmillan.

Dickinson, T. S. (Ed.). (2001). *Reinventing the middle school.* New York: RoutledgeFalmer.

Dieker, L. A. (2001). What are the characteristics of "effective" middle and high school co-taught teams for students with disabilities? *Preventing School Failure, 46*(1), 14–23.

Doll, B., Sands, D. J., Wehmeyer, M. L., & Palmer, S. (1996). Promoting the development and acquisition of self-determined behavior. In D. J. Sands & M. L. Wehmeyer (Eds.), *Self-determination across the life span: Independence and choice for people with disabilities* (pp. 65–90). Baltimore: Brookes.

Dowd, L. R. (Ed.). (1993). *Glossary of terminology for vocational assessment, evaluation, and work adjustment.* Menomonie, WI: The Rehabilitation Resource.

Dreikurs, R., Grunwold, B. B., & Pepper, F. C. (1971). *Maintaining sanity in the classroom: Illustrated teaching techniques.* New York: Harper & Row.

Dreyfoos, J. G. (1990). *Adolescents at risk: Prevalence and prevention.* New York: Oxford University Press.

Eccles, J. S., & Harold, R. D. (1993). Parent–school involvement during the early adolescent years. *Teachers College Record, 94,* 568–587.

Edgar, E., Patton, J. M., & Day-Vines, N. (2002). Democratic dispositions and cultural competency: Ingredients for school renewal. *Remedial and Special Education, 23,* 231–241.

Education for All Handicapped Children Act of 1975, 20 U.S.C. §1400, *et seq.*

Educational Resources Information Center. (2002). *Assistive technology for students with mild disabilities: Update 2002.* Retrieved June 8, 2005, from http://www.ericec.org/digests/e623html

Eggert, L. (1994). *Anger management for youth: Stemming aggression and violence.* Bloomington, IN: National Educational Service.

Elias, M., & Butler, L. B. (1999). Social decision making and problem solving: Essential skills for interpersonal and academic success. In J. Cohen (Ed.), *Educating minds and hearts: Social emotional learning and the passage into adolescence* (pp. 74–94). New York: Teachers College Press.

Elias, M. J. (1993). *Social decision making and life skills development: Guidelines for middle school educators.* Gaithersburg, MD: Aspen.

Elias, M. J. (2001). Easing transitions with social–emotional learning. *Principal Leadership, 1*(7), 20–25.

Elias, M. J., & Tobias, S. E. (1996). *Social problem solving interventions in the schools.* New York: Guilford.

Elias, M. J., Zins, J. E., Weissberg, R. P., Frey, K. S., Greenberg, M. T., Haynes, N. M., et al. (1997). *Promoting social and emotional learning: Guidelines for educators.* Alexandria, VA: Association for Supervision and Curriculum Development.

Elkind, D. (1981). *The hurried child: Growing up too fast, too soon.* Reading, MA: Addison-Wesley.

Elksnin, N., & Elksnin, L. (1998). *Teaching occupational social skills.* Austin, TX: PRO-ED.

Elliot, D., & McKenney, M. (1998). Four inclusion models that work. *Teaching Exceptional Children, 30*(4), 54–58.

Ellis, E. S. (1996). Reading strategy instruction. In D. D. Deshler, E. S. Ellis, & B. K. Lenz (Eds.), *Teaching adolescents with learning disabilities: Strategies and methods* (2nd ed., pp. 61–125). Denver, CO: Love.

Ellis, E. S. (n.d.). *Watering up the curriculum for adolescents with learning disabilities.* Retrieved June 8, 2005 from http://ldonline.org/ldusindepth/teachingustechniques/wateringup1.html

Ellis, E. S., & Lenz, B. K. (1996). Perspectives on instruction in learning strategies. In D. D. Deshler, E. S. Ellis, & B. K. Lenz (Eds.), *Teaching adolescents with learning disabilities: Strategies and methods* (2nd ed., pp. 9–60). Denver: Love.

Elmore, R. (2000). Leadership for effective middle school practice. *Phi Delta Kappan, 82*(4), 268.

Englemann, D., & Carnine, D. (1991). *Theory of instruction* (Rev. ed.). Eugene, OR: ASI Press.

Englert, C. S., Tarrant, K. L., & Mariage, T. V. (1992). Defining and redefining instructional practice in special education: Perspectives on good teaching. *Teacher Education and Special Education, 15*(2), 62–86.

Erb, T. O. (1997). Meeting the needs of young adolescents on interdisciplinary teams: The growing research base. *Childhood Education, 73*(5), 309–311.

Erb, T. O. (2001). The imperative to act. In T. O. Erb (Ed.), *This we believe … and now we must act* (pp. 1–10). Westerville, OH: National Middle School Association.

Falbo, T., Lein, L., & Amador, N. A. (2001). Parental involvement during the transition to high school. *Journal of Adolescent Research, 16,* 511–529.

Feichtel, K. R. (1997). *Developing an inclusive environment: Strategies to increase learning for all middle level students.* Westerville, OH: National Middle School Association.

Feiring, C. (1999). Other-sex friendship networks and the development of romantic relationships in adolescence. *Journal of Youth and Adolescence, 28,* 495 –512.

Ferguson, J., & Bulach, C. (1997). The effect of the "shadow" transition program on the social adjustment of middle school students. *Research in Middle Level Education Quarterly, 20*(2), 1–21.

Field, S., & Hoffman, A. (1994). Development of a model of self-determination. *Career Development for Exceptional Individuals, 17*(2), 159–169.

Field, S., & Hoffman, A. (2002). Preparing youth to exercise self-determination: Quality indicators of school environments that promote the acquisition of knowledge, skills, and beliefs related to self-determination. *Journal of Disability Policy Studies, 13*(2), 113–118.

Field, S., Hoffman, A., & Posch, M. (1997). Self-determination during adolescence: A developmental perspective. *Remedial and Special Education, 18,* 285–293.

Field, S., Hoffman, A., & Spezia, S. (1998). *Self-determination strategies for adolescents in transition.* Austin, TX: PRO-ED.

Field, S., LeRoy, B., & Rivera, S. (1994). Meeting functional curriculum needs in middle school general education classrooms. *Teaching Exceptional Children, 26*(2), 40–43.

Field, S., Martin, J., Miller, M., Ward, M., & Wehmeyer, M. (1998). Self-determination for persons with disabilities: A position statement of the Division on Career Development and Transition. *Career Development for Exceptional Individuals, 21,* 113–128.

Fisher, D., & Kennedy, C. H. (2001). Access to the middle school core curriculum. In C. H. Kennedy & D. Fisher (Eds.), *Inclusive middle schools* (pp. 43–59). Baltimore: Brookes.

Fisher, S. K. (1999). Assistive technology. In S. H. deFur & J. R. Patton (Eds.), *Transition and school-based services* (pp. 309–386). Austin, TX: PRO-ED.

Fisher, S. K., & Gardner, J. E. (1999). Introduction to technology in transition. *Career Development for Exceptional Individuals, 22,* 131–152.

Flexer, R., Simmons, T., Luft, P., & Baer, R. (2001). *Transition planning for secondary students with disabilities.* Upper Saddle River, NJ: Merrill/Prentice Hall.

Florida Sunshine State Standards HE.B.2.3 (1995).

Florida Sunshine State Standards MA.A.4.3 (1995).

Flowers, N., Mertens, S. B., & Mulhall, P. F. (2000). How teaming influences classroom practices. *Middle School Journal, 32*(2), 52–59.

Fux, J. J. (2004). Gradus ad parnassum: Monuments of music and music literature in facsimile. Hildesheim, Germany: Georg Olms Verlag.

Gallavan, N. P., & Davis, J. E. (1999). Building community with young adolescents: Practical economies for the middle school classroom. *Clearing House, 72*(6), 341–344.

Gans, A. M., Kenny, M. C., & Ghany, D. L. (2003). Comparing the self-concept of students with and without learning disabilities. *Journal of Learning Disabilities, 36,* 287–295.

Garrett, M. L., Bellon-Harn, M. L., Torres-Rivera, E., Garrett, J. T., & Roberts, L. C. (2003). Open hands, open hearts: Working with native youth in the schools. *Intervention in School and Clinic, 38,* 225–235.

George, P., Lawrence, G., & Bushnell, D. (1998). *Handbook for middle school teaching* (2nd ed.). New York: Longman.

George, P. S. (2001). The evolution of middle schools. *Educational Leadership, 58*(4), 40–44.

George, P. S., & Alexander, W. M. (1993). *The exemplary middle school.* Fort Worth, TX: Harcourt Brace.

George, P. S., & Bushnell, D. (1993). The key to successful advisement activities: What works and why? *Schools in the Middle, 3*(1), 3–9.

George, P. S., Stevenson, C., Thomason, J., & Beane, J. (1992). *The middle school and beyond.* Alexandria, VA: Association for Supervision and Curriculum Development.

Gerber, P. J., & Popp, P. (2000). Making collaborative teaching more effective for academically able students: Recommendations for implementation and training. *Learning Disability Quarterly, 23,* 229–235.

Gersten, R., Chard, D., & Baker, S. (2000). Factors enhancing sustained use of research-based instructional practices. *Journal of Learning Disabilities, 33,* 445–457.

Gibbs, J. C., Potter, G. B., & Goldstein, A. P. (1995). *The EQUIP program: Teaching youth to think and act responsibly through a peer-helping approach.* Champaign, IL: Research Press.

Glasser, W. (1997). A new look at school failure and school success. *Phi Delta Kappan, 78*(8), 597–602.

Goldstein, A. (1999). *The PREPARE curriculum: Teaching prosocial competencies.* Champaign, IL: Research Press.

Goldstein, A., & Glick, B. (1987). *Aggression replacement training: A comprehensive intervention for aggressive youth.* Champaign, IL: Research Press.

Goldstein, A., & McGinnis, E. (1997). *Skillstreaming the adolescent: New strategies and perspectives for teaching prosocial skills.* Champaign, IL: Research Press.

Greene, G., & Kochhar-Bryant, C. A. (2003). *Pathways to successful transition for youth with disabilities.* Columbus, OH: Merrill/Prentice Hall.

Greene, M. (1991). Teaching the question of personal reality. In A. Liebermann & L. Miller (Eds.), *Staff development for education in the 90's* (2nd ed., pp. 3–14). New York: Teachers College Press.

Guskey, T. (2003). What makes professional development effective? *Phi Delta Kappan, 84,* 748–750.

Halpern, A. (1993). Quality of life as a conceptual framework for evaluating transition outcomes. *Exceptional Children, 59,* 486–498.

Halpern, A. (1994). The transition of youth with disabilities to adult life: A position statement of the Division on Career Development and Transition, the Council for Exceptional Children. *Career Development for Exceptional Individuals, 17,* 115–124.

Halpern, A. S. (1985). Transition: A look at the foundations. *Exceptional Children, 51,* 479–486.

Halverson, A. T., & Neary, T. (2001). *Building inclusive schools: Tools and strategies for success.* Boston: Allyn & Bacon.

Hanna, J. W. (1998). School climate: Changing fear to fun. *Contemporary Education, 69*(2), 83–85.

Hapner, A., & Imel, B. (2002). The students' voices: "Teachers started to listen and show respect." *Remedial and Special Education, 23,* 122–126.

Hartwig, E. P., & Ruesch, G. M. (2000). Disciplining students in special education. *The Journal of Special Education, 33,* 240–247.

Harvell, P. (1999). Speech and language services. In S. H. deFur & J. R. Patton (Eds.), *Transition and school-based services* (pp. 77–115). Austin, TX: PRO-ED.

Hasazi, S., Gordon, L., & Roe, C. (1985). Factors associated with the employment status of handicapped youth exiting high school from 1970 to 1983. *Exceptional Children, 51,* 455–469.

Henry J. Kaiser Family Foundation (2003). Teen sexual activity fact sheet. Publication No. 3040. Menlo Park, CA: Author.

Hensley, J. V. (2001). Reflecting on Foxfire: The durability of the Foxfire approach. *Active Learner: A Foxfire Journal for Teachers, 6*(1), 24–29.

Hines, R. A., & Johnston, H. (1997). Inclusion. In J. L. Irvin (Ed.), *What current research says to the middle level practitioner.* Columbus, OH: National Middle School Association.

Hitchcock, C., Meyer, A., Rose, D., & Jackson, R. (2002). Providing new access to the general curriculum: Universal design for learning. *Teaching Exceptional Children, 35*(2), 8–17.

Hoff, D. (2000). WIA and One-Stop Centers: Opportunities and issues for the disability community. *The Institute Brief, 10*(1). Retrieved June 8, 2005, from http://www.communityinclusion.org/publications/pdf/wiaonestop.pdf

Hoffman, A., & Field, S. (1995). Promoting self-determination through effective curriculum development. *Intervention in School and Clinic, 30,* 134–141.

Hole, S., & McEntree, G. H. (1999). Reflection is at the heart of practice. *Educational Leadership, 56*(8), 34–37.

Holloway, J. H. (1999/2000). Extracurricular activities: The path to academic success? [Electronic Version]. *Educational Leadership, 57*(4), 87–88.

Hoover, J. J., & Patton, J. R. (1997). *Curriculum adaptations for students with learning and behavior problems: Principles and practices.* Austin, TX: PRO-ED.

Houchins, D. E. (2001). Assistive technology barriers and facilitators during secondary and postsecondary transitions. *Career Development for Exceptional Individuals, 24,* 73–88.

Hough, D. L., & St. Clair, B. (1995). The effects of integrated curricula on young adolescent problem-solving. *Research in Middle Level Education Quarterly, 19*(1), 1–25.

Hourcade, J. J., & Bauwens, J. (2001). Cooperative teaching: The renewal of teachers. *The Clearing House, 74*(5), 242–247.

Hoversten, C., Doda, N., & Lounsbury, J. (1991). *Treasure chest: A teacher advisory source book.* Westerville, OH: National Middle School Association.

Howe, A. C., & Bell, J. (1998). Factors associated with successful implementation of interdisciplinary curriculum units. *Research in Middle Level Education Quarterly, 21*(2), 39–52.

Hoyt, K. B. (1975). *Career education: Contributions to an evolving concept.* Salt Lake City, UT: Olympus.

Hudson, P. J. (1997). Learning and study skills. In M. Agran (Ed.), *Student directed learning: Teaching self-determination skills.* Pacific Grove, CA: Brooks/Cole.

Huefner, D. S. (2000). The risks and opportunities of the IEP requirements under IDEA '97. *The Journal of Special Education, 33,* 195–204.

Hughes, C., & Carter, E. W. (2000). *The transition handbook: Strategies high school teachers use that work!* Baltimore: Brookes.

Hughes, C. A. (1996). Memory and test-taking strategies. In D. D. Deshler, E. S. Ellis, & B. K. Lenz (Eds.), *Teaching adolescents with learning disabilities: Strategies and methods* (2nd ed., pp. 209–266). Denver, CO: Love.

Hunter, M. (1982). *Mastery teaching: Increasing instructional effectiveness in elementary, secondary schools, colleges and universities.* Thousand Oaks, CA: Corwin Press.

Hyjer Dyk, P. H. (1993). Anatomy, physiology and gender issues in adolescence. In T. P. Gullotta, G. R. Adams, & R. Montemayor (Eds.), *Adolescent sexuality: Advances in adolescent development* (Vol. 5, pp. 35–56). Newbury Park, CA: Sage.

Individuals with Disabilities Education Act of 1990, 20 U.S.C. § 1401 *et seq.*

Individuals with Disabilities Education Act Amendments of 1997, 20 U.S.C. § 1400 *et seq.*

Individuals with Disabilities Education Improvement Act of 2004, 20 U.S.C. § 1400 *et seq.*

Inge, K. J., Simon, M., Halloran, W., & Moon, M. S. (1993). Community-based vocational instruction and the labor laws: A 1993 update. In K. J. Inge & P. Wehman (Eds.), *Designing community-based vocational programs for students with severe disabilities* (pp. 51–80). Richmond: Rehabilitation Research and Training Center, Virginia Commonwealth University.

Irvine, J. J., & Armento, B. J. (2001). *Culturally responsive teaching: Lesson planning for elementary and middle grades.* New York: McGraw-Hill.

Jackson, A. W., & Davis, G. A. (2000). *Turning points 2000: Educating adolescents in the 21st century.* New York: Teachers College Press.

Jacobs, H. H. (1989a). The growing need for interdisciplinary curriculum content. In H. H. Jacobs (Ed.), *Interdisciplinary curriculum: Design and implementation* (pp. 13–24). Alexandria, VA: Association for Supervision and Curriculum Development.

Jacobs, H. H. (1989b). The interdisciplinary model: A step-by-step approach for developing integrated units of study. In H. H. Jacobs (Ed.), *Interdisciplinary curriculum: Design and implementation* (pp. 53–65). Alexandria, VA: Association for Supervision and Curriculum Development.

James, M., & Spradling, N. (2002). *From advisory to advocacy: Meeting every student's needs.* Westerville, OH: National Middle School Association.

Jay, J. K., & Johnson, K. L. (2002). Capturing complexity: A typology of reflective practice for teacher education. *Teaching and Teacher Education, 18*(1), 73–85.

Johnson, A. M., & Notah, D. J. (1999). Service learning: History, literature review, and a pilot study of eighth graders [Electronic Version]. *The Elementary School Journal, 99,* 453–457.

Johnson, D. R., Stodden, R. A., Emanuel, E. J., Luecking, R., & Mack, M. (2002). Current challenges facing secondary education and transition: What research tells us. *Exceptional Children, 68,* 519–531.

Johnson, D. R., & Thurlow, M. L. (2003). *A national study on graduation requirements and diploma options for youth with disabilities* (NCEO Tech. Rep. 36). Minneapolis: University of Minnesota, National Center on Educational Outcomes. Retrieved June 8, 2005 from http://education.umn.edu/NCEO/OnlinePubs/Technical36.htm

Johnson, G. M. (1999). Inclusive education: Fundamental instructional strategies and considerations. *Preventing School Failure, 43*(2), 72–78.

Kalyanpur, K., & Harry, B. (1999). *Culture in special education: Building reciprocal family–professional relationships.* Baltimore: Brookes.

Kame'enui, E. J., Carnine, D. W., Dixon, R. C., Simmons, D. C., & Coyne, M. D. (2002). *Effective teaching strategies that accommodate diverse learners* (2nd ed.). Upper Saddle River, NJ: Merrill/Prentice Hall.

Kashak, D. (2001). Flexible organizational structures. In T. O. Erb (Ed.), *This we believe … and now we must act* (pp. 90–98). Westerville, OH: National Middle School Association.

Kelleher, J. (2003). A model for assessment-driven professional development. *Phi Delta Kappan, 84,* 751–756.

Kellough, R. D., & Kellough, N. G. (1999). *Middle school teaching: A guide to methods and resources* (3rd ed.). Upper Saddle River, NJ: Merrill.

Kennedy, C. H., & Fisher, D. (2001). Building and using collaborative school teams. In H. Kennedy & D. Fisher (Eds.), *Inclusive middle schools* (pp. 27–40). Baltimore: Brookes.

Kerka, S. (1994). *Vocational education in the middle school* (ERIC Digest No. 155). Columbus, OH: ERIC Clearinghouse on Adult Career and Vocational Education. (ERIC Document Reproduction Service No. ED377314)

Kilgore, K., Griffin, C., Sindelar, P., & Webb, R. (2001). Restructuring for inclusion: A story of middle school renewal (Part I). *Middle School Journal, 33* (2), 44–51.

Kilgore, K., Griffin, C., Sindelar, P., & Webb, R. (2002). Restructuring for inclusion: A story of middle school renewal (Part II). *Middle School Journal, 33*(2), 7–13.

Kinchin, D., & Brown, E. (2001). *Supporting children with post-traumatic stress disorder.* London: David Fulton.

Kling, B. (2000). ASSERT yourself: Helping students of all ages develop self-advocacy skills. *Teaching Exceptional Children, 32*(3), 66–70.

Klinger, J. K., & Vaughn, S. (2002). The changing roles and responsibilities of an LD specialist. *Learning Disability Quarterly, 25*(1), 19–31.

Knowles, T., & Brown, D. F. (2000). *What every middle school teacher should know.* Portsmouth, NH: Heinemann.

Kochar, C. A., West, L. L., & Taymans, J. M. (2000). *Successful inclusion: Practical strategies for a shared responsibility.* Upper Saddle River, NJ: Merrill.

Kochar-Bryant, C. A., & Bassett, D. S. (2002). *Aligning transition and standards-based education: Issues and strategies.* Reston, VA: Council for Exceptional Children.

Kohler, P. (1993). Best practices in transition: Substantiated or implied? *Career Development for Exceptional Individuals, 16*(2), 107–121.

Kolstoe, O. (1996). From a perspective of forty years in the field: Retrospective and prospective. *Career Development for Exceptional Individuals, 19*(2), 111–120.

Krebs, C. S. (2002). Self-advocacy skills: A portfolio approach. *RE:view, 33*(4), 160–163.

Krudwig, K. (2000). *Earning success in school.* (Available from Due Care in Education, 3327 Queen Palm Drive, Jacksonville Beach, FL 32250)

Krudwig, K. (2003a). [Statements made by parents of children with disabilities during a family as faculty training session]. Unpublished raw data.

Krudwig, K. (2003b). [Written opinions of middle school students in response to questions about their capabilities, academic and social attitudes, and social decision-making skills]. Unpublished raw data.

Lancaster, P. E., & Gildroy, P. (1999). Facilitating transition from elementary through high school. In D. Deshler, J. Schumaker, K. R. Harris, & S. Graham (Eds.), *Teaching every adolescent every day: Learning in diverse middle and high school classrooms* (pp. 207–249). Cambridge, MA: Brookline Books.

Langer, J. A. (2000). Excellence in English, in middle and high school: How teachers' professional lives support student achievement. *American Educational Research Journal, 37,* 397–439.

Langone, J., Shade, J., Clees, T. J., & Day, T. (1999). Effects of multimedia instruction on teaching functional discrimination skills to students with moderate/severe intellectual disabilities. *International Journal of Disability, Development, and Education, 46,* 493–513.

Lee, L. E., & Ursel, S. (2001). Engaging students in their own learning. *Education Canada, 40*(4), 12–13.

Lehmann, J., Cobb, B., & Tochterman, S. (2001). Exploring the relationship between transition and educational reform initiatives. *Career Development for Exceptional Children, 24,* 185–198.

Lenz, B. K., & Deshler, D. D. (2004). Teaching and academic diversity. In B. K. Lenz, D. D. Deshler, & B. R. Kissam, (Eds.), *Teaching content to all: Evidence-based inclusive practices in middle and secondary schools* (pp. 1–18). Boston: Pearson Education.

Lenz, B. K., Ellis, E. S., & Scanlon, D. (1996). *Teaching learning strategies to adolescents and adults with learning disabilities.* Austin, TX: PRO-ED.

Lessen, E., & Frankiewicz, L. E. (1992). Personal attributes and characteristics of effective special education teachers: Considerations for teacher education. *Teacher Education and Special Education, 15,* 124–131.

Levinson, E. M., & Murphy, J. P. (1999). School psychology. In S. H. deFur & J. R. Patton (Eds.), *Transition and school-based services* (pp. 53–76.). Austin, TX: PRO-ED.

Lewis, A. C. (1999). *Figuring it out: Standards-based reforms in urban middle grades.* New York: The Edna McConnell Clark Foundation.

Lewis, R. B., & Doorlag, D. H. (2003). *Teaching special students in general education classrooms* (6th ed.). Upper Saddle River, NJ: Merrill/Prentice Hall.

Lichtenstein, S., & Michaelides, N. (1993). Transition from school to young adulthood: Four case studies of young adults labeled mentally retarded. *Career Development for Exceptional Individuals, 16,* 183–195.

Lignugaris/Kraft, B., Marchand-Martella, N., & Martella, R. C. (2001). Writing better goals and short-term objectives or benchmarks. *Teaching Exceptional Children, 34*(1), 52–58.

Lipka, R. (1997). Enhancing self-concept/self-esteem in young adolescents. In J. L. Irvin (Ed.), *What current research says to the middle level practitioner* (pp. 31–39). Columbus, OH: National Middle School Association.

Lipsitz, J., Mizell, M. H., Jackson, A., & Austin, L. M. (1997). Speaking with one voice: A manifesto for middle-grades reform. *Phi Delta Kappan, 78,* 533–540.

Loughran, J. J. (2002). Effective reflective practice: In search of meaning in learning about teaching. *Journal of Teacher Education, 53*(1), 33–43.

Lynch, E. W., & Stein, R. (1987). Parent participation by ethnicity: A comparison of Hispanic, Black, and Anglo families. *Exceptional Children, 54,* 105–111.

Maccini, P., Gagnon, J., & Hughes, C.A. (2002). Technology-based practices for secondary students with learning disabilities. *Learning Disabilities Quarterly, 25,* 247–262.

Malmgren, K. W. (1998). Cooperative learning as an academic intervention for students with mild disabilities. *Focus on Exceptional Children, 41*(4), 1–8.

Manning, M. L. (2000). A brief history of the middle school. *The Clearing House, 73*(4), 192.

Manning, M. L. (2002). Revisiting developmentally appropriate middle level schools. *Childhood Education, 78*(4), 225–227.

Manning, M., & Bucher, K. (2001). *Teaching in the middle school.* Columbus, OH: Merrill/Prentice Hall.

Martin, J. E., & Marshall, L. H. (1995). Choicemaker: A comprehensive self-determination transition program. *Intervention in School and Clinic, 30,* 147–156.

Martin, J. E., Mithaug, D. E., Cox, P., Peterson, L. Y., Van Dycke, J. L., & Cash, M. E. (2003). Increasing self-determination: Teaching students to plan, work, evaluate, and adjust. *Exceptional Children, 69,* 431–446.

Martin, J. E., Oliphint, J. H., & Weisenstein, G. R. (1994). Choicemaker: Transitioning self-determined youth. *Rural Special Education Quarterly, 13*(1), 16–23.

Mastropieri, M., & Scruggs, T. (2000). *The inclusive classroom: Strategies for effective instruction.* Columbus, OH: Merrill.

Mather, M., & Rivers, K. (2003, March). *State profiles of child well-being: Results from the 2000 census. A Kids Count report on Census 2000.* Baltimore: Anne E. Casey Foundation.

McAfee, J. K., & Greenawalt, C. (2001). IDEA, the courts, and the law of transition. *Preventing School Failure, 45,* 102–107.

McCombs, B. L. (2001). What do we know about learners and learning? The learner-centered framework: Bringing the educational system into balance. *Educational Horizons, 79*(4), 182–193.

McCombs, B. L., & Whisler, J. S. (1997). *The learner-centered classroom and school: Strategies for increasing student motivation and achievement.* San Francisco: Jossey-Bass.

McEwin, C. K., & Dickinson, T. S. (2001). Educators committed to young adolescents. In T. O. Erb (Ed.), *This we believe ... and now we must act* (pp. 11–19). Westerville, OH: National Middle School Association.

McEwin, C. K., Dickinson, T., & Jenkins, D. M. (1996). *America's middle schools: Practices and progress.* Westerville, OH: National Middle School Association.

McNally, K. M., & Harvey, M. W. (2001). Career and technical organizations: A perfect path to self-determination and successful transition. *Preventing School Failure, 45*(3), 114–118.

McPherson, K. (1997). Service learning: Making a difference in the community. *Schools in the Middle, 6*(3), 9–15.

McWhirter, C. C., & Bloom, L. A. (1994). The effects of a student-operated business curriculum on the on-task behavior of students with behavioral disorders. *Behavioral Disorders, 19*(2), 136–141.

Mee, C. S. (1997). *2,000 voices: Young adolescents' perceptions and curriculum implications.* Westerville, OH: National Middle School Association.

Mercer, C., & Mercer, A. (2001). *Teaching students with learning problems* (6th ed.). Columbus, OH: Merrill/Prentice Hall.

Merchant, D. J., & Gajar, A. (1997). A review of the literature on self-advocacy components in transition programs for students with learning disabilities. *Journal of Vocational Rehabilitation, 8,* 223–231.

Merki, M. B. (1999). *Teen health: Course 1.* New York: Glencoe McGraw-Hill.

Miller, J. L. (2003). Facilitators of their futures. *Division on Career Development and Transition Network News, 27*(2), 5–6.

Miller, J. V. (1992). *The National Career Development Guidelines.* Ann Arbor, MI: ERIC Clearinghouse on Counseling and Personnel Services. (ERIC Document Reproduction Service No. ED347493)

Miller, S. P. (2002). *Validated practices for teaching students with diverse needs and abilities.* Boston: Allyn & Bacon.

Mitchell, J. J. (1998). *The natural limitations of youth: The predispositions that shape the adolescent character.* Stamford, CT: Ablex.

Mithaug, D., Horiuchi, C., & Fanning, P. (1985). A report on the Colorado statewide follow-up survey of special education students. *Exceptional Children, 51,* 397–404.

Morris, M., Chrispeels, J., & Burke, P. (2003). The power of two: Linking external with internal teacher's professional development. *Phi Delta Kappan, 84*(10), 764–767.

Moss, S., & Fuller, M. (2000). Implementing effective practices: Teachers' perspective. *Phi Delta Kappan, 82*(4), 273–276.

Mostert, M. P. (2000). A partial etiology and sequelae of discriminative disability: Bandwagons and beliefs. *Exceptionality, 8*(2), 117–132.

Motta, R. W. (1994). Identification of characteristics and causes of childhood posttraumatic stress disorder. *Psychology in the Schools, 31*(1), 49–56.

Mount B. (2000). *Person-centered planning: Finding directions for change using personal futures planning.* New York: Graphic Futures.

Muir, M. (2001). What engages underachieving middle school students in learning? *Middle School Journal, 11,* 37–43.

Multon, K. D., Brown, S. D., & Lent, R. W. (1991). Relation of self-efficacy beliefs to academic outcomes: A meta-analytic investigation. *Journal of Counseling Psychology, 38*(1), 30–38.

Murray, C., Goldstein, D. E., Nourse, S., Edgar, E. (2000). The postsecondary school attendance and completion rates of high school graduates with learning disabilities. *Learning Disabilities Research, 15,* 119–127.

National Center for Education Statistics (1999). Community service participation of students in grades 6–12. *Education Statistics Quarterly, 1*(2), 33–35.

National Center for Education Statistics (2002). Digest of Education Statistics 2001 (Document No. NCES 2000-130). Washington DC: Author.

National Center for Education Statistics (2003, June). The condition of education 2003 (Document No. NCES 2003-067) Washington, DC: Author.

National Council on Disability (2000). *Transition and post-school outcomes for youth with disabilities: Closing the gaps to post-secondary education and employment.* Washington, DC: Author.

National Middle School Association (1995). *This we believe: Developmentally responsive middle level schools.* Columbus, OH: Author.

National Staff Development Council. (2002). *Standards for staff development.* Oxford, OH: Author.

Neubert, D. A. (2003). The role of assessment in the transition to adult life process for students with disabilities. *Exceptionality, 11,* 63–71.

Neubert, D. A., & Moon, M. S. (1999). Working together to facilitate the transition from school to work. In S. Graham & K. R. Harris (Eds.), *Teachers working together: Enhancing the performance of students with special needs* (pp. 186–213). Cambridge, MA: Brookline Books.

Newman, B. M., & Newman, P. R. (2001). Group identity and alienation: Giving the we its due. *Journal of Youth and Adolescence, 30,* 515–538.

No Child Left Behind Act of 2001, 20 U.S.C. § 6301 (2001).

Noddings, N. (1992). *The challenge to care in schools: An alternative approach to education.* New York: Teachers College Press.

Nolet, V., & McLaughlin, M. J. (2000). *The general education curriculum: Including students with disabilities in standards-based reform.* Thousand Oaks, CA: Crown Press.

Noller, P. (1994). Relationships with parents in adolescence: Process and outcome. In R. Montemayor, G. R. Adams, & T. P. Gullotta (Eds.), *Personal relationships during adolescence* (pp. 37–77). Thousand Oaks, CA: Sage.

Norton, J. (2001). A storybook breakthrough. *Journal of Staff Development, 22*(4), 22–25.

Nowacek, E. J. (1992). Professionals talk about teaching together: Interviews with five collaborating teachers. *Intervention in School and Clinic, 27*(5), 262–276.

Office of Civil Rights, U.S. Department of Education (2002). *Protecting students with disabilities: Frequently asked questions about Section 504 and the education of children with disabilities.* Retrieved March 24, 2003, from http://www.ed.gov/about/offices/list/ocr/504faq.html

Office of Special Education and Rehabilitative Services (OSERS). (2000). *A guide to the individualized education program.* Retrieved July 10, 2002 from http://www.ed.gov/about/offices/list/osers/index.html?src=mr

Olson, J. L., & Platt, J. M. (2000). *Teaching children and adolescents with special needs* (3rd ed.). Upper Saddle River, NJ: Merrill.

Orkwis, R. (1999). *Curriculum access and universal design for learning* (ERIC/OSEP Digest No. E586). Reston, VA: ERIC Clearinghouse on Disabilities and Gifted Education. (ERIC Document Reproduction Service No. ED 437767)

Orkwis, R., & McLane, K. (1998). *A curriculum every student can use: Design principles for student access.* Reston, VA: ERIC Clearinghouse on Disabilities and Gifted Education/ERIC-OSEP Special Project on Interagency Information Dissemination. (ERIC Document Reproduction Service No. ED 423654)

Ornstein, A. C. (1990). *Strategies for effective teaching.* New York: Harper & Row.

Orrill, C. H. (2001). Building technology-based, learner-centered classrooms: The evolution of a professional development framework. *Educational Technology Research and Development, 49*(1), 15–34.

Otis-Wilborn, A., Winn, J., Ford, A., & Keyes, M. (2000). Standards, benchmarks, and indicators: Designing a framework for professional development of preservice and practicing teachers. *Teaching Exceptional Children, 32*(5), 20–28.

Paez, M. (2003). Gimme that school where everything's scripted! *Phi Delta Kappan, 84,* 757–763.

Pardini, P. (2001). A good fit. *Journal of Staff Development, 22*(3), 23–29.

Patton, J. (1999). Basic concepts of the transition process. In S. deFur & J. Patton (Eds.), *Transition and school-based services* (pp. 1–13). Austin, TX: PRO-ED.

Patton, J., Cronin, M., & Wood, J. (1999). *Infusing real-life topics into existing curricula: Recommended procedures and instructional examples for the elementary, middle, and high school levels.* Austin, TX: PRO-ED.

Pearpoint, J., Forest, M., & O'Brien, J. (1996). MAPs, Circle of Friends, and PATH: Powerful tools help build caring communities. In S. Stainback & W. Stainback (Eds.), *Inclusion: A guide for educators* (pp. 67–86). Baltimore: Brookes.

Perkins, P. G., & Gelfer, J. I. (1995). Elementary to middle school: Planning for transition. *The Clearing House, 68*(3), 171–173.

Piaget, J. (1972). Intellectual evolution from adolescence to adulthood. *Human Development, 15,* 1–12.

Pierangelo, R., & Giuliani, G. A. (2002). *Assessment in special education: A practical approach.* Boston: Allyn & Bacon.

Polloway, E. A., Patton, J. R., & Serna, L. (2001). *Strategies for teaching learners with special needs* (7th ed.). Upper Saddle River, NJ: Merrill.

Powell, A. G., Farrar, E., & Cohen, D. K. (1985). *The shopping mall high school: Winners and losers in the educational marketplace.* Boston: Houghton Mifflin.

Powers, L. E., Singer, G. H. S., & Sowers, J. (1996). *On the road to autonomy: Promoting self-competence in children and youth with disabilities.* Baltimore: Brookes.

Powers, L. E., Turner, A., Westwood, D., Matuszewski, J., Wilson, R., & Phillips, A. (2001). TAKE CHARGE for the future: A controlled field-test of a model to promote student involvement in transition planning. *Career Development for Exceptional Individuals, 24,* 89–104.

President's Commission on Excellence in Special Education. (2002). *A new era: Revitalizing special education for children and their families.* Washington, DC: U.S. Department of Education.

Price, K., & Nelson, K. L. (2003). *Daily planning for today's classroom* (2nd ed.). Belmont, CA: Wadsworth.

Price, L. A., Wolensky, D., & Mulligan, M. (2002). Self-determination in action in the classroom. *Remedial and Special Education, 23,* 109–115.

Pruitt, P., Wandry, D., & Hollums, D. (1998). Listen to us! Parents speak out about their interactions with special educators. *Preventing School Failure, 42*(4), 161–166.

Pugach, M. C., & Johnson, L. J. (2002). *Collaborative practitioners, collaborative schools* (2nd ed.). Denver: Love.

Pugach, M. C., & Warger, C. L. (1993). Curriculum considerations. In J. L. Goodlad & T. C. Lovitt (Eds.), *Integrating general and special education* (pp. 125–148). New York: Macmillan.

Quaglia, R. J., & Cobb, C. D. (1996). Toward a theory of student aspirations. *Journal of Research in Rural Education, 12*(3), 127–132.

Queen, J. A. (1999). *Curriculum practice in elementary and middle school.* Upper Saddle River, NJ: Merrill.

Quenemoen, R., Lehr, C. A., Thurlow, M., Thompson, S. J., & Bolt, S. (2000). *Social promotion and students with disabilities: Issues and challenges in developing state policies* (Synthesis Report 34). Minneapolis, MN: University of Minnesota, National Center on Educational Outcomes.

Quenemoen, R. F. (2001). IEPs within standards-based reform. *Assessment for Effective Intervention, 26*(2), 75–76.

Rathus, S. A. (2003). *Voyages: Childhood and adolescence.* Belmont, CA: Wadsworth.

Rebhorn, T. (2002). *Developing your child's IEP.* National Information Center for Children and Youth with Disabilities. Retrieved April 5, 2003 from http://www.nichcy.org/parents.asp

Rehabilitation Act of 1973, 29 U.S.C. § 701 *et seq.*

Reiser, R. A., & Butzin, S. M. (2000). Using teaming, active learning and technology to improve instruction. *Middle School Journal, 32*(2), 21–25.

Repetto, J. (2003). Transition to living. *Exceptionality, 11*(2), 77–87.

Repetto, J. B. (1995). Curriculum beyond school walls: Implications of transition education. *Peabody Journal of Education, 70*(3), 125–140.

Repetto, J. B., & Webb, K. W. (1999). A model for guiding the transition process. In S. H. deFur & J. R. Patton (Eds.), *Transition and school-based services* (pp. 421–442). Austin, TX: PRO-ED

Reynolds, M. C. (1990). Education teachers for special education students. In W. R. Houston (Ed.), *Handbook of research on teacher education* (pp. 423–436). New York: Macmillan.

Rice, R. P., & Dolgin, K. G. (2002). *The adolescent: Development, relationships, and culture* (10th ed.). Boston: Allyn & Bacon.

Richards, T., & Bates, C. (1997). Recognizing posttraumatic stress in children. *Journal of School Health, 67*(10), 441–443.

Richardson, R. C. (2000). Teaching social and emotional competence. *Children & Schools, 22*(4), 246–251.

Rivera, D. P., & Smith, D. D. (1997). *Teaching students with learning and behavior problems* (3rd ed.). Boston: Allyn & Bacon.

Roberts, D. F., Foehr, U. G., & Rideout, V. (2005). *Generation M: Media in the lives of 8- to 18-year-olds.* Henry J. Kaiser Foundation report. Retrieved July 21, 2005 from http://www.kff.org/entmedia/7251.cfm.

Robinson, S. M., Braxdale, C. T., & Colson, S. E. (1985). Preparing dysfunctional learners to enter junior high school: A transitional curriculum. *Focus on Exceptional Children, 18*(4), 1–12.

Roja, D. A. (1994). *How a bill becomes a law: An AskERIC lesson plan* (Lesson Plan No. AELP-GOV0015). Retrieved May 10, 2003, from http://www.eduref.org/cgi-bin/printlessons.cgi/Virtual/Lessons/Social_Studies/US_Government/GOV0015.html

Rosenberg, M. S., O'Shea, L., & O'Shea, K. J. (1998). *Student teacher to master teacher: A practical guide for educating students with special needs* (2nd ed.). Upper Saddle River, NJ: Merrill.

Rosenshine, B. (1983). Teaching functions in instructional programs. *The Elementary School Journal, 83,* 335–351.

Rosenshine, B. (1987). Explicit teaching and teacher training. *Journal of Teacher Education, 38*(3), 34–36.

Ross, A., & Olsen, K. (1995). *The way we were … The way we can be: A vision for the middle school.* Kent, WA: Susan Kovalik.

Rusch, F., & Chadsey, J. (1998). *Beyond high school: Transition from school to work.* New York: Wadsworth.

Rusch, M., & Miller, D. (1998). Emerging transition best practices. In F. Rusch & J. Chadsey (Eds.), *Beyond high school: Transition from school to work* (pp. 36–60). New York: Wadsworth.

Rutherford, C., Chipman, J., Digangi, S., & Anderson, K. (1992). *Teaching social skills: A practical instructional approach.* Ann Arbor, MI: Exceptional Innovations.

Sabornie, E. J. (1994). Social–affective characteristics in early adolescents identified as learning disabled and nondisabled. *Learning Disability Quarterly, 17,* 268–279.

Salend, S. J., Gordon, J., & Lopez-Vona, K. (2002). Evaluating cooperative teaching teams. *Intervention in School and Clinic, 37*(4), 196–200.

Santrock, J. W. (2001). *Adolescence* (8th ed.). Boston: McGraw-Hill.

Sax, C. L. (2002). Person-centered planning: More than a strategy. In C. L. Sax & C. A. Thoma (Eds.), *Transition assessment: Wise practices for quality lives* (pp. 13–24). Baltimore: Brookes.

Sax, C. L., & Thoma, C. A. (2002). *Transition assessment: Wise practices for quality lives.* Baltimore: Brookes.

Scales, P., & McEwin, C. (1994). *Growing pains: The making of America's middle school teachers.* Columbus, OH: National Middle School Association.

Schave, D., & Schave, B. (1989). *Early adolescence and the search for self: A developmental perspective.* New York: Praeger.

Schloss, P. J., Smith, M. A., & Schloss, C. N. (2001). *Instructional methods for secondary students with learning and behavior problems* (3rd ed.). Boston: Allyn & Bacon.

Schumacher, D. (1998). *The transition to middle school.* Champaign, IL: ERIC Clearinghouse on Elementary and Early Childhood Education. (ERIC Document Reproduction Service No. ED 422119)

Schumaker, J. B., & Deshler, D. D. (1984). Setting demand variables: A major factor in program planning for the LD adolescent. *Topics in Language Disorders, 4*(2), 22–40.

Schumm, J. S., Vaughn, S., & Harris, J. (1997). Pyramid power for collaborative planning. *Teaching Exceptional Children, 29*(6), 62–66.

Schunk, D. H. (1985). Participation in goal setting: Effects on self-efficacy and skills of learning disabled children. *The Journal of Special Education, 19,* 307–317.

Schunk, D. H. (1987). Peer models and children's behavioral change. *Review of Educational Research, 57,* 149–174.

Secretary's Commission on Achieving Necessary Skills (SCANS). (1991). *What work requires of schools: A SCANS report for America 2000.* Washington, DC: U.S. Department of Labor. (ERIC Document Reproduction Service No. ED 332 054)

Serna, L. A., & Lau-Smith, J. (1995). Learning with PURPOSE: Self-determination skills for students who are at risk for school and community failure. *Intervention in School and Clinic, 30*(3), 142–146.

Shepherd, J., & Inge, K. J. (1999). Occupational and physical therapy. In S. H. deFur & J. R. Patton (Eds.), *Transition and school-based services* (pp. 117–166). Austin, TX: PRO-ED.

Shortt, T. L., & Thayer, Y. (1999). Block scheduling can enhance school climate. *Educational Leadership, 56*(4), 76–81.

Simon, M., Cobb, B., Norman, M., & Bourexis, P. (1994). *Meeting the needs of youth with disabilities: Handbook for implementing community-based vocational education programs according to the Fair Labor Standards Act.* Fort Collins: Colorado State University.

Simpson, S. (1999). Early adolescent development. In C. W. Walley & W. G. Gerrick (Eds.), *Affirming middle grades education.* Needham Heights, MA: Allyn & Bacon.

Sitlington, P. L., & Clark, G. M. (2006). *Transition education and services for students with disabilities* (4th ed.). Boston: Allyn & Bacon.

Sitlington, P. L., Clark, G. M., & Kolstoe, O. P. (2000). *Transition education and services for adolescents with disabilities* (3rd ed.). Needham Heights, MA: Allyn & Bacon.

Sitlington, P., & Frank, A. (1993). Success as an adult: Does gender make a difference for graduates with mental disabilities? *Career Development for Exceptional Individuals, 16,* 171–182.

Sitlington, P. L., & Frank, A. R. (1999). Life outside of work for young adults with learning disabilities. *The Journal for Vocational Special Needs Education, 22*(1), 3–22.

Sitlington, P. L., & Neubert, D. A. (1998). Assessment for life: Methods and processes to determine students' interests, abilities, and preferences. In M. Wehmeyer & D. J. Sands (Eds.), *Making it happen: Student involvement in educational planning, decision making, and instruction* (pp. 75–98). Baltimore: Brookes.

Sitlington, P. L., Neubert, D. A., Begun, W., Lombard, R. C., & Leconte, P. J. (1996). *Assess for success: Handbook on transition assessment.* Reston, VA: Council for Exceptional Children.

Sitlington, P. L., Neubert, D. A., & Leconte, P. (1997). Transition assessment: The position of the Division on Career Development and Transition. *Career Development for Exceptional Individuals, 2,* 69–79.

Skinner, B. F. (1970). *Science and human behavior.* New York: Knopf.

Skinner, B. F. (1984). The evolution of behavior. *Journal of Experimental Analysis of Behavior, 3,* 217–222.

Slavin, R. E. (1996). Cooperative learning in middle and secondary schools. *The Clearing House, 69*(4), 200–204.

Smith, D. D. (2006). *Introduction to special education: Teaching in an age of opportunity* (6th ed.). Boston: Allyn & Bacon.

Smith, D. D. (2004). *Introduction to special education: Teaching in an age of opportunity* (5th ed.). Needham Heights, MA: Allyn & Bacon.

Smith, J. (1997). Effects of eighth-grade transition programs on high school retention and experiences. *The Journal of Educational Research, 90*(3), 144–152.

Smith, T. C., Polloway, E., Patton, J. R., & Dowdy, C. (2004). *Teaching students with special needs in inclusive settings* (4th ed.). Boston: Pearson.

Smith, T. E. C. (2001). Section 504, the ADA, and public schools: What educators need to know. *Remedial and Special Education, 22,* 335–343.

Smith, T. E. C., & Patton, J. R. (1999). *Section 504 and public schools: A practical guide.* Austin, TX: PRO-ED.

Smith-Horn, B., & Singer, G. S. (1996). Self-esteem and learning disabilities: An exploration of theories of self. In L. E. Powers, G. H. S. Singer, & J. Sowers (Eds.), *On the road to autonomy: Promoting self-competence in children and youth with disabilities.* Baltimore: Brookes.

Snodgrass, D. M. (1991). The parent connection. *Adolescence, 26,* 83–87.

Solodow, W. (1999). The meaning of development in middle school. In J. Cohen (Ed.), *Educating minds and hearts: Social emotional learning and the passage into adolescence* (pp. 24–42). New York: Teachers College Press.

Southern Regional Education Board. (2000). *A middle grade message: A well-qualified teacher in every classroom matters.* Atlanta, GA: Author.

Staub, D., & Hunt, P. (1993). The effects of social interaction training on high school peer tutors of schoolmates with severe disabilities. *Exceptional Children, 60*(1), 41–57.

Stein, M., Carnine, D., & Dixon, R. (1998). Direct instruction: Integrating curriculum design and effective teaching practice. *Intervention in School and Clinic, 33*(4), 227–233.

Steinberg, L. (1999). *Adolescence* (5th ed.). Boston: McGraw-Hill.

Sternberg, R. J. (1997). The concept of intelligence and its role in lifelong learning and success. *American Psychologist, 52,* 1030–1037.

Stevenson, C. (1998). *Teaching ten to fourteen year olds* (2nd ed.). New York: Longman.

Storms, J., O'Leary, E., & Williams, J. (2000). *The Individuals with Disabilities Education Act of 1997 transition requirements: A guide for states, districts, schools, universities, and families.* Stillwater, OK: National Clearinghouse of Rehabilitation Training Materials.

Swanson, H. L. (2001). Research on interventions for adolescents with learning disabilities: A meta-analysis of outcomes related to higher-order processing [Electronic Version]. *The Elementary School Journal, 101,* 331–348.

Tanner, J. M. (1991). Adolescent growth spurt. In R. M. Lerner, A. C. Petersen, & J. Brooks-Gunn (Eds.), *Encyclopedia of adolescence.* New York: Garland.

Taylor, H. E., & Larson, S. (1999). Social and emotional learning in middle school. *The Clearing House, 72*(6), 331–336.

Taylor, R. L. (2000). *Assessment of exceptional students: Educational and psychological procedures* (5th ed.). Boston: Allyn & Bacon.

Thoma, C. A. (1999). Supporting student voices in transition planning. *Teaching Exceptional Children, 31*(5), 4–9.

Thomas, D. R., Becker, W. C., & Armstrong, M. (1968). Production and elimination of disruptive classroom behavior by systematically varying teachers' behavior. *Journal of Applied Behavior Analysis, 1,* 35–45.

Thurlow, M. L. (2000). Standards-based reform and students with disabilities: Reflection on a decade of change. *Focus on Exceptional Children, 33*(3), 1–16.

Thurlow, M. L. (2002). Positive educational results for all students. *Remedial and Special Education, 23,* 195–202.

Thurlow, M. L., House, A. L., Scott, D. L., & Ysseldyke, J. E. (2000). Students with disabilities in large-scale assessments: State participation and accommodation policies. *Journal of Special Education, 34,* 154–163.

Thurlow, M. L., Lazarus, S., Thompson, S., & Robey, J. (2002). *2001 state policies on assessment participation and accommodations* (Synthesis Report No. 46). Minneapolis: University of Minnesota, National Center on Education Outcomes. Retrieved June 10, 2005, from http://education.umn.edu/NCEO/OnlinePubs/Synthesis46.html

Tralli, R., Columbo, B., Deshler, D. D., & Schumaker, J. B. (1999). The Strategies Intervention Model: A model for supported inclusion at the secondary level. In S. Graham, K. R. Harris, & M. Pressley (Series Eds.) & D. D. Deshler, J. Schumaker, K. R. Harris, & S. Graham (Vol. Eds.), *Advances in teaching and learning—Teaching every adolescent every day: Learning in diverse middle and high school classrooms* (pp. 250–280). Cambridge, MA: Brookline Books.

Tucker, B., Hafenstein, N. L., Tracy, K., Hillman, L., & Watson, A. (1995). Integrating middle school curriculum: A two-tiered development model. *Research in Middle Level Education Quarterly, 19*(1), 43–58.

Turner, S., & Lapan, R. T. (2002). Career self-efficacy and perceptions of parent support in adolescent career development. *The Career Development Quarterly, 51*(1), 44–55.

Ukpokodu, N. (2002). Breaking through preservice teachers' defensive dispositions in a multicultural education course: A reflective practice. *Multicultural Education, 9*(3), 25–33.

University of Kansas Center for Research on Learning. (2001). *Strategic instruction model: Learning strategies and teaching routines* [Electronic Brochure]. Retrieved June 10, 2005 from http://www.ku-crl.org/htmlfiles/simbrochure.pdf

U.S. Census Bureau. (2000). Profile of General Demographic Characteristics: 2000. Data Set: Census 2000 Summary File 1 (SF1) 100-Percent Data. Geographic Area: United States. Retrieved from http://factfinder.census.gov/

U.S. Department of Education. (2002). *Twenty-fourth annual report to Congress on the implementation of the Individuals with Disabilities Education Act.* Washington,DC: Author.

U.S. Department of Health & Human Services (2002, November). *Profile of America's youth.* Retrieved June 10, 2005 from http://www.acf.dhhs.gov/programs/fysb/youthinfo/profile.htm

Van Hoose, J., Strahan, D., & L'Esperance, M. (2001). *Promoting harmony: Young adolescent development and school practices.* Columbus, OH: National Middle School Association.

Van Reusen, A. K. (1999). Developing social competence in diverse secondary schools and classrooms. In S. Graham, K. Harris, & M. Pressley (Series Eds.) & D. D. Deshler, J. Schumaker, K. R. Harris, & S. Graham (Vol. Eds.), *Advances in teaching and learning—Teaching every adolescent every day: Learning in diverse middle and high school classrooms* (pp. 106–145). Cambridge, MA: Brookline Books.

Van Reusen, A. K., Bos, C. S., Schumaker, J. B., & Deshler, D. D. (1994). *The self-advocacy strategy for education and transition planning.* Lawrence, KS: Edge Enterprises.

Van Voorhis, F. L. (2001). Interactive science homework: An experiment in home and school connections. *NASSP Bulletin, 85*(2), 20–32.

Vars, G. F., & Beane, J. A. (2000). *Integrative curriculum in a standards-based world.* Champaign, IL: ERIC Clearinghouse on Elementary and Early Childhood Education. (ERIC Document Reproduction Service No. ED 441618)

Vaughn, S., Bos, C. S., & Schumm, J. S. (2003). *Teaching exceptional, diverse, and at-risk students* (3rd ed.). Boston: Allyn & Bacon.

Wagner, M., & Blackorby, J. (1996). Transition from high school to work or college: How special education students fare. *The Future of Children, 6*(1), 103–120.

Walker, D. M., & Lirgg, C. D. (1995). Growth and development during middle school years. In M. J. Wavering (Ed.), *Educating young adolescents: Life in the middle* (pp. 53–78). New York: Garland.

Walker, H. M., Colvin, G., & Ramsey, E. (1995). *Anti-social behavior in school: Strategies and best practices.* Pacific Grove, CA: Brooks/Cole.

Walsh, J. M. (2001). Getting the "big picture" of IEP goals and state standards. *Teaching Exceptional Children, 33*(5), 18–26.

Walther-Thomas, C., Korinek, L., & McLaughlin, V. (1999). Collaboration to support students' success. *Focus on Exceptional Children, 32*(3), 1–18.

Walther-Thomas, C., Korinek, L., McLaughlin, V. L., & Williams, B. T. (2000). *Collaboration for inclusive education: Developing successful programs.* Boston: Allyn & Bacon.

Ward, M. J., & Kohler, P. D. (1996). Teaching self-determination: Content and process. In L. E. Powers, G. H. S. Singer, & J. A. Sowers (Eds.), *On the road to autonomy: Promoting self-competence in children and youth with disabilities* (pp. 275–290). Baltimore: Brookes.

Wasburn-Moses, L. (2003). What every special educator should know about high stakes testing. *Teaching Exceptional Children, 35*(4), 12–15.

Wavering, M. J. (1995). Cognitive development of young adolescents. In M. J. Wavering (Ed.), *Educating young adolescents: Life in the middle* (pp. 111–130). New York: Garland.

Webb, K., Repetto, J., Beutel, A., Perkins, D., Bailey, M., Schwartz, S. E., & Perry, L. J. (1999). *Dare to dream* (2nd ed.). Tallahassee, FL: Bureau of Instructional Support and Community Services, Florida Department of Education.

Webb, K. W. (2000). *Transition to postsecondary education: Strategies for students with disabilities.* Austin, TX: PRO-ED.

Weddle, M. (1999). Waldo Middle School's endangered species project: A model for community based integrated instruction. *Clearing, 104,* 7–13.

Wehman, P. (1996). *Life beyond the classroom: Transition strategies for young people with disabilities* (2nd ed.). Baltimore: Brookes.

Wehman, P., & Kregel, J. (1997). *Functional curriculum for elementary, middle, and secondary age students with special needs.* Austin, TX: PRO-ED.

Wehmeyer, M. (2002). *Self-determination and the education of students with disabilities* (ERIC Digest No. E632). Reston, VA: The Council for Exceptional Children. (ERIC Document Reproduction Service No. ED 470036)

Wehmeyer, M. (2003). The impact of disability on adolescent identity. In M. Sadowski (Ed.), *Adolescents at school: Perspectives on youth, identity, and education* (pp. 127–139). Cambridge, MA: Harvard Education Press.

Wehmeyer, M., Morningstar, M., & Husted, D. (1999). *Family involvement in transition planning.* Austin, TX: PRO-ED.

Wehmeyer, M. L. (1992). Self-determination as an educational outcome. *Impact, 6*(4), 16–17, 26.

Wehmeyer, M. L. (1996). Self-determination as an educational outcome: Why is it important to children, youth and adults with disabilities? In D. J. Sands & M. L. Wehmeyer (Eds.), *Self-determination across the life span: Independence and choice for people with disabilities* (pp. 17–36). Baltimore: Brookes.

Wehmeyer, M. L. (2001). Self-determination and transition. In P. Wehman (Ed.), *Transition strategies for young people with disabilities* (pp. 35–60). Baltimore: Brookes.

Wehmeyer, M. L., Agran, M., & Hughes, C. (1998). *Teaching self-determination to students with disabilities: Basic skills for successful transition.* Baltimore: Brookes.

Wehmeyer, M. L., Sands, D. J., Doll, B., & Palmer, S. (1997). The development of self-determination and implications for educational interventions with students with disabilities. *International Journal of Disability, Development, and Education, 44,* 305–328.

Wehmeyer, M. L., Sands, D. J., Knowlton, E., & Kozleski, E. B. (2002). *Providing access to the general curriculum: Teaching students with mental retardation.* Baltimore: Brookes.

Wehmeyer, M. L., & Schalock, R. L. (2001). Self-determination and quality of life: Implications for special education services and supports. *Focus on Exceptional Children, 33*(8), 1–16.

Weimer, B. B., Cappotelli, M., & DiCamillo, J. (1994). Self-advocacy: A working proposal for adolescents with special needs. *Intervention in School and Clinic, 30*(1), 47–52.

Weinberger, E., & McCombs, B. L. (2001). *The impact of learner-centered practices on the academic and non-academic outcomes of upper elementary and middle school students.* Denver, CO: University of Denver. (ERIC Document Reproduction Service No. ED458276)

Weishar, M. K., & Boyle, J. R. (1999). Note-taking strategies for students with disabilities. *The Clearing House, 72*(6), 392–395.

Weiss, M. P., & Lloyd, J. (2003). Conditions for co-teaching: Lessons from a case study. *Teacher Education and Special Education, 26*(1), 27–41.

Wentzel, K. R. (1997). Student motivation in middle school: The role of perceived pedagogical caring. *Journal of Educational Psychology, 89,* 411–419.

West, L., Corbey, S., Boyer-Stephens, A., Jones, B., Miller, B., & Sarkees-Wircenski,. (1999). *Integrating transition planning into the IEP process* (2nd ed.). Arlington, VA: Council for Exceptional Children.

White, A. E., & White, L. L. (1992). A collaborative model for students with mild disabilities in middle school. *Focus on Exceptional Children, 24*(9), 1–10.

Widom, C. S. (1989). The cycle of violence. *Science, 244*(4901), 160–166.

Wigfield, A., & Eccles, J. S. (1994). Middle grades schooling and early adolescent development: An introduction. *Journal of Early Adolescence, 14*(2), 102–106.

Wiles, J., & Bondi, J. (2001). *The new American middle school: Educating preadolescents in an era of change* (3rd ed.). Upper Saddle River, NJ: Merrill/Prentice Hall.

Will, M. (1984). *OSERS programming for the transition of youth with disabilities: Bridges from school to working life*. Washington, DC: Office of Special Education and Rehabilitative Services, U.S. Department of Education.

Workforce Investment Act, 29 U.S.C. § 2938 (1998).

Wormeli, R. (2001). *Meet me in the middle: Becoming an accomplished middle-level teacher*. Portland, ME: Stenhouse.

Wright, P. W. D., & Wright, P. D. (2002). Wrightslaw: *Special education law*. Hartfield, VA: Harbor House Law Press.

Yell, M. L., & Shriner, J. G. (1997). The IDEA Amendments of 1997: Implications for special and general education teachers, administrators, and teacher trainers. *Focus on Exceptional Children, 30*(1), 1–19.

Yoder, D. I., Retish, E., & Wade, R. (1996). Service learning: Meeting student and community needs. *Teaching Exceptional Children, 28*(4), 14–18.

Yuan, F. (1994). Moving toward self-acceptance: A course for students with learning disabilities. *Intervention in School and Clinic, 29*(5), 301–309.

Zetlin, A., & Hosseini, A. (1989). Six postschool case studies of mildly learning handicapped young adults. *Exceptional Children, 55*, 405–411.

Zhang, D. (2001). The effects of "Self-Directed IEP" on student participation in IEP meetings. *Career Development for Exceptional Individuals, 24*, 121–132.

Zigmond, N., & Magiera, K. (2001). A focus on co-teaching: Use caution. *Current Practice Alerts, 6*. Division for Learning Disabilities and Division for Research, Council for Exceptional Children.

Zimmerman, B. J. (1996). Enhancing student academic and health functioning: A self-regulatory perspective. *School Psychology Quarterly, 11*(1), 47–66.

About the Authors

Dr. Jeanne B. Repetto has taught undergraduate and graduate courses in special education, families, and transition services in the Department of Special Education, University of Florida, Gainesville, since 2000. Prior to 2000 she directed grants and taught undergraduate and graduate courses at the University of Missouri–Columbia and the University of Illinois, Champaign–Urbana. Her university work was preceded by 10 years of teaching students with disabilities in public school sytems. In addition to teaching, Dr. Repetto has oversight of The Transition Center at the University of Florida, which is a statewide research and dissemination center in the area of transition for adolescents and adults with disabilities. Other research interests center on middle school education, transition service provision, and student outcomes.

Dr. Kristine W. Webb is a faculty member in the Department of Special Education at the University of North Florida in Jacksonville. She teaches undergraduate and graduate courses in transition, curriculum, and parent partnerships. Previously, she served as the director of the Florida Network: Information and Services for Adolescents and Adults with Special Needs, housed at the University of Florida. Her interest in teacher preparation began with a 4-year assignment as the coordinator of a collaborative special education intern program at the University of New Mexico. Prior to this assignment, Kris was a high school teacher for 17 years. Along with her interest in teacher recruitment, retention, and preparation, she has a long-standing interest in postsecondary education for individuals with disabilities, family involvement and collaboration, and transition to adult life for individuals with disabilities.

Dr. Debra A. Neubert has taught undergraduate and graduate courses in secondary special education and transition services in the Department of Special Education, University of Maryland at College Park since 1986. She is currently involved in a number of grant-supported projects, which focus on personnel preparation for transition specialists and on outreach activities for school systems implementing age-appropriate programs for students with disabilities on college campuses. Other research interests center on transition assessment, case management, and program evaluation.

Dr. Christina Curran has been a member of the special education faculty at Central Washington University, Ellensburg, since 1997. She has taught a variety of undergraduate and graduate courses in special education. Her research and content interests include curriculum planning and effective instructional practices for students with disabilities, preservice preparation of special educators, middle school-level education, collaboration and co-teaching models, and social skills strategies and behavioral supports. Additionally, she has worked as a special educator of students ages 3 through 21 with both high- and low-incidence disabilities and as a novice special educator supervisor for 10 years. Her closest encounter with early adolescents involves her own children, both currently middle schoolers.